My friend, Samuel Lee, has given the body of Christ a remarkable spiritual tour de force. Drawing profound insights from book after book of the Bible, he has distilled practical knowledge from his broad leadership experience to draw us a road map for our spiritual lives. Journey to Grace is a fresh, moving book that I wish every Christian believer could read!

C. Peter Wagner, Chancellor
Wagner Leadership Institute

I wish every Christian believer could read this book!
-C. Peter Wagner

JOURNEY TO GRACE

A Spirit-filled Survey of the Old Testament

Samuel Lee

JOURNEY TO GRACE

By Dr. Samuel Lee
Published by MinistryHouse
A part of MinistryHouse Press
31 Verrijn Stuartweg
Diemen 1112 AW
The Netherlands
www.ministryhouse.com

Cover and interior design by John H. Olsen

Royal Library Catalog Card Number: 02014249
International Standard Book Number: 90-76077-01-3

03 04 05 06 – 11 10 9 8
Printed in the United Kingdom

“My people are destroyed from lack of knowledge”
Hosea 4:6

To my beloved wife Sarah,
Filled with Grace!

To my precious team,
Filled with love!

Shaba
John
Shakila
Myrna
Thomas
Marsha
Kwame
Charles
Tony
Joseph
Daniel

ACKNOWLEDGMENT

My team has always been my constant motivator, and source of inspiration and encouragement. This book would not be made possible without their participation and input! I have a team who believes in me and in my abilities. This motivates me to work harder and prove myself worthy of their love and trust!

I could never have this book published without the tireless editing of my secretary, Marsha Namdar and the creative team of my publisher, John Olsen in the Ministry House! Thank you so much!

Finally, I would like to thank the precious Holy Spirit for without His guidance, I would not be able to write it or even dare writing it. Truly, He is the best friend and excellent Teacher we could ever have in our lives!

INTRODUCTION

There was a time when I was meditating the words of Jesus in Matthew 7:24-29, urging us to build our house upon a rock so that when the rain comes down, or when streams rise and the wind blows against its roofs and walls, that house will never be shaken nor destroyed.
Conventionally speaking, this can be interpreted such that the house represents our lives which must be built upon the Rock, who is Jesus Christ, so that when the hardships of life hit us, represented by the rain, streams of water and wind, we will not be moved.

However, the Spirit of God changed my paradigm over this passage: the house represents the Church. The wind, the streams of water and the rain are symbols of Revival!
Are we ready when the wind of revival start to blow, when the streams of water start to rise and when the new rain begin to shower the Church? Revival has two edges. The first one is the Restoration and the second one is Destruction! The churches which are built upon the Rock will take pleasure in the sweetness of revival, but those churches which are not built upon the Rock will be destroyed, instead of being renewed!

What does "building upon the Rock" means? It means having a balanced Christian life based upon the guidance of the Holy Spirit and the Word of the Living God combined with prayer!
I have studied revivals all around the world, and there is one thing I have noticed. I have noticed that those churches which didn't have a strong foundation in the Word of God burned out soon because of their lack of knowledge! Many of them misinterpreted the move of the Holy Spirit and began to look, act and think weird and as a result, many stumbled along the road of their spiritual journey. Revival can build up, but it can also burn down!

For this reason, the Word of God and the knowledge thereof is a must for every Spirit-filled Christian. When we know the truth and when we have Spirit-filled knowledge of the Word of God, the Holy Bible, we will never be destroyed!

Consequently, it took me three years to finish this book. My intention of writing is not by itself to generate another theological survey of the Bible. I rather tried to explore the Old Testament in simple but yet Spirit-filled manner so that everyone will benefit from reading it and may have a broader understanding of the Old Testament.

Knowing the Old Testament is essential for every Christian because the Old Testament is a journey that both God and man took toward Grace. Every page of the Old Testament is a road toward peace given by Jesus Christ for all men through His death and resurrection. Without the Old Testament, we cannot understand the New Testament!

This book is designed for all those who hunger for Spirit-filled knowledge. Each lesson contains main scriptures, reference scriptures and questions at the end of each lesson. It is suitable for cell groups and bible study meetings. As you read Journey to Grace, you must also realize that what I have written is only an interpretation. By all means the Word of God is living but it does not necessarily mean that my interpretations are the only correct ones! It is only one of the thousands of books at present that offers a humble support in understanding God's plan and His Grace revealed in the Old Testament!

Each chapter of this book is a road towards Christ! Are you ready to join me in this journey? Come on and let's go!

Samuel Lee
Amsterdam, the Netherlands

Table of Contents

. PART I .

Journey With Law

LESSON 1

The Creation

Genesis 1–2

INTRODUCTION TO THE BOOK OF GENESIS

Genesis is the first book of the Holy Bible. "Genesis" is a Greek word which means "origin" or "source." In the original Hebrew this book is titled *Bereshith*, which means, "in the beginning."

Christians and Jews believe that God's Spirit revealed this book along with the other four books written by Moses—Exodus, Leviticus, Numbers, and Deuteronomy. Genesis was written almost fifteen centuries before Christ.

This book is called "in the beginning" or "Genesis" because it tells us about the origin of our world, the origin of men, the origin of different nations, and the like. We also read how sin entered the world and how the love of God acts toward sinful man.

Genesis can be divided into two main parts:

A. The early history of the human race (chapters 1–11)
1. The Creation
2. The Fall
3. The Flood
4. The Nations

B. The history of Abraham's families (chapters 12–50)
1. Abraham
2. Isaac
3. Jacob
4. Joseph

In the coming eight lessons we will study the above-mentioned subjects that are found in Genesis.

TODAY'S JOURNEY

Genesis 1 speaks about the creation of the heavens and earth by God our Father. God created this world. He is almighty and everything is possible with Him. He created this world by His spoken word. God said, "Let there be light" and there was light (Gen. 1:3). This shows us the power of God. In this chapter we must focus on two important things that are related to creation:

1) "In the beginning. . ."
2) "Let there be. . . "

In the Beginning

God is our beginning. It is He who created this world. Genesis 1 teaches us that the beginning of everything starts with God. Let me give you an example:

In our world today there are many children who have problems with their identity. They do not know who their father or mother is. When they grow up they manifest psychological problems because they do not know who their biological parents are. As a result, they become miserable or end up attempting suicide.

It is exactly the same with societies today. They have forgotten who the real Father is and who is the BEGINNING. That is why our societies today are sick. They are filled with hatred, adultery, anger, wars, poverty, criminal activity, and the like. When people start to ignore God as the beginning of everything, they ignore the commandments of God the Beginner, and they ignore the teachings of His prophets, His Word, and His Son Jesus Christ. When this happens the children will not be raised according to the teachings of God. This causes a chaotic family, a chaotic society, and a chaotic world. That is why most children use prohibited drugs. Families break up mainly because men ignore the beginning: GOD AS THE CREATOR.

When a person knows his beginning no one can deceive that person. When you know your beginning, you also know your present and you know your end. You also know where you are going.

The Bible teaches us that even before the creation of the world, the Trinity already existed:

> *In the beginning was the Word, and the Word was with God and the Word was God. He (Jesus) was with God in the beginning. Through him all things were made; without him nothing was made that has been made.*
>
> (John 1:1-3)

Jesus also said: "I tell you the truth, before Abraham was born, I AM" (John 8:58).

This means that we cannot know our God, who is our beginning, without knowing Jesus. The difference between Jews and Christians is that Jews do not believe that Jesus Christ is God. You cannot know, though, your beginning without believing, knowing, and obeying Jesus Christ. Further, "in the beginning" was (is) the Holy Spirit. Genesis 1:2 says that the Spirit of God was hovering over the waters. We cannot know our Father without knowing His Spirit. We must acknowledge the existence of the Holy Spirit and obey His voice because He is our Counsellor and Teacher.

Creation of Men

In Genesis 1 we read that God first created the heavens and the earth. Then He created the light and separated the waters. And then He created the plants and animals. After the world was ready, God then made man. God gave all these things to the hand of man and told him to rule over them. God prepared the world for man like soon-to-be parents prepare their house for the arrival of their newborn child, including the baby's room, clothes, and bed. Everything is ready when the child is born. Genesis 2 teaches us about the creation of Man (Adam):

> *The Lord God formed the man from the dust of the ground and breathed into his nostrils the breath of life and man became a living being.*
>
> *(Genesis 2:7)*

> *Then the Lord God said, "It is not good for the man to be alone. I will make a helper suitable for him." . . . So the Lord caused the man to fall into a deep sleep; and while he was sleeping; he took one of the man's ribs and closed up the place with flesh. Then the Lord God made a woman from the rib he had taken out of the man, and he brought her to the man.*
>
> *(Genesis 2:18-22)*

Man has always been looking for his origin. Just how did he come into the world? Just what is a human being?

Firstly, human beings are created in the image of God. God created man in His own image. The evolutionists tell us that we are the advanced form of an intelligent kind of monkey. They tell us that we came from monkeys and that our forefathers were monkeys. This is wrong because God made us in His own image.

We just learned that God breathed His breath into man. “Breath” in Hebrew is *neshamah* which means “energy,” “wind,” or “spirit.” So you are made in a special way. God is the biggest artist and you are a very beautiful work of art by God. God enjoys when He sees you because He loves you the way you are. You are a unique person with a unique body. No one is like you in the entire world. This is very pleasant in the eyes of God.

Secondly, because of man’s likeness with God, the human being is a Moral Being. Every man and woman knows what is right and what is wrong—what is good and bad. Even the non-believer knows these things because man is made in the image of God. I believe that even in the heart of a criminal, there is something good hidden within—that which is from God.

Thirdly, the human being is a Rational Being because God is also rational. Our God is a creator and so is man. Look at our world now. Human beings have achieved tremendous technological, scientific, and artistic goals: man flies, man discovers, man makes things. All these happen because man is made in the image of God.

Fourthly, the human being is an Eternal Being because God is eternal. After the fall of man sin came to this world and man became mortal. Nevertheless, man is created as an eternal being. The Bible says that after death there are two kinds of life. There is eternal peaceful life in heaven and there is eternal life which is filled with gnashing of teeth, condemnation, and punishment in hell. Those who believe and obey God the Father, Jesus Christ, and the Holy Spirit, will forever live in eternal peace and joy. But those who do not believe in the Father, Son, and Holy Spirit will forever be tormented in hell. Jesus said:

> *I am the resurrection and the life. He who believes in me will live, even though he dies; and whoever lives and believes in me will never die.*
>
> *(John 11:25-26)*

Lastly, the human being is an Authoritative Being with a Free Will. God created this world and told Adam to rule over it. He also gave him free will. If God did not give us free will then we would be like robots. He gave us free will so we could choose Him or not choose Him. It is up to us whether we accept Him or not. See how patient our God is. But we have abused our free will and our authority because we ignore God and His teachings and His commandments by rejecting Jesus Christ as our Saviour. We abuse our authority and our free will because we mess up our world. That is why we have wars and environmental destructions and the like.

Let There Be . . .

In Genesis God said, "Let there be . . ." and the ensuing thing was formed just as God wanted it to be. Yes, this means that our God is able. Through His Word, Jesus Christ, and the Holy Spirit, He is able to do exceedingly and abundantly above all that we ask or think, according to the power that works in us (Eph. 3:20).

Nothing is impossible with God. When you have a problem in your life; when you think that there is no hope in your future; you must change something. You must change your paradigm about God. You must come back to your Creator (God the Father, God the Son, and God the Holy Spirit), and that Creator will say, "Let there be. . ." That is the solution for your life. Our God is able! In times of trouble, come to your Creator.

> *Call to me and I will answer you, and show you great and mighty things, which you do not know.*
>
> (Jeremiah 33:3)

MAIN SCRIPTURES
Genesis 1–2

REFERENCE SCRIPTURES
Jeremiah 33:3
John 1:1-3; 8:58; 11:25-26

TO MEMORIZE AND MEDITATE UPON
Jeremiah 32:27

I AM THE LORD, THE GOD OF ALL MANKIND. IS THERE ANYTHING TOO HARD FOR ME TO DO?

QUESTIONS:

1. Explain why God created Man after He had created all other things?

2. Try to find out some characteristics of God and then relate them to your own character.

NOTES:

LESSON 2
The Fall of Man

Genesis 3–5

INTRODUCTION

In the last lesson we learned about the creation of the world and the first people, Adam and Eve. We also learned that we are made in the image of God. God gave authority to Adam and to us to rule over everything that God created.

In this lesson we are going to study the most tragic event in human history—the beginning of sin and the fall of man. How did these things happen? Why did God allow them to happen? How do they affect us today? These are the leading questions in this lesson.

TODAY'S JOURNEY

In Genesis 3, we read about the first sin that took place in the history of mankind. We read that God put Adam and Eve in a wonderful garden called Eden and He gave them the right to eat from the fruits of any tree they wanted except from the tree in the middle of the garden. God did this because He gave man the freedom to choose. Man could choose to obey Him and not eat from the fruit, or he could choose to disobey Him and eat from the fruit. In short, God gave man the free will to choose between obeying and disobeying Him.

Obeying or Disobeying God

By establishing the rule of not eating the fruit of the tree in the middle of the garden, God gave man a choice. But He also told Adam what the result would be for eating from the tree. The woman said to the serpent, "We may eat from all the trees in the garden, but God did say 'You must not eat from the tree that is in the middle of the garden, and you must not touch it, or you will die (Gen. 3:2-3).

The same thing happens in our world today because God gives us the chance to choose. Shall we choose for love or for hate? Shall we choose for war or for peace? Most of the time wrong things happen in the world because people make the wrong choices. Most of the things that happen in the world are the result of human choices. For example, God never created people for hating each other; on the contrary, He created them for love. So when people beat each other up and hate each other, it is because of people, not God. This is mainly because of man's choices. God never made this world for miseries and problems. God never meant to give us trouble; the only trouble is man himself.

Right now, God is again putting us in a place to choose whether to obey Him and believe in His Son Jesus Christ, or to reject Him and live according to our own rules and regulations. It is a choice that every human being must make. Either believe in Jesus or reject Him and live a life according to one's own will.

Jesus said:

> *Everyone who listens to the Father and learns from him comes to me. No one has seen the Father except the one who is from God; only he has seen the Father. I tell you the truth he who believes has everlasting life.*
>
> *(John 6:45-47)*

The will of God is for us to have eternal life, and that comes only through His Son Jesus Christ. The will of God is for us to live a holy life:

> *Therefore, I urge you, brothers, in view of God's mercy, to offer your bodies as living sacrifices, holy and pleasing to God – this is your spiritual act of worship. Do not conform any longer to the patterns of this world, but be transformed by the renewing of your mind. Then you will be able to test and approve what God's will is – His good, pleasing and perfect will.*
>
> *(Romans 12:1-2)*

In Genesis 3:3 God said to Adam, "Do not eat from the fruit." And in Romans 12:1-3 God says to us, "Do not be conformed to the patterns of this world." These two are the same. The patterns of this world are many: dishonesty, hate, lies, orgies, drunkenness, drugs, gossip, fighting, sexual immorality, and many other things. Have nothing to do with these things. Do not even touch them. In Genesis 3:3, God said, "Do not touch the tree.".

Do Not Touch

God does not want us to even touch or come near the patterns of the world. Never forget that touch is the beginning of temptation; temptation is the beginning of sin; and sin is the start of fall and death. So if you do not want to fall like Adam and Eve, and you do not want sin in your life, stop touching, meeting, or having things in your life that cause you to sin and fall. Let me give you an example: God said that we should avoid getting drunk. God hates it. So if you have friends around you who are drinking too much alcohol and you are going with them, then you are actually in touch with them. Sooner or later they will also cause you to get drunk and sin. God said, "Do not be involved in sexually immoral activities." Nowadays, many things happen that are not according to the will of God: man sleeps with man; woman lies with woman; mothers physically and emotionally abuse their children; fathers sexually abuse daughters. Do you know why? One of the reasons is television. Television is filled with junk and dirty things that people watch. Worse than that, people get crazy and pass it on to the young ones. So if you as a Christian have some TV stations in your house that show any form of immorality and you watch them, then you are in touch with these things. Therefore, before these things tempt you, get away from the things shown on TV. Avoid anything that brings temptation. Do not go even near it.

The Temptation

As discussed above, touch is the start of temptation. In Genesis 3:4-5, we read that the woman saw that the fruit of the tree was good for food, was pleasing to the eye, and was desirable for gaining wisdom.

"The woman saw first." This means that she was near the tree. Symbolically this can be the touch. After the "touch" she saw that the tree was good for many things. She got three kinds of temptation:

1. Good for food
2. Pleasing to the eyes
3. Desirable for gaining wisdom

1. Good for food is one of the biggest temptations that man can receive. Because of food, people kill each other and destroy each other. In our life we can apply "food" not only to food, but also to money, possessions, and wealth. Do not let these things tempt you. Don't be blind to the will of God.

In Matthew 4:1-11, Jesus received the same temptation. The serpent tempted Him to change the stones into bread so that Jesus would commit a sin. But Jesus rebuked Satan by quoting the scriptures and saying, "Man shall not live by bread alone but by every word of God."

2. *Pleasing to the eyes* is the second temptation that Eve received. She saw that the fruits were very pleasing to the eyes. We can apply the same things to our daily lives. There are many things that are pleasing to the eyes but are dangerous. Sex can seem pleasing to your eyes, but it is equally dangerous when misused. Money seems pleasing to the eyes but it is also dangerous. Pleasure seems good for the eyes but it can destroy your life. The beautiful cigarette advertisements can be very enticing. They are packaged in beautiful boxes with eye-catching colors so that even if you are not a smoker you will be tempted. But when you start smoking it will be very difficult to stop.

The devil knows that one of the weak points of human beings is the area of "pleased eyes." That is why with television there are so many advertisements for products that seem so pleasing, but actually they are dangerous for us, especially for our children.

Proverbs 5:2-5:

> *The lips of an adulteress drip honey, and her speech is smoother than oil, but in the end she is bitter as gall, sharp as a double-edged sword. Her feet go down to death; her steps lead straight to the grave.*

3. *Desire for wisdom* is another big temptation that man can receive like Eve did.

The Human Being has always had the desire to know more. There is nothing wrong with that. But if we try to put our knowledge higher than God's wisdom then we are headed toward destruction. God has given us knowledge to glorify Him, not to deny Him. Because of so much technology, science, and wisdom, man ignores the existence of God. Man says there is no God and that the human being is God. This is a very foolish thought. And for this reason, God will destroy all the wisdom of the wise and confuse the philosophers of the world who claim that there is no God (see 1 Corinthians 1:1-26).

The Sin and the Fall

With the temptation in Genesis 3:3, the woman took the fruit and ate it. She committed sin and tempted Adam to do the same. He took a bite, and together with Eve, they disobeyed God. Eve could have avoided this sin from the beginning by refusing to go near the tree. Even at the second level she could have stopped the process. But no, she was blinded because of the three above mentioned temptations, and thus, she sinned. So as I said before, let us live a holy life and avoid any unholy touch and temptations by using our own strong will and relying upon the help of the Holy Spirit. If you see something around you that is tempting you, throw it away before you fall.

Then we read in Genesis that God became angry with both Adam and Eve and He judged them. And we read in Genesis 3:8-12 that God asked three major questions from Adam:

Where are you? (3:9)
Who told you that you are naked? (3:11)
Have you eaten . . . ? What have you done? (3:11)

God is going to ask every sinner these three questions. He wants to hear their answers from their very own mouths. Those who believe in Jesus Christ will be forgiven, but those who do not, will not be forgiven. God is asking the human being, “Where are you?” We are in the middle of a miserable world that is filled with hatred and war. The human being has messed up this world because of his own sinful activities. God also asks us, “Where are you?” Are we in Jesus Christ or are we in the world? Have you ever asked yourself these questions?

Further, God will ask them, "Who told you to sin?" Or, "Why did you listen to others?" My brothers and sisters, temptation always comes through someone or something. For Eve, it came from the serpent; for Adam it came by Eve. Maybe for you it can enter through your friends or through the TV or any other thing. Avoid these things.

Lastly, God will ask the sinners, "Did you commit a sin? What have you done?" This means that God gave them so many chances to come back to Him and they disobeyed Him.

After Adam and Eve sinned, God was grieved. God rejected them from the garden and cast them out. God cursed them both and He cursed their children and everything on earth. So by the fall of Adam and Eve the curse of God entered the world, and until now, our world and people are cursed. The only way to break the curse is to believe in Jesus Christ and obey Him.

> *Christ redeemed us from the curse of the law by becoming a curse for us.*
>
> *(Proverbs 5:2-5)*

After the fall we read that Adam and Eve begot children: Abel and Cain. In Genesis 4 we read the story of Abel and Cain and how Cain sinned by killing his brother. In this chapter, we read that Abel was a flock-keeper and his brother Cain was a farmer. Furthermore, we read that Abel gave the best of his property to God as a sacrifice: the first born of his flock. God was very pleased with this.

God wants us to give the best of what we have to Him. These are our tithes and offerings. God wants us to pay one tenth of our income to the temple where we worship Him for this will please God and He will bless us abundantly.

In Malachi 3:8-10, God says to the people:

> *Will a man rob God? Yet you rob me. "But how do we rob you?" In tithes and offerings. You are under a curse – the whole nation of you - because you are robbing me. Bring the whole tithe in the storehouse, that there may be food in my house. "Test me in this," says the Lord Almighty. "And see if I will not throw open the floodgates of heaven and pour out so much blessing that you will not have room enough for it."*

Cain was one of these people. He did not give his best for God. God was not pleased with this so He gave favour to Abel and not to Cain. That is why God did not bless the work of Cain's hands, but, instead, He blessed Abel. Abel gave his best for his God.

Dear friends, give to God and become like Abel. When you do this, God will bless you so much that you will not have enough space for the blessing. Even if you have very little, give it to God. When God sees this He will change your little possessions into big blessings.

Because God accepted Abel more than Cain, Cain became jealous and killed his brother. And for the first time in the history of the human race, the blood of an innocent man was shed on earth. This was the beginning of all the wars, all the anger, and all the hate.

Further, we read that Cain killed his brother. God gave us life, and it is God's choice as to when He will take it away from us. Those who kill others will be judged by God unless they repent and become born again by believing in the death and resurrection of Jesus Christ. Otherwise they will be judged and thrown into eternal condemnation in hell. That is why a person must not:

Commit suicide
Kill others
Abort unborn children

MAIN SCRIPTURES
Genesis 3–4

REFERENCE SCRIPTURES
Proverbs 5:2-5
Malachi 3:8-10
John 6:45-47
Romans12:1-2
Galatians 3:13

TO MEMORIZE AND MEDITATE UPON
Romans 12:1-2

THEREFORE, I URGE YOU, BROTHERS, IN VIEW OF GOD'S MERCY, TO OFFER YOUR BODIES AS LIVING SACRIFICES, HOLY AND PLEASING TO GOD- THIS IS YOUR SPIRITUAL ACT OF WORSHIP. DO NOT CONFORM ANY LONGER TO THE PATTERNS OF THIS WORLD, BUT BE TRANSFORMED BY THE RENEWING OF YOUR MIND. THEN YOU WILL BE ABLE TO TEST AND APPROVE WHAT GOD'S WILL IS- HIS GOOD, PLEASING AND PERFECT WILL.

QUESTIONS:

1. In Matthew 4:1-11, we read about the temptation of Jesus Christ. Compare this with the temptation of Eve. What similarities do you find there? Mention at least two.

2. Why is abortion against the will of God? Explain.

NOTES:

LESSON 3
Noah and the Flood

Genesis 6–9

INTRODUCTION

In the previous lesson we learned about the fall of man and the first sin that took place in the history of the human race. We also learned why God placed the tree of knowledge in the Garden of Eden and why He allowed the fall to take place. Furthermore, we studied the ways in which the devil tempts us to fall.

In this lesson, we are going to study about God's grief and His mercy to human beings. We see this in the Great Flood that destroyed every living thing on the face of the earth except for Noah and his family. God used Noah for the beginning of His plan with mankind. And most importantly, we are going to study the relationship of this lesson with Jesus Christ and its implication for our daily lives.

TODAY'S JOURNEY

Genesis 6 teaches us that after the fall men began to increase in number on earth. We also read that man became more wicked than ever before. Of course, everything started with one person who sinned—Eve. This sin was committed by Adam and it was passed on to the children of Adam and to the children of his children until our time today.

The Wickedness of Man

When God saw that man became wicked and evil, He became very sorry that He created man! But what is the wickedness of man in the eyes of God? In Genesis 6, three major things are mentioned about the wickedness of man:

1. *The evil thoughts and desires of the heart (6:5)*
2. *The corrupted ways of life (6:11)*
3. *The violence (6:11)*

1. The evil thoughts and desires of the heart was one of the reasons why God wanted to destroy the world. Actually, all evil starts with the heart. It is in the heart that a person decides to destroy another; it is in the heart that sin develops. Many people can praise and worship God, but if their hearts are not with God and they are filled with evil and hate, then God is not pleased at all.

In our day, there are many people who have evil desires and thoughts. That is why we have things such as pornography, murder, child abuse, and wars. All these things originate from the heart.

In Noah's time, men had evil desires and thoughts. Neighbors could not trust their neighbors. Friends could not trust their friends. Fathers could not trust their sons. All this happened because people had evil hearts

.

These things are happening right now in our world, and much worse is sure to come. For this reason keep your mind fresh with the Word of God; renew your mind with the Holy Bible (Romans 12:2); have good desires for others—both to your friends and to your enemies. Jesus Christ told us that we must bless those who curse us (Luke 6:28).

2. The corrupted ways of life was another important factor that made God very angry. As a result, He sent the Great Flood to destroy mankind. What can be understood by "the corrupted ways of life"? The best answer is found in Romans 1:18-32. In this passage we can find what "the corrupted ways of life" means.

It means:

Idol worship in place of God's glory (1:23)
Sexual impurity: homosexuality, lesbianism, and bestiality (1:24, 26)
Exchanging God's truth for lies (1:25)

These illicit and perverted activities, which took place in the time of Noah, are also happening in our world today. Nowadays, many people are worshipping idols and many different things in the place of God the Father. In our time, idols do not exist in the form of stones. They come in the form of other things such as money, fame, jobs, other people, and so on. Even in the Christian faith, some people worship certain idols more than the Word of God and the Lord Jesus Christ Himself.

Sexual impurity is increasing day by day. Fifty years ago it was not possible to talk about sex on TV in Europe. But nowadays it is very common for primetime television programs to show illicit sex and pornography. Unfortunately, our children are exposed to these things.

Homosexuality is rising. Man is with man; woman is with woman. Today sex with animals is becoming more accepted. The world we live in today parallels the world of Noah's time. Even children are the victims of sexual impurities.

Exchanging God's truth for lies is another characteristic of our modern society. By rejecting God's truth man starts to believe in things that are made by man. Evolution is one of these things. Also, with the coming of the New Age Movement and many eastern religions, our youth are being deceived.

But what then is the truth?

The only truth is Jesus Christ. No man can know the truth if he does not know and believe in Jesus Christ (John 1:17).

Jesus said:

> *I AM THE WAY, THE TRUTH AND THE LIFE. NO ONE COMES TO THE FATHER EXCEPT THROUGH ME.*
>
> (John 14:6-7)

3. The violence of man is another category of wickedness that aroused God's anger and led Him to destroy the earth. What can violence mean in this case? Violence can mean different things. It can mean the rebellion of children against their parents (Rom. 1:30), or killing and destroying. It means fighting.

Again, all these things are happening in our world today. We are seeing things unseen in the past two thousand years. We have experienced two world wars as in the twentieth century. There are racial wars in Africa and Asia and mass-killings of children and elderly people like never before. We now possess the most advanced weapons that can kill many innocent people in the world. With the rise of terrorism it seems as if our world is getting worse and worse.

Violence means individuals who harm each other. In many families women are beaten by their husbands or husbands are beaten by their wives. We are now witnessing that even a small kids can commit murder.

All these atrocities happened in the time of Noah, and I believe that even worse things are happening now. Because the time of Noah was so terrible, God decided to destroy the earth and everything in it.

God Decided to Destroy the Earth

When God saw that the wickedness of men was increasing day by day and had reached the highest level, He was tremendously grieved (Gen. 6:5). God decided to wipe mankind from the face of the earth, and every animal, every plant, and every other living thing were destroyed.

However, in the midst of all these wicked people in the world there was only one man who was blameless and righteous—NOAH.

God only wanted to save Noah and his family. God commanded Noah to build an ark because He was going to open the gates of heaven and let the waters stream on the earth to destroy every living creature. God said:

> *I am surely going to destroy both them and the earth. So make yourself [Noah] an ark of cypress wood; make rooms in it and coat it with pitch inside and out. . . .*
>
> *(Genesis 6:13-14)*

Noah obeyed God and started to build an ark, following the exact description given to him by God. What can we learn from Noah?

Noah:

Lived righteously (6:9)
Walked with God (6:9)
Obeyed God (6:22)

The righteousness of Noah meant that he was a just man. In the Hebrew language "righteous" is called *tsaddiyq*. This word means "someone who has a clear self, a lawful person who knows what is right and what is wrong in his life."

Are you righteous too? Do you know how to be righteous in our age and time? The Bible says that the righteous man believes in the

Lord Jesus Christ and puts his faith in God and not on other things (Rom. 1:17).

Righteousness comes through Jesus Christ. Those who believe and put their faith in Him and follow His teachings can be called "righteous."

Noah lived according to the faith and love of God the Father. Righteousness is the opposite of having evil thoughts of the heart.

> *So whatever you eat or drink, whatever you do, do it for the glory of God.*
>
> *(1 Corinthians 10:31)*

To walk with God means to live a life according to God's planning and will. This means that in your heart, at home, at your work, in your business, and in raising your children, you should consider God first. To walk with God means to live with Jesus Christ. He is the way and the truth.

Many people do not walk with God. In fact, to walk with God is exactly the opposite living a corrupt life.

Noah obeyed what God commanded him to do. God told him to make a big ark. Building an ark is not an easy job. These days you would need a factory to build an ark. Noah could have said, "How can I find wood?" "How can I build the ark?" Or, "What will the people think about me?" But Noah did not look at the circumstances; rather, he looked at God and His planning. He obeyed God.

We must obey God's requests. God can ask us many things that may seem ridiculous to the eyes of others; nevertheless, we must obey Him.

God destroyed the earth and saved only Noah and his family (Gen. 7). When Noah was finished building the ark, God opened the gates of water and destroyed all the inhabitants on the earth except Noah, his family, and every pair of animals on the ark. After everything was destroyed, God stopped the rain and provided a land for Noah and his family. The flood lasted for forty days. Every living thing perished and was destroyed.

After several weeks God said to Noah, "Come out from the ark with your family and the animals" (Gen. 8:15). Noah obeyed God. After that, the children of Noah started to multiply and God built the nations upon Noah, his children, and his grandchildren.

The first thing Noah did after the flood was build an altar to worship God (Gen. 8:20). Nowadays we do everything except build an altar for the Lord. In our age, the New Testament Age, God does not need altars made by the hands of man anymore, but He needs the altar of our heart, a heart that worships God in Spirit (John 4:23).

Whatever you do in your life, do it with prayer and thanksgiving to the Lord: God the Father, God the Son and God the Holy Spirit.

After the flood was finished, God made a covenant with Noah that He would never destroy earth by water again, and He gave Noah and his descendants the authority to rule over everything on the earth (Gen. 9:11).

SUMMARY

In this lesson we learned about the wickedness of men, the story of Noah and his ark, and how can we apply the principles in these accounts to our daily lives in our time today. As I told you, our world is getting more terrible. Wickedness, violence, and corruption are rising day by day. Jesus Christ said a time was coming when men would deceive men, when nations would fight against nations, and when Christians would be persecuted. All these are signs of His return (see Mark 13). But He also said that wickedness will grow simultaneously with righteousness. While wickedness increases, righteous men and women will also rise up. So both bad and good will increase at the same time.

In Genesis 7:17-19, God sent the waters and they continued to pour upon the earth non-stop while the ark of Noah stayed afloat on the great water. As the water poured greatly, the ark continued to lay over it. This has symbolic meaning for us. Water symbolizes the wickedness of man that is growing. The ark can mean the church of Jesus Christ. This means that wickedness and evil are under the feet of the church of Christ just like the waters and all the wicked and dead things were under Noah's ark.

Yes, Jesus Christ has given us the authority to step upon scorpions and snakes. He has also given us the power to shake the principalities and the powers of this age.

As Jesus said, while the world is enslaved to wickedness and happy in sin, drinking and eating with no regard of God, He will return like a thief in the night.

In Matthew 24:36-39, Jesus said:

> *No one knows the day or hour, not even angels in heaven, nor the Son, but only the Father. As it was in the days of Noah, so it will be at the coming of the Son of Man. For in the days before the flood, people were eating and drinking, marrying and giving in marriage, up to the day Noah entered the ark, and they knew nothing about what would happen until the flood came and took them all away.*

The ark symbolizes the Body of Christ. The Body of Christ consists of those who have chosen seriously for Christ Jesus and are on the spiritual ark of Jesus Christ. Those who believe in Christ will not perish but will live eternally. If you want to live according to the will of God, live like Noah lived; walk with Jesus Christ until the last days of your life; try to win souls for Christ until Jesus returns.

MAIN SCRIPTURES
Genesis 6–9

REFERENCE SCRIPTURES
Matthew 24:37-39
Luke 6:28
Mark 13
John 1:17; 4:23; 14:6-7
Romans 1:17, 32
1 Corinthians 10:31

TO MEMORIZE AND MEDITATE UPON
1 Corinthians 10:31

SO WHATEVER YOU EAT OR DRINK, WHATEVER YOU DO, DO IT FOR THE GLORY OF GOD.

QUESTIONS:

1. Why do you think God saved Noah and his family?

2. What is the relationship between Noah's Ark and the church of Jesus Christ?

3. Evaluate your own life with the life of Noah. What similarities and differences do you have with the life of Noah?

NOTES:

NOTES:

LESSON 4

The Nations and The Tower of Babel

Genesis 10–11

INTRODUCTION

Last lesson we learned about the wrath of God against mankind and how He destroyed the world and everything in it with water. Among all these people, God only saw Noah as righteous; He saved him and his family through the ark that Noah made.

In Genesis 9, we read that God made a covenant with Noah in which He promised that never again would He destroy the world by water. We read that God's grace came upon His children.

In this lesson we are going to learn about the sons of Noah and the beginning of different nations and languages. We are also going to study how mankind failed again and sinned.

TODAY'S JOURNEY

Genesis 7 teaches us that Noah had three sons, Shem, Ham, and Japheth. We also learned in the last lesson that the sons of Noah also entered the ark and came out safely when the flood was finished.

When Noah and his sons and their families came out of the ark, the first thing Noah did was build an altar for the Lord. He worshipped God and sacrificed offerings to God. When God saw this and smelled the aroma of the offerings, He decided to never again curse the land even though He knew that every inclination of a man's heart was evil. He will never destroy all living creatures by water again (Gen. 8:20-21).

God knew that even Noah and his children were sinners and their hearts were not pure. Every inclination of their hearts was evil, even from their childhood.

Sons of Noah

Shem, Ham and Japheth were the three sons of Noah. In Genesis 9:18-28 we read about the story of Noah when he became drunk and lie uncovered inside his tent. Ham, his son, saw his nakedness and told his other brothers. Because of this Noah cursed Ham and his children. This was the first time that a human being cursed a fellow human being. Noah blessed Shem and Japheth because they covered the nakedness of their father and turned their faces back when they saw their father's nakedness.

The Bible says that these three sons begat children who were scattered over the earth (Gen. 9:19). All the different nationalities and races that exist today are the descendants of the three sons of Noah. In Genesis 10, you can read the names and the list of the descendants of Noah and his children.

Japheth's descendants were Gomer, Magog, Madar, Javan, Tubal, Mescheck and Tiras. You can read about the children of these descendants in Genesis 10:2-5.

The Bible says that these people spread from the coastland and made their own countries. Some scholars think that the European people are the descendants of Japheth.

Ham's descendants were Cush, Egypt, Put, and Canaan. Cities like Babylon, Erech, Accad and Calneh in Shinhar, Nineveh, Rehoboth, Sodom, Gomorrah, etc. were built by the descendants of Ham. You can read in Genesis 10:6-20 about the descendants of Ham. Shem's descendants were Elam, Ashur, Arpachshad, Lud, and Aram. And in Genesis 10:21-32, you can read about the nations that were built upon the children of Shem.

In the following table you can see the nations that are mentioned in Genesis 10.

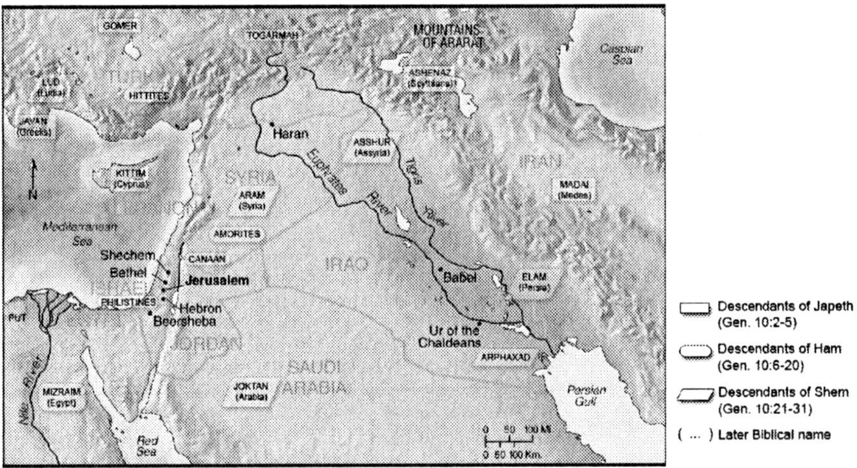

The Nations and the Tower of Babel

We just learned about the different nations that came from Noah's children. Genesis 11 teaches us that after the flood, the whole world had one language with a common vocabulary. As the people moved towards the east they found a plain in Shinhar (Babylonia) and they settled there. The people decided to make a tower that would reach to the heavens so they could make a name for themselves. When God saw this He became angry. He knew that if mankind had one language, they would become united and mess up the world and God's will. He confused the languages so that no one would understand each other. They were so confused that they could not finish the tower. God called this tower "Babel," which means "confusion" (Gen. 11:1-9).

Babel: the Tower of Egoism

In Genesis 11:3, men said to each other: "Let us make bricks and bake them thoroughly . . . and let us build ourselves a city."

By nature, man is egoistic. The word "ego" is a Greek word for self. An egoistic person is a person who puts himself above everything and does not look at the interests of others. An egoistic person talks only about himself, cares only for himself, and takes every advantage for his own advantage.

Genesis 11:3-4 shows us the ego of man. Man wants to be higher than God. In the story, they built the tower with wrong motivations. There was actually nothing wrong with the building of a tower; what was wrong was their selfish motivation, the egoistic motivation. Generally there are two kinds of Egoism:

-Ego towards other people
-Ego towards God

Egoism towards others means that a person does not look and pay attention to his fellow human beings. We are living in a time in which this kind of egoism grows day by day. Everything that man does is so mixed up with his personal interests that we can see the difference between a self-centered man and the opposite. For example, imagine two people who love each other and decide to marry. There are two things that can possibly happen: (a) the couple truly love each other from the deepest of their hearts and persevere in times of difficulties and crises, or (b) one or both of them are lovers because of their personal motivations and egoistic motivations. "I love the person, because she gives me good feelings," says the man.

But what if she does not give you good feelings after a while? Will you still love the person? For many the answer is, no. That is why so many families break up and 25% to 30% of marriages end up in divorce.

The human being is egoistic; he is self-centered. Look at the situation in the world today; people kill and destroy and build and create because of their own interests and not for the interests of others.

Egoism towards God is even worse than the previous case. Because this kind of egoism does not consider God as the Sovereign Lord of the entire world and it does not consider that everything in it belongs to God. Nowadays, human beings have reached a level where they even ignore the existence of God. They believe that they themselves are gods. Whatever man does should be based upon God. But no! Man went far from God and pursued his own interests and left Him behind. Whatever we do, we do not consider Him as the Lord. Man does whatever pleases him regardless of the consequences.

The actual building of the tower of Babel was not the main issue. The main issue was that man had the wrong motivation to build it. Imagine if they built the tower for God and His glory; God would never have been angry with them. God would never have confused them. But on the contrary, they built the tower for themselves and their own names. The builders of the tower were the foolish builders whom Jesus described in Matthew 7:24-27. "A wise man will build his house on a rock," says Jesus. The builders of the Tower of Babel did not use the stones God gave them. Instead, they used baked bricks made by the hands of man (Gen. 11:3). This is a symbolic teaching for us. Do we build upon the things that are made by man, or do we build upon the rock, the stones that God gave us? These stones are the words and the will of God in our life.

If you are going to do something, first ask these questions: Is this the will of God? Is this according to the Bible? How can this glorify

God? What good will it do to my fellow human beings? Jesus Christ taught us that we must love the Father with all of our hearts and love our neighbours with all our hearts. These two things should both be visible in a Christian.

Babel, the Tower of Competition and Rebellion

In Genesis 11:3 the people said, "Let us build a tower which reaches the heaven." In this case, heaven does not only mean the sky, but it refers to where God is. The Bible says that God is in heaven.

The people wanted to reach a level equal to God's level, and this made God angry. Never forget this point: God is the head of everything in the world. He gives life and takes it away. God always has the last word.

We are living the twenty-first century where technology and science are developing day by day. Man flies, goes into the deepest waters, launches to the moon, makes artificial children and organs, and does other things like that. Because of these achievements, there are desires in some people to reach the level of God, which is impossible. The Bible says in 1 Corinthians 1:19:

> *I will destroy the wisdom of the wise; the intelligence of the intelligent I will frustrate.*

Focus on the word "frustrate." God also confused the people who wanted to build the tower. That is why God called it the Tower Babel, which means confusion.

Human beings wants to make a name for themselves by competing and rebelling against God, and yet the Bible says that every knee will bow before the name of the Lord and every tongue will confess that Jesus is Lord (Rom. 14:11).

Babel, the Tower of Pride

The people decided to build the tower in order to reach heaven. This is an act of pride. Everything that is made with pride will be confused and broken by God. Pride is the beginning of a fall according to Proverbs 16:18.

As Christians, let us not build our lives upon pride. Let us not be proud because of our jobs, positions, families, education, or whatever. When you have pride, whatever you may have now can be taken away from you by God.

Pride can bring you higher and higher but before you reach the last point you will fall. Many families break because of pride. Many churches close down because of pride. Many kings fall because of pride. Consequently, the builders of Babel labored in vain because of their pride.

THE TOWER OF BABEL

SUMMARY

This section teaches us not to be egoistic and selfish towards other people and God. We learned that we should base our life upon the Lord's will and God's Word, which comes through Jesus Christ. We learned that we should not compete and rebel against God. Rather, we should acknowledge Him as the Sovereign Lord of everything including our projects and plans.

Further, we learned that we should not be proud because pride will lead us to fall and confusion.

Now what are your towers that you want to build in your life? A tower can be your business, your family, or your job. It can be your ambition and all your projects. The best way to manage the "tower" is the following:

It must be based upon the Word of God through Jesus Christ

It must be for the good of other people

It must be without any pride

It must be for the glory of God

If you use these techniques you will be successful to accomplish the goals of your life and God will bless you in building your "tower."

MAIN SCRIPTURES
Genesis 10–11

REFERENCE SCRIPTURES
Proverbs 16:18
Matthew 7:24-27
Romans 14:11
1 Corinthians 1:19

TO MEMORIZE AND MEDITATE UPON
Proverbs 16:18

PRIDE GOES BEFORE DESTRUCTION, A HAUGHTY SPIRIT BEFORE A FALL.

QUESTIONS:

1. Compare the tree of temptation in the Garden of Eden with the Tower of Babel. What similarities do you find?

2. What are the differences between the builders of the Tower of Babel and Adam and Eve when they were still in Paradise?

NOTES:

LESSON 5
Abraham

Genesis 12–25

INTRODUCTION

Abraham is one of the most important figures in both the Old and the New Testament. Outside of Genesis, his name is mentioned 115 times in the Bible.

Sometimes Abraham is regarded as the Father of Faith; some call him the Father of Nations.

Last lesson we learned about the nations of the world in general; we also learned that these nations were the descendants of the three sons of Noah. Genesis 11 teaches us that Abraham was the descendant of one of Noah's sons, Shem. The father of Abraham was Terah. In the beginning Abraham's name was Abram, which means, "exalted father." But later, God changed his name to Abraham, which means, "the father of many." God loved Abraham because of his faithfulness and obedience. Romans 4:3 says that Abraham believed God, and it was credited to him as righteousness. This means that Abraham did not receive God's credit of righteousness and love because of his deeds. Instead he received it because of his faith in God, for he was also a man of mistakes. Abraham lived 175 years. His two sons were Ishmael (from Hagar) and Isaac (from Sarah) (see Gen. 25).

The nation of Israel came from Isaac's side, not Ishmael's. This is because the mother of Ishmael, Hagar, was an Egyptian (Gen. 16:1).

Abraham married Hagar, the maidservant of Sarah, because Sarah could not conceive.
The life of Abraham was filled with adventures. First, he left his birthplace, then his father's family, and then his only relative, Lot. He saw many dangerous situations like wars and the destruction of Sodom and Gomorrah.

In this lesson we are not going to study the historical aspects of Abraham's life, but we will mostly examine the spiritual part as an example for ourselves as Christians.

TODAY'S JOURNEY

God calls Abraham (Abram) Genesis 12

Abraham's name was Abram when God called him. God called Abram and told him that he must leave his father's family and go to the land He would show him (12:1). During that time, Abraham had built his own family already. He had his own household. He was married to Sarai who later changed her name to Sarah.

It would be very difficult for them to leave their own households and go to an unknown land. How much more difficult was it for Abraham to leave his household and listen to the voice of God?

Like Abraham, every person has a call in his or her life and that call is the call of God. God is constantly calling us for His purposes. God has a perfect plan for our lives, the same way He had a beautiful plan for Abram. God told Abram that if he obeyed His call, He would make him into a great nation and he would be blessed. God would bless those who bless him and all the people of the world would be blessed through him.

This is a wonderful plan of God. God promised to Abram:
a) A great nation

b) A great name

c) Blessings for others

Are these three things that we want in our lives? At the end of our lives, will people talk about how much we were a blessing for others and how we had made a great name as a righteous person? Hebrew 6:13 says God wants to give you the same blessings that He promised to Abraham and to all those who believed in Christ.

Perhaps you want to be a great nation yourself. This starts with your family. Nowadays, our world is filled with broken families. Either the father is on drugs or the mother is battered. The children are on the streets with guns and the parents are divorced. This is not the plan of God for our lives. God wants to make a great family from His children. Whoever believes in Him will be blessed including his children and the children of his children. He will be blessed in health, in love, in finances, by having a good job, by obtaining a good education, by a good marriage life, and so on and so forth. God is calling His people now to come to Him and return to Him. We cannot receive this blessing of a great family through our own activities and plans. The only secure way to do it is to hear the calling of God like Abraham did.

Having a great name was another promise that God gave to Abraham, but God also gives a great name to those who believe Him. Many people die everyday but what remains in this world are their names. Some people die with a bad name which stays as a negative memory in the hearts of men. Take Adolph Hitler as an example. Whoever hears his name instantly thinks about the horrible things he did. No one considers him a good person. So what do you want? Do you want a name that brings smiles and love to the hearts of many people even in the next generations? You cannot achieve these things by your own power; the best thing is to hear the calling of God in your life. This is the first step to receive this blessing.

Another blessing that God gave Abram was that he would be a blessing for others. Is this not something you would want? Through you do you want many people to be blessed and get help from God? If a person has never been a blessing for others then there is a problem with that person. You can be a blessing for someone. If you want this then you must hear and obey the voice of God.

How can we hear the call of God? The call of God can only be heard through the Holy Spirit. God has a specific calling and a specific blessing for every person. This can only be heard, though, through the Holy Spirit. And the Holy Spirit can only be heard by believing Jesus Christ and following Him. If you want to hear the call of God, the first thing you must do is come to Jesus Christ. He is the key to hearing the calling of God in our lives. God's plan for every man is unique. Let me illustrate it this way: God wants to lead you to a "land" that is filled with blessings. In this "land" the Holy Spirit is your guide. But for this travel you need Jesus Christ as your passport.

If you do not believe in Jesus Christ and do not obey His commands, you have already rejected the call of God.

Jesus says in Revelation 3:20:

> *Here I am! I stand behind the door and knock [He calls you], if any one hears my voice and opens the door, I will come in and eat with him and he with me.*

The words "eat" and "drink" refer to the blessings that God wants to give us. Abram obeyed and left his household together with Sarai, his wife, towards the unknown Promised Land that God would give him. Likewise, we must obey the Word of God because it is the sign on the road leading us towards a blessed life.

To use another illustration, the Father is the Caller, Jesus is the Way, the Holy Spirit is the Leading Partner, and the Word of God is the Traffic Sign on the road of life.

Abram Passed Through Trials

When God called Abram and promised him the blessings mentioned above, Abram was bewildered. It was actually too great for Abram to believe. Sarai, his wife, was a barren woman, thus she could never give birth. The promise of the land of Canaan also seemed impossible. It seemed impossible for Abram because Canaan belonged to the Canaanites (Gen. 12:7). Abram considered himself to be too ordinary compared with the great plan God had intended for him. God told him once that his wife would become pregnant and would give birth to a child; both of them could not believe this 100%. They thought that God was making a joke. Abram even laughed at the promises (Gen. 17:17). But all these promises came true. God never makes jokes with His people. God loves His children. When He promises something, He will make sure that it comes to pass.

> *For no matter how many promises God has made, they are "YES" in Christ. And through him the "AMEN" is spoken.*
> *(2 Corinthians 1:20)*

Perhaps God gave you some promises through dreams, or visions, or prophecies that looked impossible in your eyes. You might even have thought that these promises were not from God. Then you are wrong because God wants to bless you more than you could ever think or imagine, for there is nothing impossible for God. All these things can be done through Jesus Christ.

When God gave His promises to Abram, Abram passed through a lot of trials and temptations; he even made mistakes. Sometimes he would lose his hope, but in the middle of all these things, he persevered and he fixed his eyes on God.

> *When God made his promise to Abraham, since there was no one greater for him to swear by, he swore by himself, saying "I will bless you and give you many descendants."*

> *And so after waiting patiently, Abraham received what was promised.*
>
> *(Hebrews 6:13-15)*

However, God cannot keep His promises if you do not pass the tests. God needs your perseverance. Again it is said:

> *We do not want you to become lazy, but to imitate those who through faith and patience inherit what has been promised.*
>
> *(Hebrews 6:12)*

If you want to see the promises of God come true, you need patience and faith. Abraham was patient. It took him almost a lifetime to see the promise of God come true. He never cursed because of God's seeming tardiness. You might think God has been late, but God is never late. He is always on time.

You might feel insecure and hopeless today. You have the visions and the promises, but it seems the opposite of the promises are happening. Or you might think that God has forgotten His promises. Stop thinking this way because God is a covenant-keeping God; He never forgets what He has promised. Rather, He fulfils it in His time.

For this reason you need faith. According to Hebrews 11:1, faith is being sure of what we hope for and certain of what we do not see. Abraham had faith in God; he never stopped worshipping God. He always put his trust in the Lord and His promises. He went through terrible times; he saw wars and battles. Even his own life was endangered, but he always had faith in God.

What about you? Are you in the middle of a very difficult situation? Are you facing sickness, family problems, and financial brokenness that are destroying your life? Never look at your present situation, but look at the promises God has given you. The end of this is already known. You will receive what God promised you a long time ago. This is faith in action.

God Promotes Abram (Genesis 17)

After many years of perseverance and passing through trials and hard times, God saw that Abram still worshipped and followed Him. Therefore, God decided to promote Abram. God gave Abram a new name, ABRAHAM. Likewise, God gave Sarai the name SARAH, which means, "princess." Abraham means, "the Father of many."

What is the name that God will give you? Or, what name has He already given you? The Bible says that those who believe in Christ are a new creation; the old has gone, and the new has come. So when God touches you and give you His promises, He will give you a new identity. That identity is based upon God's plan for your life. What kind of identity do you have? If you are in Christ, you have Christ as your identity. You must change your attitudes toward your past and focus on your new identity. You are a new person in Christ.

God Tested Abraham (Genesis 21–22)

After God gave Abraham his new identity, God fulfilled His promise. Sarah became pregnant and gave birth to Isaac (see Gen. 21).

When Isaac grew, he became the beloved of his father. God saw how much Abraham loved his son, so He decided to test Abraham to see whether Abraham loved God even more than his son Isaac (Gen. 22).

So God commanded Abraham to sacrifice Isaac as a burnt offering. It was a terrible request from God—that Abraham should kill his only beloved son. But what could he do? God was calling him. He decided to obey God and sacrifice his own son for the glory of God. He brought his son Isaac on a mountain and prepared to kill him. But before he could so God stopped him. God saw how much

Abraham loved Him. God then provided a ram for Abraham so that Abraham could offer it as a sacrifice to God. Isaac's life was spared.

Who is important in your life? The Triune God (the Father, the Son, and the Holy Spirit) should be placed in the most important position in your life. He should be number one. After God blesses you, what are you going to do? Would you still worship Him as best you can? Some people who live in poverty worship and praise God, but as soon as they receive financial blessings from God, they slowly forget Him as their Master and turn to worldly pleasures and desires.

Abraham passed the test. You can pass the tests in your life too. Always be ready to be tested by God and pass those tests.

SUMMARY

Every person has a calling from God and we should respond to it by believing in Jesus Christ. The calling of God has some consequences and blessings when we follow it. God always has big promises as part of His wonderful plan for us. His promises will be fulfilled no matter how impossible they may seem in our eyes. We need faith and patience in this spiritual journey. When we are able to pass the trials, God will give us a new identity in Jesus Christ. "The old has passed, the new has come. . . . "
Furthermore, when God fulfils His promises to us, He will also test us to see whether we fear Him and whether we will still love Him.

God puts big blessings upon your life, do not miss them!

MAIN SCRIPTURES
Genesis 12–25

REFERENCE SCRIPTURES
2 Corinthians 1:20
Galatians 3:14
Hebrews 6:12-13
Revelation 3:20

TO MEMORIZE AND MEDITATE UPON
2 Corinthians 1:20

FOR NO MATTER HOW MANY PROMISES GOD HAS MADE, THEY ARE "YES" IN CHRIST. AND SO THROUGH HIM THE "AMEN" IS SPOKEN.

QUESTIONS:

1. Read Genesis 13—the story of Lot and Abraham. What temptations or trials can you find in this story?

2. Read Genesis 12–25 and find some mistakes that Abraham made in his life. Think about your own life and evaluate your calling from God? What is God's purpose for you?

3. Read the story of Sodom and Gomorrah in Genesis 19. What similarities do you find between the life of Abraham and the Tower of Babel?

NOTES:

NOTES:

LESSON 6
Isaac

Genesis 21–28

INTRODUCTION

Isaac was the son of Abraham and Sarah, whom they received in their old age. Isaac was very precious to Abraham because Isaac was the only son he begot with Sarah.

In this lesson we are going to study the highlights of Isaac's life including his birth, his marriage, and his sons. Isaac was the continuation of God's promise to Abraham.

TODAY'S JOURNEY

The birth of Isaac, the seed of a promise!
The birth of Isaac was a miracle because when Sarah begot Isaac, she was an old lady and barren.
Isaac was the beginning of God's promise to Abraham. Through Isaac a great nation would spring forth. When Isaac was born a new nation was actually born. Because out of Isaac's lineage, Israel would be born.

The birth of Isaac brought tremendous joy to his family, especially to his mother. For this reason he was named Isaac, which means, "he laughs."

When God promised Abraham that he would be the father of many nations, it was quite impossible for him to be what God had called him to be. But God gave him the beginning of the promise—a child, Isaac. Maybe God has given you many promises. Our God is a promise-keeping God. But every promise starts with small beginnings. Every travel begins with a first step. For Abraham it was Isaac; for you it may be something else. If God wants to give you a nation, He will give you a child first. If God wants to give you a bigger gift, He will give you a smaller one first. If God wants to bless you with financial prosperity, He will give you a little money first to see whether you can handle it or not.

Therefore, be faithful with what you receive and always give thanks to God. All big things start with small beginnings.

Later on when Isaac grew, God tested Abraham by asking him to offer Isaac. Abraham obeyed the Lord and was ready to sacrifice his son, but God stopped him just in time. Yes, Abraham was going to sacrifice the key to God's promise, his very precious son. By this obedience, Abraham showed that he was ready to sacrifice his blessing for the sake of God.

Sometimes God tests us to see whether we love God because of the blessings we receive or because He is God. There are many people these days who love God because of the blessings they receive. But what if God does not bless them anymore?

Our love for God must be unconditional.

The Marriage of Isaac

The marriage of Isaac is a miracle from God. In Genesis 24 we read about a wonderful love story. Abraham was very old and was praying for a good wife for Isaac from among his own relatives. At that time they were living in the land of the Canaanites and did not want Isaac to marry one of the Canaanite girls (Gen 24:1-4).

Abraham was not a racist; he only wanted his son to marry one of his own relatives because the Canaanites did not worship the same God he worshiped. For this reason, Abraham commanded his servant to travel back to Abraham's country so he could meet Abraham's relatives and find a wife for Isaac.

So the servant left for the town of Nahor. He asked God to show him a sign to know which woman Isaac should marry. He prayed for this and God answered him. The sign was this: the girl who would voluntarily offer him and his camels water to drink would be the one God intended Isaac to marry. His request from God came true and he met Rebekah. Rebekah was ready to leave her home and marry Isaac. In the same way, Isaac obeyed the will of God and his father by marrying Rebekah.

As I mentioned above, Isaac was the key to God's promise to be a big nation. This marriage was the second biggest step to that promise. But what can we learn from the marriage of Isaac and Rebekah?

In this event four people were involved, namely Abraham, his servant, Isaac, and Rebekah.

Abraham was the one who sent his servant to find a wife for his son, Isaac. Isaac could have disobeyed his father because Canaan also had beautiful girls. He could say, "No father, I want a Canaanite girl." Instead, he obeyed his father. So in the same way, symbolically, God had a plan for his Son, Jesus Christ. Jesus Christ obeyed the will of the Father no matter how hard it was for Him. He was nailed to the cross. He was rejected by all because the will of God needed to be done. We learned before that Adam did not obey God and he failed. But with the coming of Jesus Christ the New Adam was born (Rom 5:12-20).

What would you do in times of decision-making? Would you obey God's will in your life? Will you obey it even in cases like marriage, work, or big decisions? The secret to receive God's promise is to obey His will just like Isaac obeyed his father's will. For this reason God promised Isaac the same blessings He promised his father Abraham.

Furthermore, we have the servant of God who travelled to find a bride for Isaac. He asked God for a sign to find the chosen lady. Likewise, we can see symbolically that God has sent His Holy Spirit to the world to find out who the brides of Jesus are. The Holy Spirit is moving all over the world to see who is open to be a bride of Jesus.

This means sacrifice. Sacrifice is another key to the fulfilment of God's promise. When the servant asked Rebekah for water, she did not refuse to give it to him but also offered to give water to the camels of the servant. Now to give water to one camel is not an easy job, let alone providing water to all ten. Besides, she was not totally ready to do the work since she did not have the proper tools, but still she decided to do it.

In the same way, the Holy Spirit is looking for people who want to sacrifice themselves and their possessions.

Jesus said in Luke 6:30:

> *If someone takes your cloak, do not stop him from taking your tunic. Give to everyone who asks you, and if anyone takes what belongs to you, do not demand it back.*

If Jesus gives this command we should do it to our fellow man, (like Rebekah did to the servant). How much more is this command valid for the Holy Spirit?

Maybe the Holy Spirit is asking something from you today. What are your possessions? Do you want to obey Him regardless of what He may ask? Or would you rather reject Him? The Holy Spirit can ask for your time; He can ask for your availability, your willingness, or even your money and possessions. Are you ready to sacrifice them? Read about the Holy Spirit in John 14:15-31. Believing in Jesus Christ will not make you His bride if you do not obey and do what the Holy Spirit asks you to do. Nowadays, there are many people who refuse the power of the Holy Spirit and reject Him. This is not the way it should be, otherwise the churches will not grow and they will soon lose the anointing and die.

Rebekah symbolically represents you and me, and the church of Jesus Christ around the world. If you want to be blessed it is better for you to obey the Holy Spirit. When you do this, the Holy Spirit is going to bless you, use you, and give you gifts. And through you, your family will be blessed as well. For Rebekah, Abraham sent a lot of gifts such as gold and silver jewelry and clothing. He also gave her family some gifts (Gen 24:52-53). In the same way God wants to bless you if you do what the Holy Spirit is asking you to do today.

Here we learned that God's promise will come to fulfilment only if we believe in Jesus Christ and become His bride by giving the Holy Spirit what He asks from us.

The Children of Isaac and the Power of Prayer

In Genesis 25:19-34, we read about the birth of Isaac's sons, Esau and Jacob. We learned in verse 21 that Rebekah, like Sarah, was also barren. But God listened to Isaac's prayer and He gave them two sons: Esau and Jacob. The Lord said to Rebekah that two nations were in her womb. The oldest son (Esau) and his descendants would serve the youngest one (Jacob) and his descendants. Again, we see that God keeps His promise and His promise endures forever.

In the next lesson we are going to study Esau and Jacob. What we will learn here is that God's blessings and covenant are not only intended for you but also for the generations that will come after

you. This is like how the generations that came after Abraham were blessed by virtue of the promise God gave him. Isaac received and passed the blessings on to Jacob.
On the other hand, we also learned that the devil is busy cursing, and most of the time his curses pass through generations. Abraham's wife, Sarah, was barren. Rebekah had the same sickness. Isaac broke the curse and he begat Esau and Jacob.

Therefore, always break the curses by prayer through the blood of Jesus Christ so that you can receive the blessings.

SUMMARY

In this lesson we learned about the birth of Isaac, his marriage, and the symbols they represent. We also learned how we could apply the faith of Abraham and Isaac in our daily lives. In short, I would like to summarize this lesson in the points listed below.

If you want the promises of God to be fulfilled in you, you should acknowledge the following:

1. Acknowledge that all big promises start with small beginnings.
2. Be satisfied with the small things you receive because they are the keys to the big ones.
3. Be ready to sacrifice what the Holy Spirit is asking you to give.
4. Pray always and break any possible curse that you think may have been transferred to your life. It may come from your mother and father or from your grandparents. You can only break these curses by prayer in Jesus' name and through His blood.

MAIN SCRIPTURES
Genesis 21–28

REFERENCE SCRIPTURES
Luke 6:30
John 14:15-30
Romans 5:12-20

TO MEMORIZE AND MEDITATE UPON
Luke 6:30

IF SOMEONE TAKES YOUR CLOAK, DO NOT STOP HIM FROM TAKING YOUR TUNIC, GIVE TO EVERY ONE WHO ASKS YOU, AND IF ANYONE TAKES WHAT BELONGS TO YOU, DO NOT DEMAND IT BACK.

QUESTIONS:

1. Read the parable of the Ten Virgins in Matthew 25:1-13. Relate this parable to the story of Isaac's marriage.

2. Explain why God usually works from small to big and not vice-versa.

NOTES:

NOTES:

LESSON 7
Jacob

Genesis Chapters 25–36; 49–50

INTRODUCTION

In the last lesson we learned about the life of Isaac. We also learned that God gave him twin sons, Esau and Jacob.

Jacob is one of the most important figures in the Bible. He was chosen by God, but yet he committed many mistakes including rebellion. His life is a lesson for both young and old.

In this lesson, we are going to analyze some important parts of Jacob's life and learn how we can apply them to our spiritual lives.

TODAY'S JOURNEY

A. The Birth of Jacob (Genesis 25:19-27)

Rebekah bore twin sons after twenty long years of being married to Isaac. They were Esau and Jacob. Esau was the first one to come out from her womb. Jacob came next and he held Esau's heel. Because he grabbed his brother's heel, they gave him this name, which means, "the holder of heel." In the original language and custom a person who keeps the heel means somebody who cheats.

Later, we will learn what influence this name had on Jacob's character. Since Esau's skin was covered with hair, he was given this name, which means "hairy."

When the sons were born God promised His blessing to Jacob and not to Esau. This blessing was very important because it was the continuation of Abraham's blessing which came to Isaac and passed to Esau because he was the first born. However, God said Jacob would be the one to receive the Abrahamic blessing and out of him a mighty nation would come. God said that the older would serve the younger, which meant that Jacob would be elevated above Esau. God had a purpose and a plan for this.

B. The Stolen Blessings (Genesis 25:27-34)

The Bible says that when the boys grew Esau became a skilful hunter while Jacob was a quiet man who remained mostly in the tents. One day while Jacob was cooking, Esau came back from hunting and was terribly hungry. He saw Jacob cooking some stew and he asked Jacob to give him some. Jacob, however, used the situation and told Esau to give him his birthright in exchange for the stew. The birthright is very important because through it the first born could inherit God's blessings, and in this case, Esau had the right to receive God's blessings given to their grandfather Abraham. And because Esau was hungry he swore and exchanged his birthright with food (25:33).

So now you can understand why God said Jacob would receive the blessing. God knew the future and Esau's character. Hence the responsibility was given to Jacob, the younger brother.

God is our Creator. He knows who we are. He has counted the hairs on our heads even before He formed us in our mother's womb. Jesus said in Luke 12:7:

> *Indeed, the very hairs of your head are all numbered.*

Nowadays, many people try to be leaders and pastors without God calling them. God knows that these people are neither ready nor are they qualified for these jobs.

By cheating Esau, Jacob inherited the firstborn rights which were the blessings from God to his grandfather Abraham. However, he still needed his own father's blessing.

One day Rebekah heard that Isaac wanted to bless Esau, his beloved son. He loved Esau more than Jacob. But Rebekah loved Jacob, so when she heard it, she and Jacob planned to cheat Isaac.

Genesis 27 tells us that Isaac was old. He could not see properly and he was weak. Rebekah and Jacob took advantage of his weaknesses to steal Jacob's blessings that were intended for Esau. While Esau was out hunting for his father's favorite food, Jacob covered himself with goatskin. He did this because Esau had hairy skin. Isaac would think that Jacob was Esau. Jacob also wore Esau's clothes. When Jacob went to his father's side, Isaac believed that he was Esau. Therefore, Isaac blessed him (see 27:27-29).

Afterwards, Esau knew what had happened but he could not change it anymore. He could not receive any blessing from his father, but only a curse (27:39-40).

C. The Results of Jacob's Mistake

Jacob, who in the beginning was promised the Abrahamic blessing, made a huge mistake. He lost his patience and tried to claim the blessing by his own abilities. He could no longer wait for God to act, thus, he and his mother devised an evil plan to claim what was supposed to be Esau's.

How often do people try to solve their problems by their own efforts to no avail? Indeed, it is better to be humble, patient, and to wait faithfully for God's action.

Of course, God's planning is God's planning. No one can stop it and even our mistakes and our immature actions will never be able to stop the will of God from happening. Everything will pass away but the Word of God will remain the same forevermore.
Jacob did a silly mistake, but because God had spoken to him the blessings. It could not be changed, not even by Jacob's own mistakes. On the other hand, God did not sit quietly because of Jacob's mistakes. The results of Jacob's cheating came back later in his life.

It Started With His Marriage

After cheating his brother he was terribly afraid that Esau would kill him. Because of this Jacob went to Haran where Rebekah's brother lived.

There he met Rachel and fell in-love with her. When he asked for Rachel's hand, her father said that he needed to work for him for seven years before Jacob could marry her. But when seven years had passed, Laban, Rachel's father, cheated Jacob and gave him his oldest daughter Leah, who had "weak eyes." On the night of the wedding, Jacob did not know that he was with Leah. He realized only in the morning that the girl was not Rachel and he became very angry at Laban. Laban suggested that Jacob work for him for another seven years so he could marry Rachel.

Can you see the similarity? Leah could not see well, the same as Isaac who could not see? Can you also see that Leah was the first-born and that is why she should have been married first before Rachel? Esau was the firstborn, like Leah.

Jacob's Children Were the Second Punishment

Jacob also married Bilhah, the servant of Rachel, because Rachel herself could not conceive at that time. Later on, God granted Rachel's prayer and gave her two sons, Joseph and Benjamin. Leah, after giving birth, stopped having children and she let her maidservant marry Jacob.

All in all by these marriages Jacob received 12 sons: Reuben, Simon, Judah, Zebulun, Levi, Issachar, Dan, Gad, Asher, Napthali, Joseph and Benjamin.

These twelve sons represent the twelve tribes of Israel. Judah was the line from which David and Jesus descended.

As his sons grew older, they all rebelled against Jacob. They disobeyed him many times (Gen. 34). Jacob loved Joseph the most. That is why his sons became very jealous. They lied to him and said that Joseph was dead while in fact they threw him into a pit and sold him as a slave. They took his robe and mixed it with an animal's blood and pretended that he was attacked and died in the process.

Can you see the similarity between the clothes from Joseph and the clothes of Esau that Jacob wore when he went to cheat Isaac?

What Can We Learn?

We must be honest. We must try our best not to cheat people for our own benefit. The wrong things that we do to others will come back to us.

> *If a man digs a pit, he will fall into it; if a man roles a stone, it will roll back on him.*
>
> *(Proverbs 26:27)*

The very same thing happened to Jacob. Everything he did wrong rolled back at him. Nevertheless, this does not mean that God does not love Jacob anymore. On the contrary, God still loves him. That is why He gave him the blessings. The only thing that God tried to do was discipline Jacob to teach him a lesson.

> *. . . the Lord disciplines those he loves, and he punishes everyone he accepts as a son..*
>
> *(Hebrews 12:6)*

If you have done someone wrong; if you have cheated someone, ask forgiveness from God in the name of our Lord Jesus Christ.

Israel Begins

One night when Jacob was left alone, a man wrestled with him until daybreak. When the man saw that he could not overpower Jacob, he touched the socket of his hip so that it was wrenched as he wrestled with the man. Jacob, upon discovery that the man he was wrestling with was from God, kept him until he received blessings from him. The angel blessed him and changed his name to “Israel,” which means, “he struggles with God.”

He said this because Jacob had struggled with God and man. Until today the descendants of Jacob are called “Israel.” Truly they still struggle with God because they do not recognize Jesus Christ as the Messiah.

This was actually the beginning of the nation of Israel. Jacob died in Egypt but he was buried in the land of Canaan (Gen. 49–50). Before Jacob died, he blessed all his sons (Gen. 49) who each represented a tribe of Israel. The blessings that Jacob spoke came true later.

IN CLOSING

When you read the story of Jacob, you can see that he was looking for a blessing all throughout his life.

Blessing is a spoken word by God or by a person. Jacob's struggles and acts of cheating were purposed primarily to receive the blessing word.

We learned here that Jacob gave a lot of attention to the word. We learned that spoken words are very important. For example, when Isaac spoke the blessing by mistake to Jacob, he could not change it anymore.

The same is true with the Word of God. Whatever He has spoken will not change.

What about you? Do you use your tongue in a proper way? What kinds of words do you use in your daily life? Try to use good words and avoid filthy words. What comes out of your mouth will influence your life.

SUMMARY

In this lesson we learned about the life of Jacob, including the mistakes he made. We learned about his sons and his marriages, and most importantly, we learned that we should not cheat others. We should wait for God's perfect time to give us His blessings. Further, we learned that the word we speak is very important. It is better for us to use proper words than dirty words. Lastly, we also learned some information about the nation Israel, which started with Jacob.

MAIN SCRIPTURES
Genesis 25–36; 49–50

REFERENCE SCRIPTURES
Proverbs 26:7
Luke 12:7
Hebrews 12:7

TO MEMORIZE AND MEDITATE UPON
HEBREWS 12:7

THE LORD DICIPLINES THOSE WHOM HE LOVES, AND HE PUNISHES EVERYONE HE ACCEPTS AS A SON.

QUESTIONS:

1. Read Genesis 34 and 37. How did Jacob's sons dishonor him?

2. Find out, through the scriptures, how many wives Jacob had and the number of sons he had by them.

NOTES:

NOTES:

LESSON 8
Joseph

Genesis 37–50

INTRODUCTION

Last lesson we learned about Jacob's life including his children and the blessing he stole from his brother, Esau. We learned about his sons and their disobedience. In this lesson we are going to study the life and times of Joseph. Joseph was the most beloved son of Jacob for a number of reasons. First, he was the son of his old age. Second, Joseph was the first born son by Rachel. And third, Joseph was an obedient son.

The life of Joseph is filled with adventures and sorrows which came through his own brothers. At the age of seventeen, he was thrown into a pit by his brothers and they sold him to traders travelling to Egypt. In Egypt he became a slave, was falsely accused, and was put in prison. Nevertheless, God had other plans for him. God raised him and gave him one of the highest positions in the Egyptian government.

In this lesson we are not going to dig into the historical facts of Joseph's life, however, we are going to focus on the spiritual part of his life and try to learn how we can effectively apply it.

TODAY'S JOURNEY

Joseph is loved by his father but hated by his brothers. Actually, the story of Joseph starts in Genesis 37 when he had two dreams. The dreams made his brothers jealous of him. They were also jealous because their father made a richly ornamented robe for Joseph.

When his brothers saw that their father loved him (Joseph) more than any of them, they hated Joseph and they could not talk a kind word to him.

(Genesis 37:4)

So one day when his brothers went to graze their father's flock, Jacob called Joseph and told him to find his brothers and inspect whether they were doing well, and to give him a report afterwards. Joseph left his father to find the brothers in the wilderness. He found them, but when his brothers saw him coming from the distance, they plotted to kill him. Reuben tried to rescue Joseph by suggesting that Joseph be thrown into a pit.

> *So when Joseph came to his brothers, they stripped him of his robe he was wearing and they took him and threw him into the cistern. Now the cistern was empty and there was no water in there.*
>
> *(Genesis 37:23)*

Then we read that they sold him to the Ishmaelite traders for twenty shekels of silver. Then told a lie to their father and said that Joseph was dead.

This story reminds us about our Lord Jesus Christ. Jesus Christ was loved tremendously by His Father, God the Father. While we were sinning, God sent his only Son into the world. Jesus is just like Joseph who was sent by his father to check the flock and the flock keepers. But his brothers, because of jealousy and hatred, threw him into a pit.

The same thing happened with Jesus. His own people rejected Him. They stripped Him and crucified Him on the cross and then they threw Him into a pit. Jesus was also sold for thirty shekels of silver; Joseph was sold for twenty coins. There are important similarities between Joseph's story and the life of our Lord Jesus Christ.

Joseph Feared God

The fear of the Lord is the beginning of wisdom.
(Proverbs 1:7)

In Genesis 39, we read about the story of Joseph as a slave in the house of Potiphar, the Egyptian high official. Joseph worked in his house as a slave. God blessed Joseph there and Potiphar was highly satisfied with Joseph. He entrusted Joseph with his household affairs. But the wife of Potiphar had an evil eye on Joseph, and because he was handsome she wanted to lay with him. Joseph however, resisted her, and in turn, she falsely accused him of rape. As a result, Joseph was put in prison.

Joseph was a man who feared God. He did not want to sin against God. The woman came to him and said, "Come to bed with me" (Gen. 39:7). She tried to do this a couple of times (Gen. 39:7).

These days we Christians are also tested with temptations in life. Some of us are being tempted with money, power, sex, and all the other things that lead to sin. The society is sick. There are people who tempt Christians to lay with them and to do evil things other than sexual wrongdoings.

For example, when a person kills his fellow man because of money, he lays in bed with murder. And if a person chops his own brother's money, then he lays with money.

Yet, these days the world is too sweet for people. People cannot stop unhealthy pleasures. People sin without asking the question, "What would God think about this?" People kill because they feel like killing. People hate because they want to hate. People commit sins because they want to and it's normal for them.

But Joseph was not like any of these. Joseph feared God and for that reason he did not submit himself to sin; he resisted it.

Imagine if Joseph had slept with the woman to make his power stronger. If he takes the woman, after a while he would have become the boss in the house. He could have easily thrown Potiphar out of the house. Jacob could have used the situation for his own advantage, but he did nothing of the sort. Joseph did not listen to the voice of the devil.

Whose voice do you listen to today? Do you listen to lust? Then you are wrong. It's better for you to listen to the voice of God like Joseph did.

When a person has victory over the temptation, God will raise that person up and bless and reward him like he did with Joseph.

> *Consider it pure joy, my brothers whenever you face trials of many kinds, because you know that the testing of your faith develops perseverance. Perseverance must finish its work so that you may be mature and complete, not lacking anything.*
>
> *(James 1:2-4)*

The Lord Was With Joseph

When you study the life of Joseph there is one sentence that appears regularly through the chapters of Genesis: "The Lord was with Joseph and whatever he did prospered."

The Lord was with Joseph and he prospered, and he lived in the house of his Egyptian master. His master saw that the Lord was with him (Joseph) and that the Lord gave him success in everything he did (Gen. 39:3).

When a person chooses for God and fears God, then that person will have God on his side. All big men of faith have God on their sides. Let us take Noah as an example. He walked with God and was saved from the Great Flood.

There is a conditional aspect in the sentence. The Lord was with Joseph, therefore, he prospered.

These days, everyone desires prosperity and because of this they ignore their root, which is God. People are so engrossed with climbing the ladder of success that they forget the call of God through His Son Jesus Christ. People are so busy with finding prosperity that they ignore God's commands.

A person can look prosperous and successful, but if he does not have God with him, his success will not last forever. A person can live in prosperity, but spiritually he can be very poor. A person can have a palace and lots of properties but still live in sadness and sorrow because he has no God with him.

The opposite is also possible. You can live below the average, but because you have God with you, you are prosperous. Look at Joseph. His brothers beat him, threw him into a pit, and sold him as a slave, but he still prospered.

-In the pit, he was saved because the Ishmaelites came and rescued him; God was with him.

-In the house of his Egyptian master, he became a slave but he prospered; God was with him.

-In the prison in Egypt, he prospered; God was with him.

-In the Egyptian government, he prospered; God was with him.

These days God has left many people, many families, many cities, many countries and many nations because they left Him first with their sinful activities. When God leaves a person or a family, disaster and problems will follow them. But God will change any disaster or problem if a person is with God. What is your position today? Is God with you?

> *Woe to those who call evil good and good evil.*
> *Woe to those who put darkness for light and light for darkness.*
> *Who put bitter for sweet and sweet for bitter?*
> *(Isaiah 5:20)*

Yes, societies are changing and forgetting their godly roots. In place of normal sexual relationships they tolerate homosexuality. In place of tolerating life they proclaim death by promoting abortion. In placc of peace they bring war.

Another key to success is hardship, perseverance, and forgiveness. It starts with the dream.

When you look at the life of Joseph, you see that God gave him a promise that he would become a big person through the dreams he had. His family took his dreams for granted and they became jealous of him.

Perhaps you have dreams about your future too. But unfortunately, people have no respect for them and they are even jealous. Do not give up.

Joseph was thrown into the pit and he became a slave. He was faithful in all that he had and he gave thanks to God for His position.

Further, we read that Joseph forgave his brothers and his enemies, and because he forgave them, Joseph prospered all the more. Nowadays, many people look for success, but if they have unforgiveness and hate against someone, success will not come but they will end in failure.

If you are looking for success and prosperity forgive all those who did you wrong and bless them like Joseph did with his brothers.

SUMMARY

Joseph married an Egyptian woman and had two children. He prospered and held the second most important position in Egypt next to the Pharaoh.

You can read in Genesis how the children of Jacob entered Egypt and how Joseph tested them and released his forgiveness on them. There are moral aspects that we can find in the life of Joseph such as fearing God, trusting God, choosing for God, humbleness, and forgiveness.

However, our Lord Jesus Christ is not from the lineage of Joseph but from the lineage of Judah. I believe God chose this way because Joseph married an Egyptian and Judah had a sinful background. God wanted to show us His grace in which He can use even a sinful person to bless us.

MAIN SCRIPTURES
Genesis 37–50

REFERENCE SCRIPTURES
Proverbs 1:7
Isaiah 5:20
James 1:2-4

TO MEMORIZE AND MEDITATE UPON
PROVERBS 1:7

THE FEAR OF GOD IS THE BEGINNING OF WISDOM.

QUESTIONS:

1. According to Romans 8:28, "All things work together for good to them who love God, to the one who is called according to his purpose." How can you relate this promise to the life of Joseph?

2. Read the entire life of Joseph from Genesis 37–50 and try to find five characteristics of Jesus Christ in Joseph. Find also some situations that happened to Joseph that are also similar to what happened to Jesus.

NOTES:

NOTES:

LESSON 9
Redemption

Exodus 1–18

INTRODUCTION TO THE BOOK OF EXODUS

Exodus is the second book of the Holy Bible. It derived its name from a Greek word, which means "going out" or "departure." This refers to the departure of the people of Israel from Egypt where they were slaves. It is good to know that this book in Hebrew has a different name. It comes from the first two words by which the book starts: *we'elleh shemoth*, which means, "these are the names of those Israelites."

Exodus is an important book because for the first time in the history of mankind, God revealed His Law to His people. The origin of Law was written in this book.

Further, when we talk about the Law we should automatically remember Moses, the redeemer of the Israelites, from the bondage of Egypt.

In this book, God did not only reveal His laws, He also revealed His name and His character to His nation and to us.
Many believe that the Holy Spirit used Moses to write this book.

Exodus can be divided into two major areas namely:
The Redemption of Israel from Egyptian bondage
The Law

In total, we are going to spend three lessons discussing the book of Exodus.

In this lesson we are going to study the story of redemption and see how God planned to redeem His people from the yoke of Egyptian dictatorship and slavery.

TODAY'S JOURNEY

The book of Exodus is a book of great adventures. In Genesis, we learned how the children of Jacob entered the land of Egypt, how they were received by their brother Joseph, and how they persecuted and betrayed him. We also read how Joseph, because of his fear of the Lord, was raised by God to the highest governmental position in Egypt after the Pharaoh.

By entering the land of Egypt, the nation of Israel started to multiply and become prosperous. Exodus 1 teaches us that they became a mighty nation in Egypt. After Joseph's generation, many generations came from him and his brothers.

The book of Exodus starts with the Israelites residing in Egypt for 430 years. We also read in Exodus that the Pharaoh in power forgot the good deeds of Joseph and he became jealous of Israel. Therefore, he decided to make the Israelites his slaves. The Israelites were forced to work under very harsh conditions. They were oppressed and mistreated (Exod. 1:8-11).

The Cry of Israel

Exodus 2:23 describes the highest point of their sufferings and their desperate pleas for help. During that long period, the king of Egypt died. The Israelites groaned in misery and their cries for help went up to God.

The Israelites, whom God chose to be His nation, became slaves and lived in bondage, sorrow, and pain. Suffering was their daily yoke. They lived in oppression.

They had nowhere to go. They had no agencies to help them. And they had no facilities to run to. Egypt was a superpower; there was no chance of escaping. For this reason they cried, they wept, and they shouted for help. That was the only thing they could do. Exodus 2:23 says that they cried for help; they cried out to God, their Creator.

The Cry of Man Today

Earlier we read that the Israelites were living under the bondage of slavery. We saw how much they cried to the Lord to save them. The Lord heard them and decided to send them a redeemer—Moses. He would set them free and lead them to a land flowing with milk and honey.

What about the world today?

Today, there are also many people who are living in bondage. They suffer in an 'invisible Egypt.' People are suffering because of family/marriage problems; some are suffering because of hard labor and low wages; some people are suffering because of various sicknesses. Perhaps you are oppressed. Perhaps you are asking yourself, "Lord why should I suffer? Why should I be oppressed and live under this yoke?"

Yes, there are people who live under slavery because of drugs, alcohol, or other bad habits. Some people are the slaves of sicknesses. In the same way the Israelites were the slaves of the Egyptian superpower. Maybe they tried to get out of their poor condition but to no avail. They started to cry to the Lord for help.

Yes, even now there are many people under bondage who are trying many things but to no avail!

What is the position of the crying man? Can the United Nations or other human organizations give stability to a world where there is war, hunger, and social injustice?

Man is under depression and suffering. Families and individuals live with problems. Who can help us? To whom should we cry? Maybe you can associate your situation with one of these problems. To whom do you want to cry?

The Israelites cried to God. The man of the twentieth-century should likewise cry to God for help. God is the biggest Help-provider. He can break the yoke of any bondage and suffering. He can heal you from any sickness. He can bless you and bring you out of the bondage of poverty or marriage problems. LET GOD HEAR YOUR CRY.

> *The eyes of the Lord are on the righteous, and His ears are attentive to their cry.*
>
> *(Psalm 34:15)*

God's Response to Israel's Cry

Exodus 2:24-25 teaches us that God heard the cries of the Israelites:

> *God heard their groaning and their cry for help and he remembered his covenant with Abraham, with Isaac and with Jacob. So God looked on the Israelites and was concerned about them.*

The book of Exodus teaches us that God saw the sufferings and heard the cries of the Israelites and He decided to rescue His nation and bring them out of Egypt to the Promised Land. God made up

His mind. He decided to help His nation and no one could change that.

For this reason, He decided to choose a person who would bring redemption to His people. God always has His answers; God has His own ways and approaches for helping mankind. The help and the solution always come from places where man would never think. That's why God chose Moses to rescue His people from Egypt.

Moses grew up in the royal family of the Pharaoh. He was educated in the Egyptian life and culture. In Exodus 2, we read the story of Moses' birth. He was born when the Pharaoh commanded that every Israelite boy in Egypt be slaughtered. Moses was born in a Levite family which belonged to the nation of Israel. His mother could not let her child be killed, so she hid him and placed him in a papyrus basket to be carried away by the river streams. The daughter of the Pharaoh found him in the river and took him as her own child. She called him Moses, which means, "drawn out of water."

Later we read how a tragic event turned the course of Moses' life. Moses killed an Egyptian soldier and because of that he escaped to the land of the Midians where he married the daughter of Jethro. Moses became a shepherd of his father-in-law's flock.

One day, while he was tending the flocks in Mount Horeb, an angel of the Lord appeared to him in a burning bush.

We read in Exodus 3 about God's calling on Moses to redeem His people from bondage. No one could ever think that God would choose Moses to do this great task. He was called to lead almost two million people with their children, flocks, and all their possessions out of the land of Egypt.

Even Moses himself could not believe this. He asked many questions of God.

But God had already made His covenant:

> *I have indeed seen the misery of my people in Egypt. I have heard them crying out because of slave drivers, and I am concerned about their suffering. So I have come down to rescue them from the hand of the Egyptians and to bring them up out of that land into good and spacious land, a land flowing with milk and honey . . . . And now the cry of the Israelites has reached me, and I have seen the way Egyptians are oppressing them. So now go, I am sending you to Pharaoh to bring my people the Israelites out of Egypt.*
>
> *(Exodus 3:7-11)*

> *Then God revealed His name to Moses;* ***I AM WHO I AM.***
>
> *(Exodus 3:14)*

God promised that He would rescue and prosper them when they left Egypt. God also warned Moses that it would be difficult but the end result would be good.

We can read about the grief of Pharaoh in Exodus 3–11 since he didn't want to give freedom to the Israelites. There were already ten plagues that came upon his kingdom and destroyed it, but still his heart was hardened. He had grief in his heart towards the Israelites.

The ten plagues showed the anger of God toward Pharaoh and the Egyptians. God demonstrated His power and showed them how mighty He was.

Here Come the Ten Plagues That Took Place at That Time:

1. *The Nile River turned into blood (Ex. 7:14-25)*
2. *Frogs overran the countryside (Ex. 8:1-15)*
3. *People and animals were infested with gnats (Ex. 8:16-19)*
4. *Swarms of flies covered the land (Ex. 8:20-32)*

5. *Diseases killed the livestock of Egypt (Ex. 9:1-7)*
6. *Boils and sores infected the Egyptians and their animals (Ex. 9:8-12)*
7. *Hail destroyed crops and vegetation (Ex. 9:13-35)*
8. *Swarms and locusts covered Egypt (Ex. 10:1-20)*
9. *Thick darkness covered Egypt for three days (Ex. 10:21-29)*
10. *The Egyptian firstborn, including both people and animals, were destroyed by God's angel of death (Ex. 11-12:1-30)*

Yes, this happens when man does not answer the call of God. God called Pharaoh to obey Him and to let the nation go. But because he did not listen and was extremely stubborn, God sent these disasters to the Egyptians.

Today we are also living in a world where people do not listen to the call of God. That is why families have problems, marriages are in danger of breaking up, and hunger and war are killing the nations. This time it is not the plague of locusts or the plague of frogs, but worse than these, we have the plagues of incurable diseases and natural and environmental disasters. Our world is sick because we do not hear the call of God.

> *Today when you hear His voice do not harden your hearts.*
> *(Psalm 95:7b-8)*

The Passover

The last plague that God sent on the Egyptians was the death of all the firstborn sons. Every firstborn son would be killed by the angel of death. When the right time came, God told Moses that every Israelite family should take a lamb and slaughter it. Further, they should put its blood on the sides and on top of their doorframes (Exod. 12:70). Also, they were told to eat bread made without yeast.

Then God commanded them to do these things on the fourteenth day of the month at midnight. They should not leave their houses until morning. The angel was going to pass through Egypt in the night and every house that had the blood of the lamb on the doorframes would be saved. The angel of death would not enter that house. He would pass over these houses, but the houses of the Egyptians would be attacked and all the firstborn sons would be killed.

Departure and Crossing the Sea

After this they were ready to head toward the Promised Land. So they left. Exodus 14 teaches us that after Pharaoh let the people go, he then changed his mind. He wanted the Israelites to return to Egypt, so he sent his chariots after them.

Now the Israelites camped by the sea near the Pi Hahiroth. When they saw that the Egyptian soldiers were approaching they became terrified and cried out to the Lord. They rebelled against God and Moses. They told Moses that it was entirely his fault. He brought them to the desert to die at the hands of the Egyptians. They wanted to go back to Egypt. But Moses raised his staff and stretched out his hand over the sea and it became divided. The Israelites could pass through the sea to the other side. When the last Israelite crossed the sea, the Egyptians entered the divided sea and then God closed it. All of Pharaoh's soldiers died in the water. The people of God walked in freedom from slavery and bondage.

God's Response to the Cry of Man

When a person, family, country, nation or society does not respond to the call of God many dreadful things can happen. This happened to Pharaoh and his nation because they did not listen to the call of God through Moses. Perhaps at this point you are wondering how the story of Moses is relevant to your life today. Here's why it is.

The Bible says that every one has sinned. There is nobody in the world without sin. Further, the Bible says that those who live in sin are slaves of sin. Romans 6:16-23 teaches us that before we knew Christ, we were slaves to sin and death. What does this slavery mean? What are the borders of this "spiritual-Egypt slavery"? Our world is full of misery. Who then is our redeemer?

The Bible says that while we were slaves to sin, God sent His Son Jesus Christ to make us free from the bondage of sin. Two thousand years ago, God heard the cry of man, not only of Israel, but of all of the nations. For that reason He decided to send His Son Jesus Christ so that through Him redemption and freedom could enter the world. Jesus Christ did not come for a vacation. He had a task. He came to make us free and because of His resurrection He is still alive. So He is still the redeemer of the world. He is also your redeemer.
He came to make us free from:

The Slavery of Sickness and Disease
Jesus Christ healed the sick; He gave sight to the blind, healing people with leprosy and other illnesses. Jesus Christ hated sickness, but He loved the sick. No one could heal the sick like Jesus. We have our own technology and science, but there are still so many sicknesses that cannot be cured. AIDS, for example, is the burden of twentieth-century man. AIDS is conquering and destroying families. How many children have died because of AIDS? How many has lost their loved ones because of AIDS? How many people have been and are now being discriminated against because of this disease?

But the Bible says that Jesus Christ is the same yesterday, today and forever (Hebrews 13:8). I have seen people get healed from AIDS, cancer, and other sicknesses because of the power of Jesus Christ. Jesus is alive and when a person gives his life to the Eternal Redeemer, he will be saved. His healing is free and His love cannot be bought.

The Slavery of Unforgiveness

We all have our wrongdoings. There is no one who can say, "I never did wrong." Just look back at your own life, from your birth until the present time. You can find many mistakes, some small and some big. Sometimes you cannot forgive yourself; sometimes others cannot forgive you.

Some people are afraid of death and hell. They are afraid to be judged. The Bible says every one will be judged by God. But if you believe in your heart that Jesus Christ is the Son of God and believe in the Holy Spirit and ask for forgiveness, then you will be forgiven and He will give you eternal life in paradise. God is your forgiver through Jesus Christ.

When you study the life of Jesus, you will notice that He lived with the sinners; He forgave the prostitutes and the corrupt tax collectors. Salvation comes only through Jesus Christ.

The Slavery of Sin

Many people think that sin is doing bad things such as killing or stealing. No, these are not sin; they are the results of sin. What is sin? To sin is to disobey God. It is when a person hears the word of God and Jesus Christ but rejects Him. Sin is rejecting Jesus Christ and His Holy Spirit. For this reason, Jesus revealed Himself to us so that we can know and believe in Him and be free from the wages of sin which is eternal punishment in hell.

The Slavery of Poverty

When God created the world, He never wanted Adam to suffer under poverty. That is why He told him to rule over the world. But because he sinned, he lost his position. But through Jesus Christ you can receive the first blessing that God gave Adam. Jesus Christ wants to bless you. He wants you to be successful and He loves you.

This does not mean that there should be no poor people in the world. Of course there are even poor Christian people, but their poverty is often caused by the mistakes and abuses of others. Do you think God wants us to suffer?

There are many kinds of slavery, but God's will for you is to believe and receive Jesus Christ, the Eternal Redeemer. When you do so you will be free.

Poverty is not only material, it is also mental and spiritual. In the West, there are many people who are rich, but they live in spiritual poverty. They lack joy, peace, and all these things. Only Jesus Christ can break all these forms of poverty.

The New Passover

God used the lamb's blood on the doors of the Israelites to save them. In a similar way, God sent His Son Jesus Christ into this world. He was slaughtered and shed His blood on the cross. Through His blood we are saved.

That is why symbolically you must have the blood of Jesus on the doors of your heart. That is why at the Last Supper He said, "This is my blood you drink . . . ." (Matt. 26:17-30).

He shed His blood for you so that you could receive life upon believing in Him as the only way to salvation and eternal life.

New Kind of Crossing the Sea: Baptism

When the Israelites crossed the sea, they were literally baptized in the sea. Today you do not need to cross the sea, but you can be baptized: (a) in the water and (b) in the living water, the Holy Spirit. Every Christian should be baptized in water. That is a duty. Further, a Christian should have the experience of the baptism of the Holy Spirit.

The baptism of the Holy Spirit is an experience that you cannot explain by words and it is highly individualised. It differs from person to person. Some people have shaking movements or some experience laughter. Some cry or have some other reaction. But most importantly, it is visible by the changes in the person's life.

Even Paul talked about the symbolism of Moses' baptism (Israel's passing through the Red Sea) and the baptism in Christ:

> *For I do not want you to be ignorant of the fact, brothers, that our forefathers were all under the cloud and that they all passed through the sea. They were all baptized into Moses in the cloud and in the sea.*
>
> *(1 Corinthians 10:1-2)*

Again we read here about the cloud which represents the baptism of the Holy Spirit in our time. The sea represents the water baptism in Jesus Christ.

SUMMARY

In this lesson we learned the story of how God rescued Israel from bondage and how He responded to their cry. Further, we learned that redemption of the modern age comes through Jesus Christ, the Son of God who is alive.

We learned how we can be rescued and freed from the bondage of spiritual Egypt.

If you live in problems; if you live in bondage and yoke; cry out to the Lord and answer His call which comes only and through His Son Jesus Christ and the Holy Spirit.

MAIN SCRIPTURES
Exodus 1–18

REFERENCE SCRIPTURES
Psalm 34:15
Psalm 95:7b-8
Matthew 26:17-30
Romans 6:16-23
1 Corinthians 10:1-2
Hebrews 13:8

TO MEMORIZE AND MEDITATE UPON
PSALM 95:7b-8

TODAY WHEN YOU HEAR HIS VOICE DO NOT HARDEN YOUR HEARTS.

QUESTIONS:

1. Read Exodus 1–18. Mention two or three similar characteristics of Jesus and Moses. Explain your answer.

2. Why does God sometimes allow bad things to happen to His people? Give some reasons.

NOTES:

LESSON 10

The Ten Commandments

Exodus 18–24

INTRODUCTION

Last lesson we spent our time studying the redemption of Israel from the yoke of slavery in Egypt. We learned a lot about the nation of Israel, their sufferings and how God saved them and brought them out of Egypt through His signs and wonders and great miracles. We learned about the Passover and the crossing of the nation through the red sea.

We also tried to relate Israel's redemption to our own world today. We learned that many people are in bondage to a "spiritual Egypt" and how we can be free from this bondage through the New Redeemer: Jesus Christ.

In this lesson we will focus on the Law that the Israelites received at Mount Sinai on the way to the Promised Land.

The Law, which was given to the nation of Israel, consisted of three major parts:

A) The Commandments
B) The Judgements
C) The Ordinances (Religious Rites)

However, it is not possible to explain all the laws given by God in one lesson. We will try to give emphasis in this lesson on the Ten

Commandments of God. The Ten Commandments are the foundation of the entire Law.

TODAY'S JOURNEY

The Hebrew word for law is "Torah," which means "teaching" or "instruction." All five books of Moses are called Law—Torah. The Israelites still rebelled against Moses and God even though they experienced so many miracles. For example, they rebelled when they had no water to drink and complained when they wanted to eat bread (Exod. 15:22-24; 16:1-3). But in all these circumstances, God's hand was with them.

When God saw His nation as rebellious He gave them the Law. The Law directed them on the road of righteousness. The Law specifically showed the Israelites what God wanted from them; the Law taught them how to live a life according to God's will.

In our time today, many Christians believe that they do not need the Law anymore because they are living in the New Testament era. This is not true because Jesus Christ said:

> *Do not think that I have come to abolish the law or the prophets; I have not come to abolish them but to complete them. I tell you the truth, until heaven and earth disappear, not the smallest letter, nor the least stroke of a pen, will by any means disappear from the law until everything is accomplished.*
>
> (Matthew 5:17-18)

Jesus Christ Himself said that He did not come to destroy the Law, but to accomplish the Law. When you accomplish something, it means that you make that thing complete. Let me explain it in this way. Whenever you read the five books of Moses (the first five books of the Old Testament), you will notice that they are mostly based on the physical aspects of the Law. For example, if someone committed a specific sin, there was a punishment for that sin. Most of the time these punishments ended in death. But that is a physical death. The focus of sin was also based on the physical or visible sins. But when Jesus Christ came, He changed the aspects of sin from the physical to the spiritual. For example, the Old Testament laws teach us that we should not murder; this counts for the physical aspect of Law. But when Jesus came He added the spiritual aspect. Man should not hate because if he does it is tantamount to killing someone.

So the Law is tremendously important for us Christians. However, there are certain laws in the Bible that are not valid anymore in physical form, but they are valid in spiritual form. For example, the Law says that if a person commits adultery that person should be stoned to death. But when Jesus Christ came, He added something to this Law which makes the other unimportant. The punishment is no longer stoning but eternal punishment in hell which is actually worse than stoning.

The Law, especially the Ten Commandments (T.C.), is important because the laws of God are holy, just, and good (Rom. 7:12). Today the Law is not condemning us because we have Jesus Christ who is the Law Himself.

The Bible says:

> *For sin shall not be your master, because you are not under the law, but under grace.*
>
> (Romans 6:14)

Why then do we need the Law since we live in grace? The answer is simple. God wants us Christians to live a holy life. You cannot say that you are a Christian and have His grace but commit stealing and killing.

God wants His children to live according to His standards, and if they fall or fail then there is grace granted to them because Jesus Christ paid the price in order to present them to the Father as blameless and without any sin.
We Christians should not be proud of our Christianity. We should not be self-righteous people. We must try to live according to the basic laws that God gave us in the T.C. All the eternal principles of right and wrong that are contained in the T.C. are also taught in the New Testament (N.T.).

Let us now study the Ten Commandments since God's will is there written for you. Furthermore, the commands of God contain practical ways to be successful in our lives.

> *Be careful to obey all the law my servant Moses gave you; do not turn from it to the right or left, that you may be successful wherever you go.*
>
> (Joshua 1:7)

Do you want the blessing of God to be poured out in your life? Then desire to live a life based on the Ten Commandments of God.

Ten Commandments

Three months after the Israelites left Egypt, they set out from Rephidim. They entered the desert of Sinai where Israel camped in front of the mountain. This was where Moses received the Law for the Israelites.

COMMAND ONE: *DO NOT WORSHIP GODS (Ex. 20:3)*

While Moses was on the mountain to receive the commandments, the Israelites became very impatient. Therefore, they made another god, a golden calf, which they worshipped. God already knew that the people of Israel had the tendency to worship other gods. That is why He gave this law as the first command.

There is only one God who is alive. God is one. There are other gods made by human thoughts and imaginations, but these gods are dead; our God is alive. Our God is God the Father, Son, and Holy Spirit. A person cannot worship God without worshipping His Son and His Holy Spirit.

COMMAND TWO: *DO NOT MAKE AND BOW DOWN BEFORE ANY IDOL (Ex. 20:4-6)*

God hates to see His people bow before things that are made by their own hands. For centuries, man made idols from stone and worshipped them; people worshipped the sun, the moon, and the stars. However, God sent His commands. He forbade any form of idol worshipping.

What about our time today? Maybe you say, "I am a Christian and I do not worship any idol." But there are also many believers who unconsciously worship other gods and idols.

Some people love money so much that they forget the calling of Jesus in their lives. Many Christians fall because of the temptation of money and wealth. If a person values money a lot, then that person worships money. Money is an idol with the image of man on it.

Some Christian loves the statues of saints like Peter, Paul or the Virgin Mary more than the Bible they have at home. God does not like these kinds of images. Now there is nothing wrong with having these kinds of pictures in your house because they will remind you of the Lord, but the moment you start to worship these things and give more value to them unnecessarily, then you are sinning.

Some people worship pastors or bishops more than God Himself. This is a sin. Jesus said that He is the High Priest, and there is no other High Priest than He.

Some people love the Pope more than Jesus, or they worship him more than Jesus. Some obey the Vatican more than what Jesus commands. They have a lot of pictures of different saints but they do not read the Bible enough. These kinds of Christians are breaking the law of God.

God wants us to worship Him in Spirit and not the material things or images.

COMMAND THREE: *DO NOT MISUSE MY NAME (Ex. 20:7)*

No one likes his name to be misused. If someone falsely used your name and your identity for wrong purposes, how would you feel? The same is true with God. The Israelites misused the name of God. They swore in God's name and broke their covenants with God many times. God's name became something cheap for them.

These days, there are also many people, including Christians, who are misusing God's name.

How can a Christian misuse God's name? An example is found in the way we live. Christianity is not only a matter of believing in the right formulas that can 'save' you. No, Christianity is a matter of living in the way Christ lived on earth. Some people describe themselves as holy Christians, but when you look at the way they live, it is filled with bad attitudes and habits. Even unbelievers do not live like this.

Let me give you a practical example:

Somebody calls himself a Christian. He says to everyone that he believes in God and His Son Jesus Christ. However, he gossips and judges others. If a person who is not a Christian looks at him, what would that person think? He would think that all Christians are gossips and judgmental. God's name will be abused by the attitude of this man.

The way we live and the way we are as the children of God is the business card of our Lord. Through us, they will know Christ. That is why Jesus says,

> *"Love each other so that the world can see you are my disciples."*
>
> *For we are to God the aroma of Christ among those who are being saved and those who are perishing .*

(2 Corinthians 2:15)

COMMAND FOUR: *KEEP THE SABBATH HOLY (Ex. 20:8-11)*

God made the heavens and the earth in six days and then He rested on the seventh day. These days, societies are trying to avoid any form of the Sabbath. For us Christians, the Sabbath is Sunday and for the Jews it is Saturday.

We have seven days a week, six of which are devoted to our daily activities. The remaining day is allotted for God; to remember Him and to praise Him. Nowadays, some believers are so busy that they neglect to worship at the house of God. But if you have time for God, He will have time for you!

COMMAND FIVE: *HONOR YOUR FATHER AND MOTHER (Ex. 20:12)*

God wants us to honor our fathers and mothers. Of course, there are always mothers or fathers who abuse their children in various ways. But generally, God wants us to respect our parents. We must love them. If they do something wrong, we must forgive them.

There are people who love God but show no respect to their mothers and fathers. God does not tolerate this attitude. There are also some people who give more value to their earthly parents than to God the Father. They put their parents first instead of God.

Every person must put God first rather than his father and mother or other priorities of life. When a person fears God he will automatically honor his mother and father too.

COMMAND SIX: *DO NOT MURDER (Ex. 20:13)*

Just like in the time of Moses, killing people is very easy for people today. There are so many wars. God gave us life, and God will take that life away from us. That is why it is not right for a person to kill. We should not tolerate the death sentence as a form of punishment. There many parents who commit abortion. God does not tolerate this either.

Maybe some of us think we have never committed murder. We become self-righteous. Jesus Christ says there is another kind of murder that is worse. This is hate and bitterness. Jesus taught us that if anyone carries hate and revenge in his or her heart then that person has committed the sin of murder.

If you are carrying hate, unforgiveness, or discrimination toward a person today, then this is the day that you should repent and ask forgiveness from God.

COMMAND SEVEN: *DO NOT COMMIT ADULTERY (Ex. 20:14)*

From the beginning God created man for woman and woman for man. The Bible teaches us that man should leave his house, marry, and start a new family.

Adultery involves husbands and wives who break their marriage covenant in any form. Adultery also has something to do with sexual immorality. God does not tolerate two people of the same sex living together or two unmarried people sharing the same bed.
Unfortunately, our societies have failed on this part of the T.C. If you look at the societies of the so-called modern world, many forms

of adultery are visible. Some governments in the world even promote these activities.

Jesus Christ completed this Law and taught us that even if someone had lust and desire in his or her own heart that person had already committed adultery.

COMMAND EIGHT: *DO NOT STEAL (Ex. 20:15)*

Stealing is one of the oldest criminal occupations. People often steal because they have no food to eat. Others steal because it is a form of adventure. There are also many other ways of stealing. I call them spiritual stealing. For example, you have the ability to help a brother of yours, but because of your own laziness, you refuse to help him. This is a kind of stealing because you could have made your brother happy in his time of need but you did not. So in that time you stole his happiness.

Some Christians think that they have never stolen. But God said, "Yet you rob me" (Mal. 3:6-12). God commanded His people to give tithes. This means that one-tenth of their income should go to the house of God. But some of us do not tithe because we are disappointed with people who have abused money. But the Law is Law. By doing this God wants to see how far you can go. We have the money to pay for many luxurious things we want, but when it comes to giving to God, we are so reluctant.

COMMAND NINE: *DO NOT GIVE FALSE TESTIMONY (Ex. 20:16)*

Giving false testimony is to lie. False testimony happens when a person does not tell the truth. God is truth; in God there is no lie. Since God has made us in His own image, we must not lie. Try always to tell the truth no matter how difficult and even dangerous it could be to your situation. Tell the truth. Because when you tell the truth God is on your side. Truth is eternal.

These days no one can trust each other anymore. Lying has become the easiest way to escape from problems. Be like Joseph; never be afraid of telling the truth.

Many people say that they have never lied in their lives. This is not true. The Bible says that not knowing Jesus Christ as Lord makes you a liar.

COMMAND TEN: *DO NOT COVET (Ex. 20:17)*

To covet means to desire someone else's property or possessions with a jealous heart. In the T.C. God says, "Do not covet your neighbour's wife and the things your neighbour has." This means to be satisfied with who you are, with whom you are married, and with what you have.

These days there are people who have everything but they still find something to complain about. The Bible, though, says to give thanks in all circumstances and be satisfied with your life.

When Jesus Christ came He gave us two commands that actually cover all the Ten Commandments and the entire Law. Jesus Christ told us to love our God with all our heart, with all our soul and with all our minds. The second command was that we must love our neighbors as we love ourselves (Matt. 22:37-40).

If you look at the first four commands, they are God-oriented commands. If you look at commands five to ten, they are people or neighbor-oriented commands.

Examine yourself. Which of these commandments are weak in your life? Ask God to help you overcome these weaknesses. But never forget that the Law brings a curse for those who are under it; but for you, the curse has no more effect because you are not under the Law anymore. You are free but you still have to do your best to live according to the teachings of the Lord.

IN CLOSING

The Law of Moses is still used in some countries as the standard law. As I wrote before, the Law given to Moses can be divided into three major areas. First, there are the "you shall" and "you shall not" rules. Next, we have the judgement laws. These are given to judge a certain person who broke one or more laws in the commands. Lastly, there are the laws about the rituals and manners of worship and religious activities. These kinds of laws are called ordinances.

SUMMARY

We learned in this lesson the basic laws that God gave to His people and to us. God still expects His children to obey these commands. If we try to obey these things God is going to give us success on this earth like He did for Joshua.

Try to live according to these laws. By doing this you will create for yourself a healthy personality, a healthy family, a healthy job career, and a healthy society.

CHANGE ALWAYS BEGINS WITH YOU!!

MAIN SCRIPTURES
Exodus 19–24

REFERENCE SCRIPTURES
Joshua 1:17
Malachi 3:6-12
Matthew 5:17-18; 22:37-40
Romans 6:14; 7:12
1 Corinthians 2:15

TO MEMORIZE AND MEDITATE UPON
JOSHUA 1:7

BE CAREFUL TO OBEY ALL THE LAW MY SERVANT MOSES GAVE YOU; DO NOT TURN FROM IT TO THE RIGHT OR LEFT, THAT YOU MAY BE SUCCESSFUL WHEREVER YOU GO.

QUESTIONS:

1. Explain why it was important for God to give the Israelites the Law.

2. Explain why it is important that we Christians should obey the Law.

NOTES:

NOTES:

LESSON 11
Tabernacle

Exodus 24–40

INTRODUCTION

We learned in the previous lesson about the Law of God that was given to the nation Israel and, by extension, to you and me. In this lesson, we are going to focus on the ceremonial laws God gave to us. But most importantly, we are going to study the relationship between the Tabernacle and Jesus Christ. What does the Tabernacle and Jesus have in common?

TODAY'S JOURNEY

When the nation of Israel came out of Egypt, God wanted to dwell with them. He also wanted them to worship no other but He. For this reason, He commanded Moses to build the Tabernacle.

In Exodus 26, God taught them how to construct the Tabernacle. The Tabernacle was the beginning of religious life and activities; it also represented the House of God where God dwelled.

The original word used for Tabernacle is the Hebrew word *Mishkan*, which means "the dwelling place" or "tent." They also called it the "Tent of Meeting." The Tabernacle was the place where the sinner had the opportunity to 'meet' God.

The Tabernacle was not a permanent place because later Solomon would build a permanent temple of God. For this reason some people called the Tabernacle, the Tabernacle of the Desert.

Later, the word tabernacle (*Mishkan*) referred to the entire area surrounding the temple in Jerusalem (Psalm 46:4; 87:2). But when the Israelites failed to remember God, and they lived without fear and submission to His commands, God made a covenant that He would not dwell in the Tabernacle (Ezekiel 10). He promised to build His people a New Tabernacle—Jesus Christ Himself.

> *When Christ came as high priest of the good things that already are he went through the greater and perfect tabernacle that is not man-made, that is to say not part of this creation.*
>
> *(Hebrews 9:11)*

What did the Tabernacle look like?

The Map of the Tabernacle

The Tabernacle was built into three major areas:
A) The Outer Court
B) The Holy Place
C) The Most Holy Place.

See the map below:

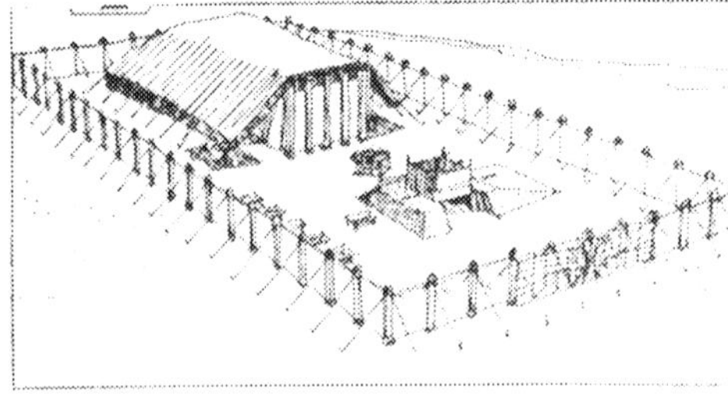

The Tabernacle was built to provide a place where God might dwell among His people. The term tabernacle sometimes refers to the tent, including the Holy Place and the Most Holy Place, which was covered with embroidered curtains. But in other places, it refers to the entire complex, including the curtained court in which the tent stood.

The Tabernacle was a large portable tent surrounded by an outer court. The tent itself was built with curtains (Exod. 26). Most people believe the Tabernacle was only a tent inside the court, but some consider the Tabernacle as the entire place including the outer court.

The tent itself consisted of two major areas: the Holy Place and the Most Holy Place.

A) The Outer Court and Jesus Christ

The outer Court, as mentioned above, was the court where the Tabernacle or the tent was placed. This Outer Court had only one entrance. Everyone who wanted to meet or worship God had no other choice except to enter through this door.

Jesus Christ said:

> *I am the door (gate), whoever enters through me will be saved.*
>
> *(John 10:9)*

Today we are living in the spiritual part of the Old Testament. Now we have a new Tabernacle which brings us a new way to approach God, a new way of worshipping and a new way of pleasing God. That is why Jesus told the Samaritan woman that the time would come and has now come when the true worshippers would worship the Father in spirit and in truth (John 4:23).

Jesus Christ is the only way to God. You cannot approach God with worldly ways because God gave His Son; those who enter through Jesus, the Gate, will have access to God.

When a person enters the court of the Tabernacle, he immediately passes through the Altar of the Burnt Offering (Exod. 27:1-8). When a person enters the place he must sacrifice an animal to the

Lord. The blood of the sacrifice was to be sprinkled on the four horns of the altar. Through this blood a person could find forgiveness.

Now we have a new Altar of Burnt Offering and that is the cross of Jesus Christ. By His death and His blood, He gave us forgiveness. The horn on which the blood of animals should be sprinkled represents the wounds of Jesus through His crucifixion. Through His blood He gave redemption and salvation to all who believe in Him.

> *He did not enter by means of the blood of goats and calves; but he entered the Most Holy Place once for all by his own blood having obtained eternal redemption.*
>
> *(Hebrews 9:12)*

After passing through the ceremony at the Altar of Burnt Offering and Sacrifices, a person was to pass by the Bronze Laver (Exod. 30:17-21). This was a large container for water made from bronze metal. It was used at the Altar of the Burnt Offering.

The Bronze Altar stood just in the front of the entrance of the tent that led to the Holy Place. It was placed here to cleanse those who entered the Holy Place.

The act of going to the Bronze Laver represents the act of baptism. Jesus Christ Himself was baptized by John the Baptist. And in the same way He commanded us to go to all the nations and baptize them in the name of the Father, Son, and the Holy Spirit.

B) The Holy Place

After the ceremonies at the Bronze Laver, a person could enter the Holy Place. In the Holy Place there were three furnishings. On the right hand was the Table of Bread (Exod. 25:23-30). It kept a constant supply of fresh food. This table always had twelve loaves

of bread available in God's presence that symbolized the twelve tribes of Israel.
Jesus Christ said that He is the Bread. At the Last Supper He took the bread and said that it was His body they were about to partake. This bread represents the Word of God. Now, we have the New Table of Bread—the Word of God. Jesus said that we must not live by bread alone but by every word that comes out of the mouth of God.

So every Christian who worships God in spirit through Jesus Christ must read the Bible constantly. In the New Tabernacle, which is Jesus Christ, our relationship to God should be realized in reading the Holy Bible, the Bread from heaven.

To the left side of the Holy Place was the Golden Lampstand (Exod. 25:31-40). This Golden Lampstand held seven lamps. It was made in such a way that the oil could constantly flow to the lamps. This lamp was the only source of light in the Holy Place.

Now we have the new Golden Lampstand which is Jesus Christ Himself. Jesus said that He is the Light of the world. This light will guide you to see the truth and help you to worship God.

The constant flowing of the oil to the lamps represents the constant anointing of the Holy Spirit. We need the constant flowing of the Holy Spirit in our lives if we want to have a perfect relationship with God. We cannot be anointed only once; we must be anointed constantly.

The last furniture in the Holy Place was the Golden Altar of Incense (Exod. 30:1-10). This was placed before a curtain that separated the Holy Place from the Most Holy Place. The incense burned on the altar was a perfume of sweet-smelling aroma. This was another aspect of worshipping God.

This time God does not need aroma which is made by man, but He needs your deeds of faithfulness. In the new Tabernacle, God does not need the Golden Altar of Incense anymore, but He needs your way of life as an aroma of Christ. This means the way you live must show that you are a Christian who belongs to God. Second Corinthians 2:15 says that we are the aroma of Christ to God.

C) **The Most Holy Place**

After the Holy Place comes the Most Holy Place which was separated from the Holy Place by a very thick curtain. This curtain was only moved once year when the high priest entered it alone on the Holy Day of Atonement. He carried the blood of the sacrifice that was to be sprinkled on the Ark of the Covenant. The Most Holy place was the place where the presence of God was highly concentrated.

The Ark of the Covenant was placed in the most Holy Place (Exod. 25:10-22). This was the most important furniture in the Tabernacle. Here the Israelites kept the Ten Commandments. The Ark of the Covenant was put there to remind the people about God's covenant with them and all the miracles that He performed.

Now we have a new Ark of the Covenant where we keep God's commands, and that is in our hearts. The Law of God is no longer written on stones but on our hearts. Our hearts must represent the altar of the covenant with God.

When Jesus was crucified the curtain that separated the Holy Place from the Most Holy Place was torn into two from top to bottom (Matt. 27:51).

As we learned before, we became enemies of God because of sin. For this reason there was a big curtain placed between God and us. Our hearts were far from God and closed to His presence, but when Jesus Christ died, we became His friends and the curtain literally and symbolically was torn in two. Now, with the new Tabernacle which is always in us, we can worship God whenever and wherever we want. Through Jesus Christ we have been forgiven.

The Three Places

The entire Tabernacle was divided into three parts: the Outer Court, the Holy Place, and the Most Holy Place.

The Holy Court represents Jesus Christ Himself.

In the Old Testament, no one could come to God unless he passed through the Outer Court. In order to enter the Outer Court, one had to pass through the door. The same is true in our time today. The only way that you can go to God is through Jesus Christ.

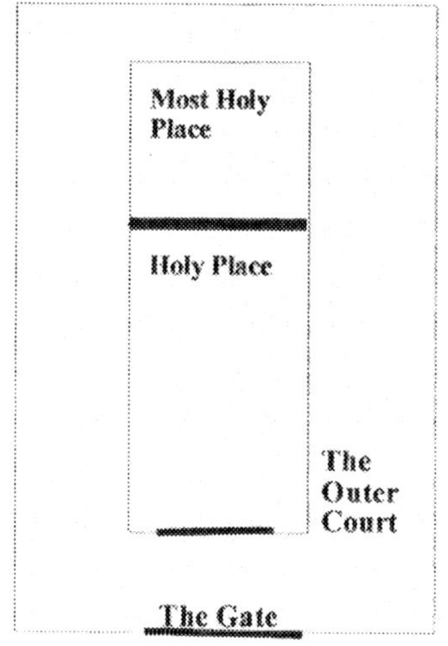

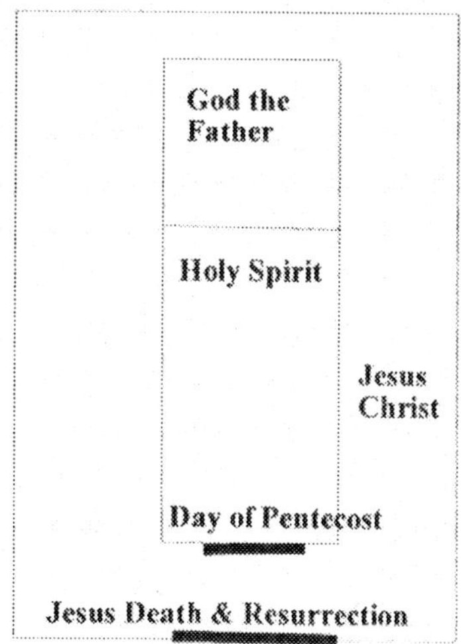

Only hanging around the court will not bring you into God's presence. You must enter the Holy Place. The Holy Place represents the baptism of the Holy Spirit. Once you have passed through the gate to the Holy Place then you are baptized in the Holy Spirit. No one can come to God if he ignores the Holy Spirit.

These days, there are many people who call themselves Christians but they ignore the Holy Spirit. These people are like those who are hanging around the Outer Court but never enter the Holy Place itself.

Next to the Holy Place comes the Most Holy Place. In our time this represents God the Father. No one can come to God the Father unless he is born again in water and spirit. To come to God the Father, we must believe in Jesus Christ as God; we must believe in the Holy Spirit as God; we must believe in God as the Father.

We believe the Outer Court as the Tabernacle, the Holy Place as the Tabernacle and the Most Holy Place as the Tabernacle. The Tabernacle exists with three parts. This is true for us Christians who believe in one God—the Father, the Son, and the Holy Spirit. We are made in three components—the soul, the spirit, and the body.
The liar is the man who ignores that Jesus is God and the Holy Spirit is God.

The Tabernacle and its Furniture

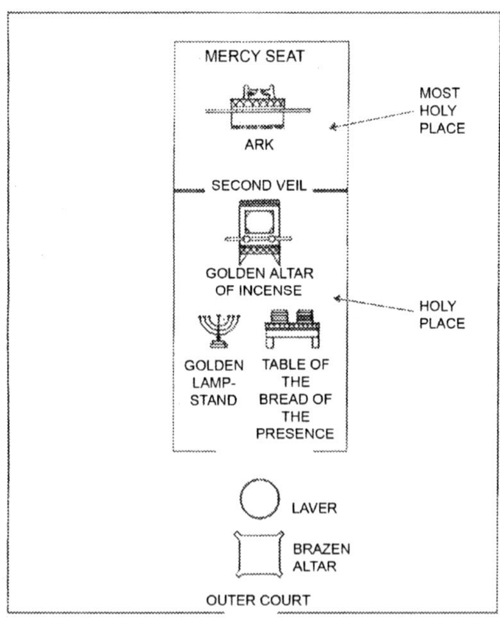

Ark of the Covenant
(ex. 25:10-22)
The ark was most sacred of all the furniture in the tabernacle. Here the Hebrews kept a copy of the Ten Commandments, which summaruzed the whole covenant.

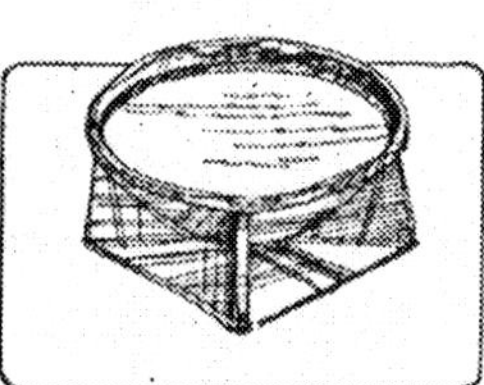

Bronze Laver
(Ex. 30:17-21)
It was to the laver of bronze that the priest would come for cleansing. They must be pure to enter the presence of God.

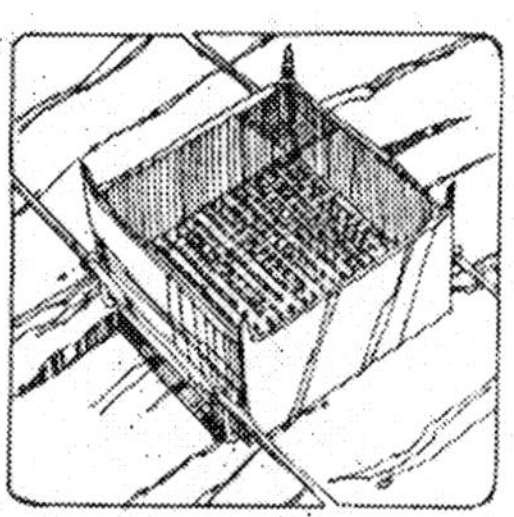

Altar of Burnt Offering
(Ex. 27:1-8)
Animal sacrifices were offered on this altar, located in the court in front of the tabernacle. The blood of the sacrifice was sprinkled on the four horns of the alar.

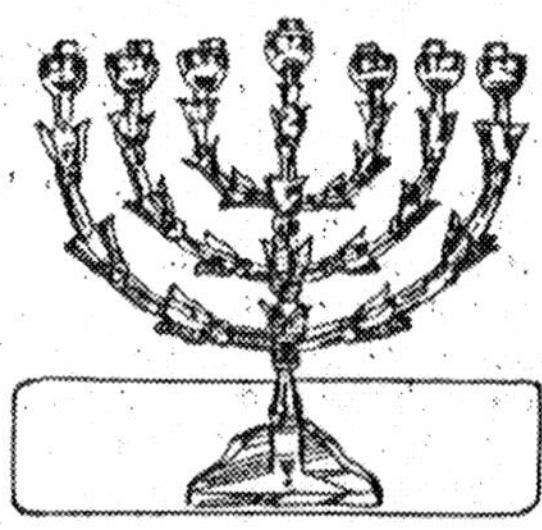

Gold Lampstand
(Ex. 25:31-40)
The gold lampstand stood in the holy place, opposite the table of showbread. It held seven lamps, flat bowls in which a wick lay with one end in the oil of the bowl and the lighted end hanging out.

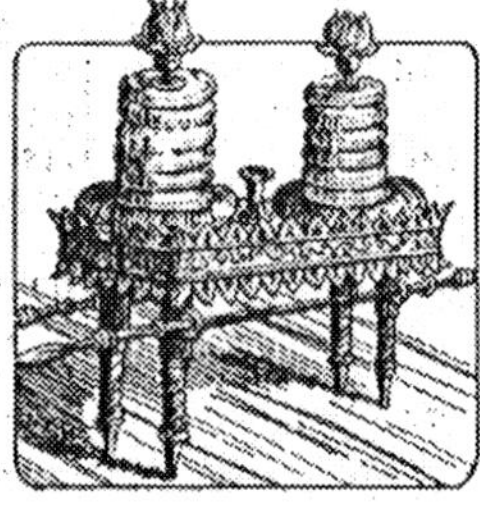

Table of Showbread
(Ex. 25:23-30)
The table of showbread was a stand on which the offerings were placed. Always in God's presence on the table were the 12 loaves of bread representing the 12 tribes.

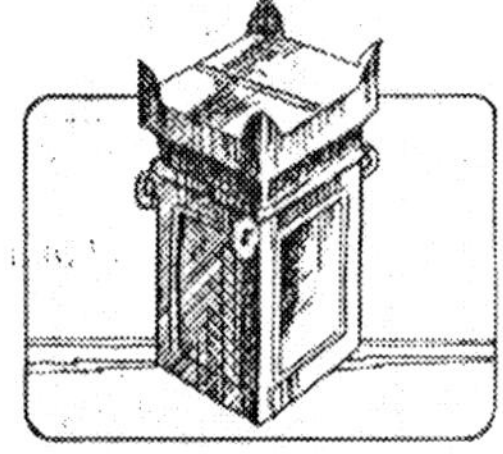

Altar of incense
(Ex. 30:1-10)
The altar of incense inside the tabernacle was much smaller than the altar of burnt offering outside. The incense burned on the altar was a perfume of a sweet smelling aroma.

SUMMARY

We have learned about the Tabernacle and its relationship with Jesus Christ and Christianity.

We learned that we must worship God in the spiritual Tabernacle, which means that we must worship Him in Spirit. We can only do this if we enter the gate, which is Jesus Himself, and be baptized in the Holy Spirit. We also need to live upon God's word which is written in our hearts and not on stones.

MAIN SCRIPTURES
Exodus 24–40

REFERENCE SCRIPTURES
Matthew 27:51
John 4:2; 10:9
2 Corinthians 2:15
Hebrews 9:11-12

TO MEMORIZE AND MEDITATE UPON
HEBREWS 9:12

HE DID NOT ENTER BY MEANS OF THE BLOOD OF THE GOATS AND CALVES; BUT HE ENTERED THE MOST HOLY PLACE FOR ALL BY HIS OWN BLOOD HAVING OBTAINED ETERNAL REDEMPTION.

QUESTIONS:

1. Why it is important for us to study the Tabernacle?

2. Write down the all the furniture in the Tabernacle and try to relate them to Jesus Christ and the Holy Spirit.

NOTES:

LESSON 12
Approaching God and Holiness

Leviticus (all chapters)

INTRODUCTION TO THE BOOK OF LEVITICUS

Leviticus is the third book of the Old Testament. It is the continuation of the book of Exodus. Actually all five books of Moses are strongly connected to each other.

The title of this book was derived from a Greek translation, which means “pertaining to Levites” (Leviticus). In Leviticus, God gave instructions to the priests who were only a small group of the tribe of Levi. Many recognize this book as a manual for the priests of that time. However, a majority of theologians and teachers consider this book as an Old Testament manual of worship for the nation of Israel. In this book, the Israelites learned how to approach and worship God.

In Leviticus we are confronted with different types of ceremonies and rituals concerning sacrifice and worship codes. Born-again Christians believe that every law and God-given code of worship and sacrifice represents something about Jesus Christ. These codes represent physical elements of something spiritual that would be revealed to mankind in the New Testament later.

Leviticus can be divided into two major areas:

Codes and Methods to Approach God (chapters 1–16): Approaching God by ceremonial codes and methods.

Codes and Methods to Holiness and Purity (chapters 17–27): Maintaining relationship with God by the codes and methods of holiness.

TODAY'S JOURNEY

Since the beginning of the human race and the fall of man, many have tried to approach God. Many nations and races have tried to come in contact with the unknown God who made the heavens and the earth. Even today, among some primitive tribes, people try to approach God. They fail however, because they do not know who the real God is.

In the previous lessons we have seen how God rescued the Israelites from the bondage of darkness and brought them out of Egypt. God revealed Himself to the Israelites through Moses and told them His name: I AM WHO I AM. The Israelites also saw the power and manifestations of God's hand on their side. Along the journey, God rescued them many times from hunger, thirst, diseases, and many other dangerous situations. They saw the loving and forgiving heart of God. For this reason they needed to approach Him, to have fellowship with Him, and to show Him their love. But how can they do this? How can a mortal and sinful man approach the immortal and Holy God? How can the poor contact the rich? How can death contact life?

For this reason God called out Moses and gave him certain laws and codes to teach the Israelites for approaching God. In these laws, God appointed a priest to be a medium between man and Himself.

To approach God the Israelites needed five ceremonies that I call sacrificial ceremonies:

1. *The Burnt Offering*
2. *The Meal (Grain) Offering*
3. *The Fellowship (Peace) Offering*
4. *The Sin Offering*
5. *The Trespass (Guilt) Offering (chapters 1–5)*

Studying all the offerings and ceremonial rules takes much investigation and research for those interested in this topic. What I will try to explain in this lesson is more than what most commentators offer. I will relate the ceremonies to our Christian lives today.

God gave these kinds of offerings so that the Israelites could approach Him.

Every relationship begins with an approach. If you want to make friends with an unknown person, you first need to approach the person. If you need a job in a company, you first need to approach the human resource director or manager of that company. The same is true with God. If you are in need of a close relationship with God, you need to approach Him. In Old Testament times this approach was not easy because it had lots of rules and regulations. Furthermore, man could never come into contact with God through his own way. Instead, this could only take place through the priests. In Leviticus these priests were Aaron and the sons of Aaron. Put simply, there were many obstacles between God and man. These obstacles include:

1. *The high priests*
2. *The priests*
3. *The law*
4. *The offerings*

The offerings and sacrifices could only take place under the authority of the high priests. They were the only designated people who could practice the ceremonies. If you read through Leviticus 1–6, you can see that with all five offerings the high priests and the priests were involved.

We also learn in Leviticus that the high priests and the priests were considered mortal and sinful; they were not perfect.

With the coming of Christ everything changed; God replaced all these high priests with one who was greater—the only supreme and High Priest who is the Lord Jesus Christ. In Hebrews 8:1-2, the writer says:

> *We do have such a High Priest, who sat down at the right hand of the throne of the Majesty in heaven, and who serves in the sanctuary, the true tabernacle set up by Lord and not by man.*

Hebrews 8 talks about a new High Priest. His name is Jesus Christ. He is without fault and He is free of sin. Also Hebrews 9:11 tells us that Christ came as a High Priest of the good things that were already here.

From the other side there were priests who were mediators between man and God in the tabernacle of the Old Testament. Since we have Jesus Christ and believe in Him, and because He lives in us through His Spirit, we automatically become fellow priests and saints with Him under His High Priesthood. The Greatest High Priest dwells in us! (1 Pet. 2:9).

Another obstacle between man and God was the Law. The Law kept human beings in the bondage of sin because nobody could keep its fullness and perfection. Because of the Law, man became the slave of sin, and for this reason he could not come into contact with God. God is holy and men are sinners. They could not meet each other. Even today many people try to live good according to the standards of the world and universal law, but that is not enough for God. God will judge them based on the Law and they will be condemned eternally. In our eyes men do some good things, but we only see a small percentage of their inner and private lives. What can make us free from the Law? The Bible says that Christ came to make us free from the Law. By believing in Him we are justified and by His grace we are forgiven. Galatians 5 teaches us that Christ came to set us free from the slavery of the Law: "It is for freedom that Christ has set us free. Stand firm, then, and do not let yourselves be burdened again by the yoke of slavery" (Gal. 5:1). Further, we read in verse 4:

> *You who are trying to be justified by the Law have been alienated from Christ; you have fallen away from grace.*

The good news for us is that Christ took our sins upon Himself and by His grace He saved us. He represents us to the Father without any fault. Truly the ways of man are more complicated than God's way.

Offerings or Sacrifices (chapters 1–16)

Lastly, there were ceremonies that led men to God. These ceremonies and offerings were skilfully and strictly given by God to the Israelites so they could approach Him. The commands and codes of the offerings were so strict that if one did not obey them exactly he could lose his life. These codes for the offerings and ceremonies worked like the pinch buttons of a bomb. Some buttons will activate the bomb and only one will deactivate it. If one chooses the wrong button, the bomb will explode. For this reason these ceremonies and offerings took place in fear.

Let me give you an example from the book of Leviticus.

> *Aaron's sons Nadab and Abihu took their censers, put fire in them and added incense. They offered unauthorized fire*

> *before the Lord, contrary to his command. So fire came out from the presence of the Lord and consumed them, and they died before the Lord.*
>
> (Leviticus 10:1-2)

This is an interesting story because here we have two priests who actually had good intentions but they did not obey what God had prescribed for the offering. The fire consumed them and they both died.

These days there are so many people who try to do their own thing. They have correct intentions and motives but they are not doing things God's way. God has only one way and that way is the Lord Jesus Christ. Jesus said: "I am the Way, the Truth and the Life." Thanks to God who has sent His own beloved Son Jesus Christ and freed us from the bondage of ceremonies and offerings because He Himself became the offering for us. We do not need any ceremonial offerings. Christ has redeemed us from these.

Below is another clear example:

> *The Lord said to Moses, speak to Aaron and his sons and all the Israelites and say to them: "This is what the Lord has commanded: Any Israelite who sacrifices an ox, a lamb or a goat in the camp or outside of it instead of bringing it to the entrance to the Tent of Meeting to present it as an offering to the Lord—that man shall be considered guilty of a bloodshed; he has shed blood and must be cut off from his people."*
>
> (Leviticus 17:1-4)

In this passage, God clearly prohibited any sacrifice outside the tent or inside the tent. Otherwise, a man would be guilty of bloodshed. Since Jesus Christ is the only door to the Father, if someone tries to approach God in any other way than Jesus Christ, then that man is guilty of bloodshed; he will be judged on the day of judgement. God only accepts our worship if it goes through Jesus Christ.

The word "camp" above means other religions because there are many beliefs that try to approach God but not through the right entrance! The outside camp means the people who make their own way of life and have their own philosophies about God and His existence! Both groups must realize that they cannot do it without Jesus Christ!

From what we have read, there were big obstacles between man and God. Jesus Christ took them all and put them aside because all these things are summarized in the person Jesus Christ (read Hebrews 10). If you want to approach God, the only way is through Jesus Christ. By accepting Jesus Christ as your Saviour you will enter into a new realm of peace and joy with God. Do not try doing it your own way!

Old Testament Offerings

As I mentioned earlier, God gave the Israelites five offering ceremonies:

1. *The Burnt Offering*
2. *The Meal (Grain) Offering*
3. *The Fellowship (Peace) Offering*
4. *The Sin Offering*
5. *The Trespass (Guilt) Offering (chapters 1–5)*

The common factor in all these offerings is that every time God gave these laws of offering, He emphasized one important thing: the offer must be without defect (Lev. 1:3). This is a fact! If you love a person you need to give him your best. The same is true with God. God gave His best for us with Jesus Christ. Now it is our turn to give the best of what we have to our Lord and Father.

These days there are many Christians who have hidden areas in their lives that they do not want to surrender to God. Christianity requires that you surrender whatever you have including your character, yourself, and everything all for the glory of God. Look, for instance, at the story of Abraham and Isaac. Abraham was ready to give away his best to God, his only beloved son, Isaac. We cannot love the world and at the same time love God. We must choose only one!

Many born-again Christians teach that these five sacrifices all represent Christ Jesus. I totally agree with them, but I would like to go further and bring a new interpretation for these sacrifices. "Sacrifice" in the Hebrew language is called *Q-urban*, which literally means, "that which someone brings near the presence of God."

I believe Jesus Christ did His job to be the ultimate sacrifice because He was sacrificed once and for all. But sacrifices and offerings are duties to the Creator. We must bring sacrifices and offerings to our Creator: the God of Trinity. But what shall we sacrifice to Him? Are meats, fruits, or grains enough to satisfy Him? No.

During the Old Testament era, animals and crops were used for sacrifice. But since the death and resurrection of Christ we are now sacrifices for God. Do not misunderstand me. I do not mean that we must die physically. No, what I mean is written in the Bible—we must be living sacrifices for God. This means every aspect of our lives must become sacrifices for God. It means our old way of life must die and the new life must begin. We must be born-again! (John 3:16).

Keeping this in our mind, let us take the Burnt Offering as an example. Burnt Offering means *Holo-Caust.*
Holo= burnt and Caust=offering.
That is why this term is used for the tragedy of the Jews during the Second World War. Six million Jews died and were turned into ashes. The scholars gave a symbolic meaning for this event and gave it the name of Holocaust.

God begins His commands in Leviticus with the Burnt Offering. A burnt offering was offered every morning and evening by all Israelites (Exod. 29:39-42). This offering needed to be from the herd and it had to be a male without a defect. It must also be presented at the entrance of the tent. A young bull must be slaughtered and the priests had to put the sacrifice on the burning wood of fire until it was totally consumed (Lev. 1).

God first gave this ceremonial sacrifice so that the Israelites could approach Him. This burnt offering was a physical shadow of what would happen later: the Baptism of the Holy Spirit.

The first encounter a Christian must have in his life after accepting Christ as Savior is the baptism of the Holy Spirit. That is why the Acts of the Apostles contained several testimonies about this very important promise of Jesus Christ. Let us compare this with the Burnt Offering:

The Lord said that the offering must be at the entrance of the tent. This means that before you approached God the Father, you must come near the entrance. This entrance is called Jesus Christ. Jesus said: I AM THE DOOR. That is the first step a person must take.

Of course before they brought the young bull to be sacrificed, they washed and cleaned it so that it would be perfect. For our time, this symbolizes baptism in water. After the bull was presented at the entrance of the tent, it had to be prepared for the burnt offering. The priest needed to lay his hands on the bull and prepare the offering to be set on fire. This looks exactly like what was written in the book of Acts. Many times people received the baptism of the Holy Spirit through the laying on of hands. After the laying on of the hands, the bull was prepared for the altar to be sacrificed as a burnt offering. It needed to be consumed by fire until it was changed into ashes.

The event of baptism itself is something familiar only on a spiritual dimension. With the burnt offering, God used a man-made fire, but with the baptism of the Holy Spirit, God used a Perfect

Fire—Himself, the Holy Spirit. Fire is one of the symbols of the Holy Spirit. On the Day of Pentecost, when the disciples were baptized with the Spirit, the Holy Spirit came like fire upon them. Yes, these disciples became living sacrifices, consumed by the fire from heaven. Further, we read that everything had to be totally burned, even the internal organs of the bull. For our case, baptism means we must allow the fire to consume every aspect of our life both inside and outside, a complete combustion! We must allow the Holy Spirit to change us just like the priests made sure that the fire burned everything: WE MUST BECOME LIVING SACRIFICES FOR CHRIST JESUS!

When God asked for the burnt offering from the Israelites, He said that the aroma of this offering would please God (Lev. 1:13). For us who believe in Jesus, it means our lives must become a pleasing aroma. This will make the heart of God rejoice. That is why God is pleased with children who obey His commands (see 2 Cor. 2:15).

If we look further to the other four offerings, they also represent other aspects of the Christian faith. For example, the Grain Offering (Lev. 2) can symbolize our Scripture reading and meditation on it through the Holy Spirit. The Fellowship Offering (Lev. 3) can represent prayer and meditation with God and also the fellowship of Christians with each other in the Church. The Sin and Guilt Offering (Lev. 4–5) can represent the confession of our sins to the Lord because even though we are Christians we still sin. But God said to be honest and to confess our sins to Him and He will hear our prayers and forgive our sins (see 1 John 1:9).

Holiness (chapters 17–27)

In Leviticus 17–27, we are confronted with different laws and regulations that kept the Old Testament Israelites holy in the eyes of the Father. We must realize that these laws and ceremonies were strongly focused on the physical level first and then the spiritual. If you read chapters 17–19, you can find various laws designed to keep the Israelites holy. Leviticus 17 focuses on how the drinking of blood and the eating of particular animals makes a person unclean. Leviticus 18 is about various physical and sexual immoralities, and Leviticus 19 discusses different offences like stealing, lying, defrauding neighbours, and the like.

In Leviticus 19:2 God said to the Israelites: "Be Holy because I, the Lord your God, am Holy." God made us in His own image, but sin separates us from God. That is why God gave the standards of holiness to bring us back to Him. But this did not satisfy God for that reason, He chose someone more effective and powerful to make us holy—Jesus Christ! By believing in Jesus Christ, we automatically become holy because He who is Holy dwells in us. But this does not mean that we will not keep the Ten Commandments. If we fail in fulfilling any of the Ten Commandments, Jesus Christ will still forgive and forget our mistakes by His grace. We are saved by grace and we are made holy by God's grace! Of course there are laws about eating that are still in the New Testament. God gave us the free will to choose whether to obey them or not. But we will not be unholy anymore simply because of what we eat or touch (see Rom. 14).

The word "Holy" in the original Hebrew language means "separated one." God is Holy because He is separated from sin and the sinful man. He does not identify with sin at all.

When God calls us to be holy this means that He wants us to be separated from sin, just like Him. When God says we must be holy, it means we must be united with Him. This unification can only take place through God the Son, Jesus Christ! Yes, in Jesus Christ we become the "called out ones," (*Ekklesia* in Greek).

For the first time in his history man was called "holy" without any ceremonial rules and regulations. This time man did not choose to be holy, but God called him to be holy through His only Son Jesus Christ.

In 1 Corinthians 1:2 Paul begins his letter with: "To the church of God in Corinth, to those sanctified in Christ Jesus and called to be holy." This means that this time you are not holy by your own deeds, but you are called holy by the spoken word of God: Jesus Christ (see John 1).

In Leviticus, there were also different kinds of feasts and festivals that reminded the people and kept them as a holy nation. The important ones were: 1. The Passover Festival; 2. The Feast of Pentecost; 3. The Feast of Booths; 4. The Feast of Trumpets; and 5. The Day of Atonement. All these days were the holy days. Sabbaths, too, were holy days. We just read that "holy" means "separated one." These above-mentioned days are separated from all other days of the year and the Sabbath is separated from all the other days of the week! That is why we call them holy days. The word "holiday" comes from this!

Passover (Lev. 23:1-8), is the great annual feast that recalls the sacrifice of a lamb in Egypt when God wanted to rescue them. It celebrates the time when the Israelites marked their doorframes with the blood of the lamb so that the angel of death would pass over their homes without harming them. Only those without the blood mark died (Exod. 12:1-13:16).

The Last Supper of the Lord Jesus Christ also took place at the Passover Festival when He said, "This is My Blood that you drink." In our time today, only through the Blood of Jesus, which was poured into our hearts, can we be saved and rescued from the hands of the angel of death!

The Feast of Pentecost (Lev. 23:15-22) is the harvest festival when the Israelites gave thanks to God for the grain and other crops harvested. They sacrificed their first fruits to the Father. Likewise, for us Christians, the Holy Spirit was poured out on the first fruit disciples of Jesus in Pentecost! This was the beginning of the church.

The Feast of Trumpets (Lev. 23:23-25) represents when the Lord commanded Moses that on the first day of the seventh month the Israelites must have a day of rest, a sacred assembly commemorated with trumpet blasts. The purpose of this feast was to present Israel before the Lord for His favor.

The Feast of Booths or the Feast of Tabernacles (Lev. 12:33-44) was held to remember the years when the Israelites wandered in the wilderness before they occupied the Promised Land. In Leviticus 23:42, God said to the Israelites: "Live in booths so your descendants will know that I had the Israelites live in booths when I brought them out of Egypt, I am the Lord your God."

The Day of Atonement (Lev. 23:26-32) is a day of fasting, humiliation, and reverence. Atonement means reconciliation of the guilty by divine sacrifice. On this day, the high priest made atonement for his own sin and then entered the most holy place of the tabernacle to make a special animal sacrifice to atone for the sins of all the people.

Thanks be to God that that we do not need all these things because our High Priest, Jesus Christ, reconciled us with the Father forever on the day of His crucifixion when the curtain between the Holy Place and the Most Holy Place was torn into two (see lesson 11).

Lastly, there were not only days which were holy but there were also certain holy years:

For the Sabbath Year (Lev. 25:1-7), after entering the Promised Land, God asked the Israelites to work in the fields for six years in a row, but on the seventh year the land was to rest. This Sabbath Year was designed so that the Israelites could devote themselves fully to the Lord.

Also there was another Sabbath year that was called the Year of Jubilee. With this the Israelites counted out seven Sabbath years (7 x 7 years is 49 years) so that on the fiftieth year there would be liberty for all the inhabitants. In this jubilee, every one returned to their clan and family. Like the Sabbath Year, no one was allowed to work.

Three Chapters in Human History

When we look at the spiritual side of man's history, we will notice three human eras. The first era is what I call, the Physical Era of Discipline. From the fall of man until the period of John the Baptist, God the Father did His best to introduce and reveal Himself to His chosen people. He focused merely on the physical aspects. God tried to discipline His people through rules and regulations, ceremonies, and traditions that were mostly focused on physical aspects.

This era can also be called the Era of Childhood where God taught His children how to live and He punished them when they disobeyed. But He also restored and encouraged them at the right time. However, when the physical discipline started to lose its purpose, God planned to introduce something spiritual. But before going to the spiritual part, He needed a bridge between His spiritual plan and His physical disciplining. The perfect bridge was Jesus Christ. In the personality of Jesus Christ, the spiritual meets the physical. God revealed Himself through Jesus Christ. God became man and lived among us.

The thirty-five year period in which Jesus Christ walked the earth is what I call the Bridge Period. In this period, Jesus Christ, God the Son, is the center of all life existence. Whatever was found in the Old Testament such as the ceremonies, tabernacle, rules, and Law were all summarized in Jesus Christ.

After the death and resurrection of Jesus Christ and the coming of the Holy Spirit on the day of Pentecost, man entered the Spiritual era, which I call the Era of the Holy Spirit. Until now we are in this

period in which the Holy Spirit reveals Himself through the Holy Spirit which can only be received through Jesus Christ!
What I am trying to say is that without the Physical Period we can never understand the Bridge Period and the Spiritual Period. The Bible says, first the physical then the spiritual. Thus, whatever you read in the Old Testament must be fulfilled in the person of Jesus Christ! Try to keep this advice in mind!

SUMMARY

In this lesson we attempted a short overview of the book of Leviticus. We did not go deeper into the ceremonial facts since I trust the student to do this on his or her own. In this lesson, I have tried to show the most important spiritual aspects of this book for our daily lives. We learned that God is not pleased with worship if it is not through Jesus Christ. Jesus is the only way to come to the Father. We also learned the symbolic meanings of the sacrifices mentioned in Leviticus and how they help us approach God. We learned that all these were summarized in Jesus Christ. Only believing in Christ is not enough, we must be baptized in the Holy Spirit and become a living sacrifice for the Lord Jesus Christ.

Lastly, we saw that what we eat or drink or touch does not make us holy. We become holy when we have Jesus Christ dwelling in us through His Spirit. We are not justified by the Law, but we are pardoned by grace. Nevertheless, we must do our best to keep the commands of God.

Keep your eyes upon Jesus because by His words, He has called you, HOLY! Amen.

MAIN SCRIPTURES
Leviticus (all chapters)

REFERENCE SCRIPTURES
John 1 and 3
Romans 14
2 Corinthians 2:15
Galatians 5:1
1 Peter 2:9
1 John 1:9
Hebrews 9:11-10

TO MEMORIZE AND MEDITATE UPON
LEVITICUS 19:2

BE HOLY BECAUSE I, THE LORD YOUR GOD, AM HOLY.

QUESTIONS:

1. How many feasts and celebrations are mentioned in Leviticus? Mention them.

2. Why are we not supposed to live by the ceremonial sacrifices anymore?

3. Are the ceremonies written in Leviticus still needed for us Christians to approach God today? Explain.

NOTES:

NOTES:

LESSON 13

In The Wilderness

Numbers (all chapters)

INTRODUCTION TO THE BOOK OF NUMBERS

The fourth book of the Old Testament is Numbers. The Greek translation gave this book its name. It was called Numbers because God began to take a census of the nation of Israel. He numbered them and chose them for specific missions and ministries. Numbers tells us that there were two occasions when the nation Israel was numbered. The first one was in the beginning of the forty years journey and the other at the end. In Hebrews, this translates as, "In the Wilderness." This book not only teaches us about the numbering and the tasks of every tribe of Israel, but it also tells us the story of an unsatisfied nation, a nation that rebelled against God. This book is about a nation who grieved God and ignored His love! Numbers contains 36 chapters. Chapter 33 is a summary of the book. Scholars divided this book into three major sections based on the geographical position of the Israelites' journey. These three major sections are:

-From Sinai to Kadesh-Barnea (chapters 1–12)
-From Kadesh through the Wilderness and back to Kadesh (chapters 13–19)
-From Kadesh to Jordan (chapters 20–36)

See the map below:

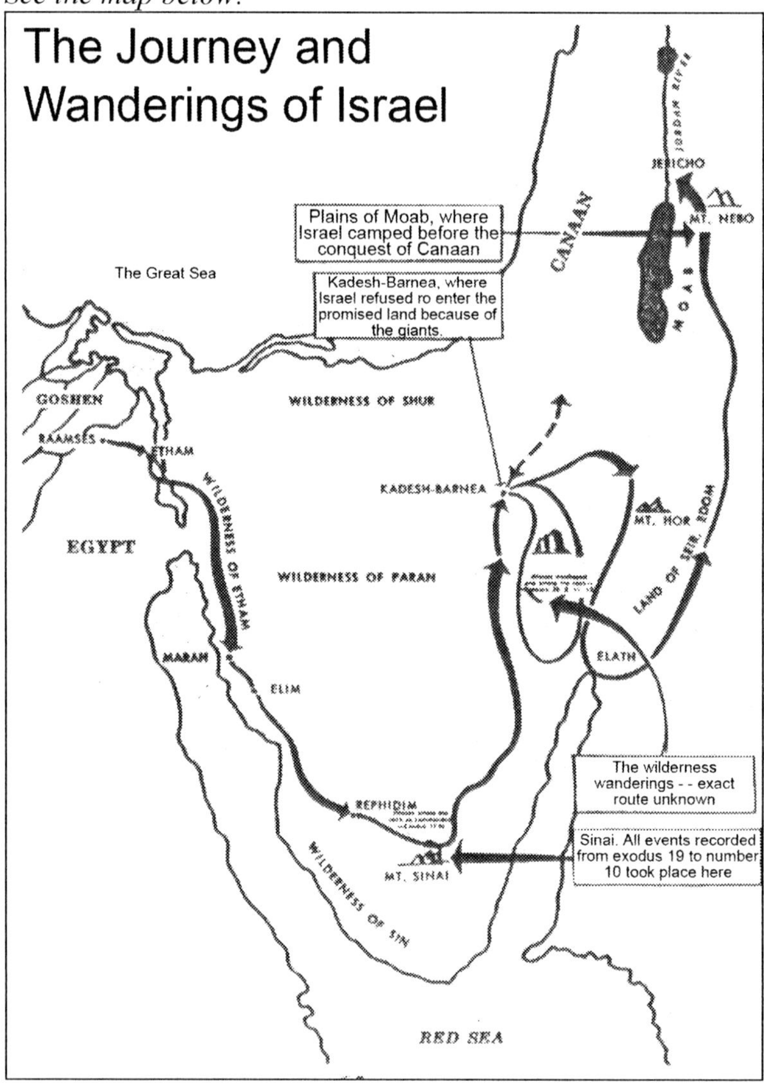

When God rescued the Israelites out of Egypt, they arrived at Sinai. Actually, the real journey began at the time they arrived at Sinai. While Israel was moving towards the Promised Land, God saw the need of taking a census or a numbering of the people (Num. 1–4).

God numbered the men from each tribe for military purposes (Num. 1) and some for other purposes. When the Israelites were called to move, they had to carry the tabernacle by themselves. So God numbered every tribe and positioned every tribe around the tabernacle and assigned the order of the march (Num. 2). God numbered the different tribes and assigned many men to do different jobs. God also gave instructions on how to set up and decorate the tabernacle. He gave instructions for putting up the lamps and how to observe the Passover. The tabernacle was to be carried exactly as God commanded. Imagine how heavy these tasks were. The numbering of these tribes is very interesting. However, I do not wish to focus on the actual numbering and ceremonial issues. Instead, I want to concentrate on the spiritual implications.

TODAY'S JOURNEY

The book of Numbers always reminds me of God's anger toward His people Israel and their journey that took forty years because of their disobedience! The nation that God chose to be a holy nation had to suffer in the wilderness! The question is why? There are many theories and reasons written in various books and theological studies. I believe there are three major factors for the forty years of punishment in the wilderness. The first factor was—*Rebellion against God.*

Rebellion against God

After God rescued Israel from Egypt, He trained and instructed them concerning the rules and regulations for setting up and carrying the Tabernacle to Sinai. God guided Israel to the Promised Land: "So they set out from the mountain of the Lord and travelled for three days. The Ark of the Covenant of the Lord went before them during those three days to find them a place to rest" (Num. 10:33). However, on the third day they began to complain about the burden that God laid upon them. Numbers 12:1-2 tells us that the people complained about their hardship, and when God heard them, He became furious. His anger came upon them and He sent fire to consume them.

1. Complaining about Hardship is one of the signs of rebellion against God. The Israelites complained about the hardship they were experiencing. If God wants to make something out of your life, He will first let you carry the load that He has given you. Jesus Christ said: "If you do not deny yourself and carry your cross and follow me, you are not worthy to be called my disciple" (Luke 14:27). These days many Christians do not want to carry their crosses. They complain about their lives. They complain a lot about the things they have and the things they don't have. The Bible, though, teaches us to be satisfied!

The Israelites got an assignment from God to carry the loads and to carry the Tabernacle. By doing this they could come to the Promised Land. So God gave them work, but they were not faithful to it. They complained! The Bible teaches us that when we Christians work for the Lord in the church or in a secular job, we must work and not complain.

It is hard to be called and chosen by God at the same time! Many people want to work for God, but when God gives them a load to carry, they complain and soon after they begin to fall out of God's plan! We receive from God according to our faith and according to our works in Him.

> *Do everything without complaining or arguing, so that you may become blameless and pure, children of God without fault in a crooked and depraved generation, in which you shine like star . . . .*
>
> *(Philippians 2:14)*

2. Material and Physical Complaints is another type of rebellion against God. Constantly, the Israelites and some rabbles (those who were not Israelites but came along with them from Egypt) complained about food and water. However, God was patient and sent them manna from heaven. Then they complained again and this time they wanted meat because they were tired of eating only manna.

God heard their rebellion and told them that they would eat so much that the meat would come out of their nostrils and they would get sick of it! (Num. 11:4-35). So God had the birds fall upon the camp and the people ate them. They ate so much that they got sick. The anger of God struck those who were complaining while they were eating!

After experiencing this, the Israelites didn't learn their lesson. They complained again because they had no water to drink (Num. 20). The Lord told Moses, "Speak to this rock and it will give water to the people." But Moses was angry and he took his staff and struck the rock twice and the water came out. God became angry with Moses and said, "Because you did not listen to what I said, in place of speaking to the rock, you struck it; you will never enter the Promised Land!" Even Moses rebelled against God by disobeying Him and dishonoring Him (see Num. 20:9-12).

As Christians we must not complain about what we receive from God. We must be satisfied and thankful with the material things we have even if we have little food and it is not so delicious! The Bible says to give thanks in all circumstances, and if you want something from the Lord, ask for it in prayer and with thankfulness (1 Thess. 5:18).

Also spiritually, be satisfied with what God has given you and ask Him gently for more but not with a complaining attitude. If you have the gift of tongues do not become jealous with someone who has the gifts of prophesying or healing. Be satisfied with what you have and God will use you mightily in your own ability and according to the gifts He has given you. Of course, you can always want more, but you must do it with love and thankfulness to God!

Rebellion against God's Man

God chose Moses to be the leader of Israel. Moses was meek and gentle towards Israel. Yet the people often rebelled against him and his leadership. Even his own family rebelled against him. Miriam, his sister, and Aaron, his brother, opposed him terribly.

Numbers 12:1-10 says that Miriam and Aaron began to talk against Moses because of his Cushite wife. "Has the Lord spoken only through Moses?" they said. "Hasn't he also spoken through us?" And the Lord heard this. At once the Lord said to Moses, Aaron and Miriam, "Come to the Tent of Meeting, all three of you." So the three of them came out. Then the Lord came down from the pillar of cloud and He stood at the entrance to the tent and summoned Aaron and Miriam. When both of them stepped forward, He said, "Listen to my words, when a prophet is among you, I reveal myself to him in dreams, I speak with him in dreams. But this is not true of my servant Moses; he is faithful in my house. With him I speak face to face, clearly and not riddle; why then were you not afraid to speak against My servant Moses?" The anger of the Lord burned against them, and He left them. When the cloud lifted from above the tent, there stood-Miriam-leprous like snow. Aaron turned towards her and saw that she had leprosy.

In every period of time God has chosen His men to proclaim the message of God and His plan for them. God spoke through Elijah, Elisha, John the Baptist, the apostles, and to other men and women of God. God used them all in their own times. God has used people like G. J. Lake or L. Moody Smith or Smith Wigglesworth. Men of God exist all around the world. God chooses for every nation His servant to lead them.

God chose Moses. God talked with him face to face. But Miriam and Aaron gossiped behind him and asked, "Why does God only talk to him? He should also talk to us!" Yes, these days many people in churches do not respect authority and the decisions of the Spirit-filled men of God. They doubt and complain regularly. "Why this?" and "Why that?" they exclaim. Why does the pastor make such and such decisions? Why does he talk that way? Why doesn't he do what all the other churches do? They probably opposed the leader and even gossiped behind his back. This act is not pleasing to God! If you belong to a Spirit-filled church and are under a Spirit-filled leader, stay with the leader. He knows what is best for you because God will guide him to lead you and because he has the Holy Spirit, the Spirit of truth.

> *Obey your leaders and submit to their authority. They keep watch over you as men who must give an account. Obey them so that their work will be a joy and not a burden, for that would be of no advantage for you.*
>
> (Hebrews 13:17)

Surely it was not an advantage for Miriam because God struck her with leprosy. Only Moses' prayer influenced God to have mercy on her. Miriam and Aaron saw the powers and miracles of God through Moses; Aaron was like an elder in the church!

Yes, these days the quarrels in churches come from those closest to the pastors and leaders, those whom the leaders would not expect trouble to come from!

Rebellion against God's Plan

God has a wonderful plan for every person. There is no one here on earth whom God has left without a plan. Especially when you are a Christian, God will reveal His plan to you. God is a good God and He wants to use you for His divine plan. The same thing happened with the Israelites. God's plan was to rescue them from Egypt and bring them to the Promised Land. God promised them a wonderful plan; a plan of giving them a land of milk and honey; to defeat all their enemies and give them the land. In Numbers 13, God asked Moses to send some men to explore the land of Canaan. So Moses built a group from every tribe and sent them to spy on the land.

When they came back on the fortieth day from spying the land, they reported that indeed the land was flowing with milk and honey. The land was blessed, they said, but they also argued that they could not possess it because the people of the land were much stronger than they. The Israelites were terrified. Everyone rebelled against God's plan and complained that God brought them to the desert to be killed by their enemies.

Only Caleb and Joshua were not terrified (see Num. 13–14). After they complained about God's plan, God became angry and said, "For forty years-one year for each of the forty days you explore the land–you will suffer your sins and know what it is like to have me against you!" (Num. 14:34).

God also promised that none of them would see the Promised Land except Joshua and Caleb. You simply cannot rebel against God's plan!

Take Jonah as another example. God asked him to go and preach repentance to Nineveh, but he did not follow God's command. Therefore, God punished him and sent him inside a fish until he repented.

The Israelites disobeyed God's plan because they feared the enemy. Today, God has a plan for your life. Do not fear the enemy. Just do what God wants you to do. The enemy (the devil) was defeated two thousand years ago. You can walk in victory and power. When God is on your side, who can be against you? God is with you through His Son Jesus Christ and the Holy Spirit.

SUMMARY

Three Lessons for Us

I believe the reason why the Israelites suffered for years in the wilderness was because they rebelled against God by complaining and being dissatisfied. They then opposed the chosen man of God. Lastly, they rebelled against God's plan. Today there are many Christians who are wandering in the desert for many years. My heart hurts when I see them without any sense of direction and motivation. They wander in their own desert and they stay nowhere. I have seen Christians who are many years in the Lord, but they still do not know their place and position in the Body of Christ. They are confused. They travel from church to church. In one or two years they have attended more than five or six Spirit-filled churches. Then when I see them again after three years, they are still wandering and doing nothing, confused and going nowhere! I see no difference that their life is "in the Lord." I have asked God to show me why there are people like this. He answered me through this teaching today: First, most of these men and women who jump from church to church and do not know where they belong after ten or twenty years are people who rebel against God.

Some people say, "I don't like this church. The music is too soft." Or "I don't like this church because I am not moved by the preacher's shouting." Or, "I don't like this church because they pray in tongues." These are the kinds of people who leave the church and transfer to another one. Sooner or later they find something to complain about and the cycle continues.

The second reason is rebellion against the man of God—the Leader! If you look at the life of confused Christians, you can tell that they think they are better than their leaders. They think they can do it better; they think that they do not need to submit under the leader's authority. Sooner or later they find another place where the leaders eventually mess up and then they go to another place. Some are even like Miriam and Aaron who gossip behind their leader's back. They say, "How come this leader doesn't do it my way?" Or, "I know better because the Holy Spirit talks to me!"

Christianity, however, means to submit to the Father, Son, and the Holy Spirit, and also to the chosen leaders.

Lastly, they rebelled against God's plan. Many confused Christians rebel against God's plan. For example, God wants a person to be an usher in the church because that is God's plan for him. But because of pride he or she wants to become a music leader. So every time his plan is frustrated he goes to another church or ministry. If your plan and God's plan do not match, you cannot be successful with your life. Submit yourself under God's plan!

My experience tells me that if God wants a person to be a leader or a pastor, God will immediately tell him and guide him. God will prepare everything for him to be so. I have seen a lot of people who, against the will of God, want to become a pastor or a leader, but after ten years they are still the same. They did not gain anything and they have no fruits. But they still want to be leaders. God is not happy with these kinds of people. That is why He confuses them until they repent and stay in one place and obey the Lord's voice. If you see yourself in this example, you need to repent and start your journey with the Lord again. Stay in one church under one authority and under God's plan for you.

MAIN SCRIPTURES
Numbers (all chapters)

REFERENCE SCRIPTURES
Luke 14:27
Philippians 2:14
1 Thessalonians 5:18
Hebrews 13:17

TO MEMORIZE AND MEDITATE UPON
PHILIPPIANS 2:14

DO EVERYTHING WITHOUT COMPLAINING OR ARGUING, SO THAT YOU MAY BECOME BLAMELESS AND PURE CHILDREN OF GOD, WITHOUT FAULT IN A CROOKED AND DEPRAVED GENERATION, IN WHICH YOU SHINE LIKE STARS.

QUESTIONS:

1. Name three major errors committed by the Israelites that led them to suffer for forty days in the wilderness. Give some examples.

2. Why do you think God punished the Israelites for forty days and not fifty six or thirty four days? Why forty days? Give Scripture references.

3. Read the book of Jonah and compare it with it the rebellion of Israel discussed in this lesson. How many similarities can you find? Mention three of them.

NOTES:

LESSON 14

Obedience and Love

Deuteronomy (all chapters)

INTRODUCTION TO THE BOOK OF DEUTERONOMY

The word Deuteronomy was derived from the Greek word, *Duetrionum* which can be translated as, “The Second Law” or “The Repetition of Law.” The book of Deuteronomy is a summary of the Law that was given to Moses almost forty years after the generation that was set free from the bondage of Egyptian tyranny. The repetition of the Law was a reminder to the present generation about God’s promise to bring them to the Promised Land. This new generation didn’t see the division of the Red Sea and the signs and wonders the Lord showed their forefathers. This new generation was a fresh generation ready to enter the Promised Land.

Personally, I’d like to call this book, “The Book of Curses and Blessings.” I say this because God gave the Israelites a choice between a blessed life and a cursed life.

One can divide this book into the following outline:

Review of the History (chapters 1–4)
Review of the Law (chapters 5–26)
Blessings or Curses (chapters 27–30)
The Last parts of Moses' Life (chapters 31–34)

TODAY'S JOURNEY

Remember the Past

Deuteronomy is interesting because it is a book that reflects the past and projects the future. In chapters 1–4 Moses reminded the Israelites about their history including the liberation of Israel from Egyptian bondage and their struggles and victories. Moses reminded them about their victories and failures. And in all these God was the central focus: "It was God who redeemed you"; "It was God who was with you"; and "It was God who disciplined you."

I believe that God, through Moses, not only reminded this specific generation about what He has done to their forefathers; He was also speaking to us today. He wants to remind us about the many good things He has done for us in the past.

As Christians, our past begins with the Gospel of Christ because He is our Redeemer from our spiritual wilderness and bondage. Jesus Christ our Savior saved humanity with His blood. We must always be reminded of what He did for us by reading the New Testament. The book of Acts is a good example of the victories and persecutions of the early church. Further, a Christian should always remember the day when he or she came to Christ and accepted Jesus as Lord and Savior. Do you remember your day? We must give thanks to God for all the things He did for us. If you read the Pauline books, you can see that Paul repeatedly shared the same stories about his encounter with Jesus Christ.

We Christians have testimonies to tell. By sharing them, we can transform people's lives just like the apostle Paul did.

THE GREATEST METHOD OF EVANGELISM AND SAVING SOULS IS TELLING YOUR TESTIMONY.

In so doing, you do not need any certificate or diploma. It was the testimony of Paul that made him an apostle to the Gentiles. Share your testimony with others.

We must learn from Moses' example. He shared the history of the past generation to the new generation of Israel. Remembering the past helps you learn from your mistakes. For instance, God gave the command to the Israelites to go and capture the Promised Land because He was with them. But the Israelites did not exactly obey what God asked them to do. They sent the spies to see the Promised Land, but when they returned they quarrelled and were terrified. For this reason, God punished them and kept them in the desert for forty years. The distance between them and the Promised Land was only fourteen days of journey, but they wandered in the wilderness for forty years. They could not even enter themselves; only their children could go in. By knowing the mistakes of the past, the new generation learned to obey God without any hesitation.

Remember and Obey Your God and His Commandments

In Deuteronomy 5–26, Moses reminded the new generation about the Law and the commandments God gave their forefathers forty years earlier. He said to them:

> *Keep His decrees and commands, which I am giving you today, so that it maybe well with you and your children after you and that you may live long in the land the Lord your God gives you for all time.*
>
> (Deuteronomy 4:40)

What do you remember about the decrees of God? Here are two very important Laws that God requires from every man and woman including you and me:

1. Love and obey the Lord your God (chapters 6 and 11)
2. Do not forget the Lord your God (chapter 8)

Love for God is the beginning of all success and prosperity. Jesus Christ taught us that the summary of all the Law is found in two things: love for God and love for our neighbors. It is the love for God that keeps us on the right path of Christian living. It is the love for God that helps us put His commands in our hearts. It is the love for God that helps us teach these commands to our children. It is the love for God that keeps us on fire to preach the Gospel to the others. The love for God is the key to a blessed living.

Secondly, as Christians we must never forget our God and His deeds for us (Deut. 6:12). Many people easily forget the good things He has done for them. Never forget that it is God who provides for your needs. The food you eat, the water you drink, the bed you sleep on are all blessings from God.

One of the reasons why societies fail is because they forget God. Let us take Europe as an example. Western Europe is one of the most advanced regions in the entire world. Technology, science and art are developed on this continent. In the beginning, the average European feared God and remembered Him as the source of inspiration for all artistic and human expressions. But today the love and fear of God are diminishing from the people. No one remembers God. No one goes to church. No one prays. No one gives thanks to God or praises Him.

The people commend their own knowledge and abilities. They are even proud of their own immoral activities which are against God's commands. In Western Europe, there is enough food for everyone. Everyone eats and drinks abundantly but only a minority prays and thanks God for it. The people even consider these kinds of activities shameful and childish (see Deut. 8:10-20).

But the Bible says differently:

> *When you have eaten and are satisfied, praise the Lord your God for the good land he has given you.*
>
> (Deuteronomy 8:10)

Forgetting the Lord also means worshipping other gods. These days many worship things other than God. Some worship money; some wealth; some their own children. The Lord our God, though, is a jealous God and He will destroy disobedient people when He returns (Deut. 8:19). What about you today? What is God's place in your life? Put God first and you shall prosper.

Blessings or Curses

Many people ask the question, "If there is a God, why is our world getting worse"? This is a very important question! God never desired that the world be cursed. God never wanted wars, hate, anger, sickness and all these things. God never intended to give us these things. On the contrary, He wants us to have an abundant life. The important thing we need to put in mind is that God is giving us the chance to choose blessings or curses. The choices we make influence people and all creatures. It is the human being who began slavery; it is the human being who began to cut trees and destroy the forests, not God. Deuteronomy 27–30 teaches us how to gain all the blessings and receive all the curses (see Deut. 28).

But even though you have been a victim, you can be free from your victimized life. There is a way to be free and that is by believing and accepting Jesus Christ as your Lord and Saviour. With Jesus Christ you are not a victim anymore; you are more than a conqueror.

Moses

The last part of Deuteronomy describes the closing of Moses' life (31–34). Chapter 32 is called the "songs of Moses" and chapter 33 deals with the blessings that Moses spoke to the tribes of Israel. The death of Moses is written about in chapter 34.

It is beneficial for us to look back at the life of Moses, an incredible man of God who led the Israelites from Egyptian oppression and slavery.
The life of Moses can be divided into three major periods, each comprises forty years. The first period is from his birth until the time he escaped from Egypt to Midian (Acts 7:23-29).

The second part begins with his return from Midian to Egypt to rescue the Jews (Exod. 7:7), and the third period is the last forty years of his life earth (Deut. 34:7).

His Birth

Moses was the third child of Amram and Jochabed. Aaron and his sister Miriam were older than he. He belonged to the tribe of Levi (1 Chron. 6:1-3).

Moses experienced extreme persecution and serious life-threats when he was a baby. The Pharaoh issued a law that every baby boy must be killed. Moses was one of them but God protected and saved him.

These days there are lots of people being killed even before they are born. Abortion is not from God. Only God should decide whether a child must live or die. The same issue happened in the time of Moses. However, in that time they did not posses the technique to kill an innocent baby before birth. Thus, they waited until the baby was born. Thank God that the one Pharaoh wanted to kill was raised in his own palace because his daughter found baby Moses in a basket being carried by the river while she was bathing. God made a way so that Moses would be raised by his own Jewish mother. The daughter of Pharaoh took Moses' mother as her maidservant to raise the child (Exod. 2:8-10).

They called the child "Moses" because he was found in the water. Moses means, "drawn out." Can you see the wisdom of God? The one whom Pharaoh wanted to kill was raised by Pharaoh himself. And even his real mother got paid to raise her own child!

No matter what situation you are in, God is going to make a way when there is no way. All the tricks of the devil against your life will return to him!

Moses killed an Egyptian man and because of that he fled from Egypt to Midian (Exod. 2:13-15). Many believe that Moses already knew that God would use him but he rushed and for this reason he became a fugitive and fled to Midian and stayed there for forty years. This was forty years of disciplining Moses. God also disciplined the Israelites during their forty years of wandering in the desert.

He married the daughter of a local chief named Jethro in Midian where he worked as a shepherd. It was during this period of Moses' life that God prepared him for the great job he had to do for God's people. God first trained him to shepherd the sheep and goats in the fields and mountains, and when the right time came, God used him to shepherd the Israelites. Moses, who was raised up to be the next prince of Egypt, had adopted himself to a shepherd's life. This happened so that he could carry on a greater work for the kingdom of God.

Eventually, Moses was ready to do his calling. He had the burning bush experience where God revealed His name and called Moses to go back to Egypt. Moses asked for a sign. God told him to throw his rod on the ground. The moment Moses threw his rod it changed into a snake. Then God told Moses to take it by its tail. This is exactly what God does with us. The rod symbolizes our human capacities and talents. When we are transformed into a new creation by believing in Jesus Christ, God will take our talents and our abilities and turn them upside down. This means that our talents will no more be used for the world but for the glory of God. Take, for example, a person with a good voice; first he sings for the world, but as soon as God change him, he will sing with a different purpose. He will glorify the Lord so that when he sings, people start to get healed.

What was your talent before? Ask God to use this talent and ability for His kingdom. This will be your rod!

The last part of Moses' life took forty years; from the time he rescued the Israelites to the time when the new generation of Israelites was ready to enter the Promised Land. Moses, however, did not enter the Promised Land because of his disobedience. After God showed him the Promised Land, he died in Moab. He died when he was 120 years old. God chose Joshua to be his successor and to lead the Israelites to the Promised Land.

SUMMARY

We learned that we must remember the past, remember the Law, and remember the goodness of God. We also learned that blessings and curses are matters of choosing between God and the enemy. We also reviewed the life of Moses and used it as an inspiration for our own personal lives.

With this lesson we come to the end of the five books of Moses (Pentateuch), the books of Law. I hope and pray that by having read these Bible studies, your life has been changed. In the coming Bible studies we will be studying the history of the nation Israel.

MAIN SCRIPTURES
Deuteronomy (all chapters)

REFERENCE SCRIPTURES
Exodus 1–3
Exodus 7:7
1 Chronicles 6:1-3
Acts 7:23-29

TO MEMORIZE ANDMEDITATE UPON
DEUTERONOMY 6:4-5

HEAR, O ISRAEL: THE LORD OUR GOD IS ONE. LOVE THE LORD YOUR GOD WITH ALL YOUR HEART AND WITH ALL YOUR SOUL AND WITH ALL YOUR STRENGTH.

QUESTIONS:

1. Why must we Christians remember the past?

2. What does "Deuteronomy" mean?

3. Read Deuteronomy 28 and make a summary of all the blessings and curses that the Lord has promised us.

NOTES:

. PART II .

Journey Through History

LESSON 15
Joshua

Joshua (all chapters)

INTRODUCTION TO THE BOOK OF JOSHUA

The book of Joshua is the continuation of the book of Deuteronomy. We read here about the location of the Israelites; they were still camping of the east side of Jordan River and were waiting for God's command in order to begin the battle. The book of Joshua is the historical beginning of the State of Israel.

One can compare this book with the book of Acts in the New Testament because just after the death and resurrection of Jesus, the church was born and warfare and persecution immediately followed the Christians. The same situation happened when Moses died. Joshua was given the leadership and the warfare immediately began. Since our warfare is not against flesh and blood anymore, I consider the book of Acts as a spiritual reflection of the book of Joshua.

The writer of Joshua is unknown. The book was named after Joshua by virtue of the leadership position given to him by God. His name was changed by Moses from Hoshea, which means "salvation," to Joshua, which means "the Lord saves" or "the Lord gives victory" (Num. 13:8, 16).

The book of Joshua and the book of Esther in the Old Testament are called the historical books of Israel.

Joshua can be divided into two major parts:

Warfare and Victory (chapters 1–12)
The Formation of the State of Israel (chapters 13–24)

TODAY'S JOURNEY

From the desert to Lebanon, from the great river to the Great Sea.

As was just mentioned, the nation of Israel was still waiting on the east of the Jordan River, ready for God's command to conquer the Promised Land. The book of Joshua begins with God's words to Joshua, the chosen one, who must lead the nation. God renewed and repeated His covenant and said to him:

> *I will give you every place you set your foot, as I promised Moses. Your territory will extend from the desert to Lebanon and from the great river. No one will be able to stand up against you.*
>
> *(Joshua 1:3-4)*

After forty years in the desert, the Israelites were ready for a great change. Specifically, they were about to leave life in the desert and start a new life in the green pastures of the Promised Land. This was a great change for them.

Today, God is calling the people of the world with the same promise; He wants us to move from a "desert-life" to a life filled with God's blessings. This can only be fulfilled through believing in His Son Jesus (Joshua) Christ. By believing in Jesus we will arrive in the great river which is the Holy Spirit and face the challenges and the hardships of life. Together, with His guidance, we will arrive in the Great Sea which is heaven.

The Israelites were never guaranteed that setting foot in the Promised Land would be easy. They had to face a lot of battles both on the spiritual and physical levels. We can go through hardships but one thing is sure: We are not alone; the Lord is with us. We are sure that Jesus is leading us from the great river to the Great Sea, which is eternal life. He guides us from mortal life to eternal life.

GOD'S COMMANDS BEFORE WARFARE

Read and Meditate

God gave Joshua a very important instruction:

Do not let this book of the law depart from your mouth; meditate on it day and night, so that you may be careful to do everything written in it. Then you will be prosperous and successful.

(Joshua 1:8-9)

Be Strong! Be Courageous! Do Not Be Terrified! Do Not Be Discouraged!

The most important thing we must do is keep the word of God in our hearts. Many Christians these days are so busy with the world, and even busy with the work of God, but they forget to read and meditate upon the Word of God. While God said explicitly that the secret to prosperity and success was meditating upon the Word of God. Without the Word of God we will lose the battle. Please notice that Jesus Christ is the greatest Word of God (John 1), and He is with us forever. But we also need the spoken and the written word, the Bible.

> *For the word of God is living and active. Sharper than the double-edged sword, it penetrates even to dividing soul and spirit, joints and marrow; it judges the thoughts and attitudes of the heart.*
>
> *(Hebrews 4:12)*

Be Strong, Be Courageous, Do Not be Terrified, and Do Not Be Discouraged

These four instructions are real commands from God. God said to Joshua:

> *Have I not commanded you? Be strong and courageous. Do not be terrified; do not be discouraged, for the Lord your God will be with you wherever you go.*
>
> (Joshua 1:9)

As God's people, we must try our best to be strong. Because greater is He who is in us than he who is in the world (1 John 4:4). Through believing in the Word of God we will be strong; God said, "Be strong." We are not a defeated people, but we are a victorious generation. We can only be strong if God's anointing is upon us, which is the Holy Spirit. God also asks us not to be terrified. We must train ourselves to put aside fear and look unto Jesus.

Another command that God gave us is to be courageous. There are many people who have lost their courage because of the heavy loads and the pressures of life that confront them. Because of this, they have no strength and courage to carry on so they fail to experience the adventures of the Lord. They are terrified to see new things and initiate new things. But God has promised us, "Whatever we do and wherever we go, it will be blessed." The devil is a liar. He tries everything to put fear in our hearts. He is up to destroying you spiritually so that great things will never happen to and through you. Therefore, rise up because Christ has redeemed you!

Crossing the River Jordan (chapter 3)

God commanded the Israelites to pass through the Jordan River before beginning their battle with the enemy. God promised to split the river so that they could walk through on dry land. But if you look at the map below, you will notice that there was no need for the Israelites to pass through the Jordan River. They could enter the Promised Land another way. But why did God want them to pass through the Jordan River and from there attack their enemies?

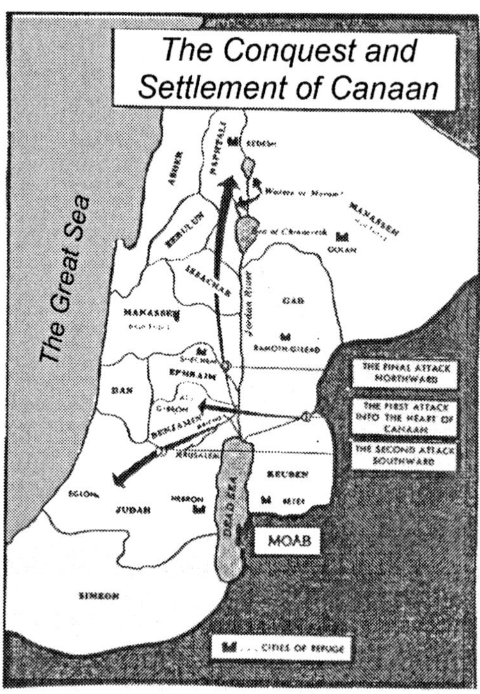

It was because God wanted the Israelites to be baptized in water before they begin their warfare. Their forefathers were baptized in the Red Sea when Moses led them out of Egypt (1 Cor. 10:2). The new generation did not experience this event, so by doing this, God not only showed His power but also symbolically baptized them in the Jordan River. Please notice that John the Baptist baptized in the same river.

One of the greatest commands of our Lord Jesus Christ for us is that we be baptized in water. This is a very important issue. We must obey all the commands of God and one of them is baptism. It is good to obey this and be baptized. There are many Christians who give no attention to baptism. If we ever want our warfare to be effective and victorious, we must learn to obey the Lord and be baptized. Baptism is a duty of every born again Christian.

Being Circumcised (chapter 5)

God also commanded the Israelites to be circumcised. He did this because all the people who came out of Egypt were circumcised, but those born in the desert were not (Josh. 5:5). Circumcision is a type of becoming born again. When a person is born again, his bad character has been removed. Through the born-again experience we are circumcised in our hearts. We are no longer the same person, but we are new in the name of our Lord Jesus Christ. This also means that we cannot serve the devil and God and at the same time go into warfare. We cannot fight the devil while we are still living in sin. We need a great change before getting into warfare. Some people live in misery because they do not fully obey God; they cannot let go of their evil desires and bad intentions. They cannot crucify their old self on the cross. That is why they live in misery. GOD NEEDS HEART-CIRCUMCISED CHRISTIANS! (read *Rom 2:29)*

The Battle (chapters 6–12)

Soon afterwards they were ready for warfare. Their enemies were terrified at them because they saw that the Lord God was with them. They also saw that God opened the Jordan River for them. So the enemies knew that they would lose the battle (Josh. 5:1). Two thousand years ago Jesus Christ finished off the devil. The devil knows that he is defeated. Remember this when reading this book.

YOU HAVE WON THE BATTLE ALREADY BECAUSE JESUS CHRIST FINISHED THE DEVIL.

The only thing you must do is claim your victory over the devil. If you do not claim it, the devil wins because you did not claim the victory that is already yours.

The Israelites went to the enemy's camp and claimed the land that God promised them. Maybe the enemy stole your family, your health, and your joy. You must claim them back. You must fight for them because Jesus is with you in the battle.

The Israelites Had Three Major Campaigns:

The Conquest of Jericho and Ai (chapters 6–8)
The Southern Campaign (chapters 9–10)
The Northern Campaign (chapters 11–12)

I would like to focus this lesson on the Conquest of Jericho.

Conquest of Jericho (chapter 6)

Jericho was a city situated in the western part of Jordan River, just above the Salt Sea. Jericho was a strategic city for the Israelites because by Jericho's conquest they would literally isolate the northern enemies from the southern part.

Jericho was a city with walls, and for a long time no one could go to or fro because the Israelites had entirely surrounded it. God commanded the Israelites to take the city by marching around it for six days with seven priests carrying the trumpets of rams' horns at the front of the Ark of the Covenant. On the seventh day, they were commanded to march around the city seven times with the priests blowing the trumpets. As soon as they heard the long blasts on the trumpets, all the people were to give a long shout and the wall of the city would collapse. They did just what God commanded them and the walls of Jericho fell down.

There is an interesting fact that is hidden in these Scriptures about the fall of Jericho. One of the commands of God is that the Jews must keep the Sabbath. But why were the Israelites instructed to fight on the seventh day to have the victory? I believe that during the six days of the week we Christians also march around our personal difficulties and problems, but on the seventh day which is Sunday, when we pray, sing, and shout God's name together repeatedly, our problems and our spiritual Jerichos will all collapse. That is why the Church of Jesus Christ must be open for singing, shouting, and crying out the name of the Lord. Because, then, the wall of the spiritual Jericho will fall. Whenever you are faced with a problem, call upon the name of God loudly, He will be there to help and answer you.

The Division of the Land (chapters 13–24)

When the battles were finished, it was time to divide the land between the tribes of Israel. Every tribe got its own parts. Chapters 13–24 prescribe the formation of the cities and Israel as a territory. The summary of the book is written below:

> *And the Lord gave them rest on every side, just as he had sworn to their forefathers. Not one of their enemies withstood them; the Lord handed all their enemies over to them.*
>
> (Joshua 21:44)

Through His Son Jesus Christ, God has prepared a place for us in heaven. He has written our names in the Lamb's Book of Life and has prepared a room for every person who has accepted Jesus as Lord and Savior. Everyone has his own reward.

Jesus said:

> *Behold I am coming soon! My reward is with me, and I will give to everyone according to what he has done.*
>
> (Revelation 22:12)

MAIN SCRIPTURES
Joshua (all chapters)

REFERENCE SCRIPTURES
Romans 2:29
1 Corinthians 10:2
Hebrews 4:12
1 John 4:4

TO MEMORIZE AND MEDITATE UPON
HEBREWS 4:12

FOR THE WORD OF GOD IS LIVING AND ACTIVE. SHARPER THAN ANY DOUBLE-EDGED SWORD, IT PENETRATES EVEN TO THE DIVIDING SOUL AND SPIRIT, JOINTS AND MARROW; IT JUDGES THE THOUGHTS AND ATTITUDES OF THE HEART.

QUESTIONS:

1. What does the name Joshua mean?

2. How can we relate the book of Joshua with the book of Acts in the New Testament?

3. Which chapter in the book of Joshua explains the division of the land?

NOTES:

LESSON 16
Judges

Judges (all chapters)

INTRODUCTION TO THE BOOK OF JUDGES

The book of Judges is the written history of the people whom God raised up in Israel. This was the period when Israel experienced many disasters and troubles. When Joshua died the love of the Israelites toward the Lord grew cold; they neglected to worship Him. For this reason, God brought them trouble as a sort of punishment, but at the same time, He also sent His judges to rescue them. These judges are the heroes in Israel's history because they functioned as military deliverers of the Israelites from the hands of their oppressors.

Further, the book of Judges describes the life of the Israelites in the Promised Land until the establishment of the monarchy in Israel. The authorship of this book remains debatable, but according to tradition, it was Samuel who wrote it. Some scholars believe it was written somewhere between 1380 B.C. and 1050 B.C. (This indication is not a sure one.)

The Book of Judges can be divided into two major areas:

1. History of Israel during the Judges (chapters 1–16)
2. Religious and Moral Confusion (chapters 17–21)

TODAY'S JOURNEY

The book of Judges begins with the death of Joshua. During this historical moment, Israel was looking for a new leader. God gave them Judah as the successor of Joshua. Judah immediately began to attack the enemies and conquer their territories. Chapter 1 explains the wars that took place in Israel. Generally, we consider the book of Judges as the written account of the formation of Israel in geographical terms.

God asked Israel to capture the land He promised them. He also gave them assurance of winning the battle because He was with them. The first generation failed to comply because fear overcame them. Due to their disobedience and lack of faith, they suffered for forty years in the desert. After that, the second generation came to power and to them was given the authority and power to conquer the lands. They booked various victories under the leadership of Joshua; however, the love and faith of the people grew cold when Joshua died.

Do Not Compromise

In Joshua 1, every tribe of Israel began to take the land God promised them. They fought but they could never destroy their enemies fully. So they compromised with them, and they lived together in one land and worshipped their gods. They mixed their pagan religion with their own faith and way of life (Judges 1:19-36).

This was not God's plan. God's plan was that the Israelites should defeat all their enemies without sparing anybody. Due to lack of confidence in the Lord, they once again failed to fully obey God.

That is why in Joshua 2 we read that the angel of the Lord went up from Gilgal to Bokim and said,

> *I brought you out of Egypt and led you into the land that I swore to give your forefathers. I said I will never break my covenant with you, you shall not make a covenant with the people of this land, you shall break down their altars. Yet you have disobeyed me. Why have you done this? Now therefore I tell you that I will not drive them out before you; they will be thorns in your sides and their gods will be a snare to you.*
>
> (Judges 2:1-3)

The Bible teaches us not to conform to the patterns of this world.

> *Do not conform any longer to the patterns of this world, but be transformed by the renewing of your mind. Then you will be able to test and approve what God's will is-his good, pleasing and perfect will.*
>
> (Romans 12:2)

We are living in a time where some Christians are not obeying God fully. By believing in Jesus Christ we are new creations; the old has gone and the new has come. And by becoming a new creation, we must have faith and the power to drive out certain things in us that separate us from God.

AS CHRISTIANS WE SHOULD NEVER COMPROMISE WITH SIN AND THE SINFUL WAYS OF LIFE. FOR LIGHT HAS NOTHING TO DO WITH DARKNESS AND TRUTH HAS NOTHING IN COMMON WITH A LIE.

In the same way the Israelites, the Holy nation, were supposed to have nothing to do with unclean nations who worshipped other gods! We are living in a time where different cultures and different nationalities meet each other. The world has become smaller especially through the digital world where we can exchange huge amounts of information in a very short time. There are Christians who try to mix Christianity with other types of religions, especially those from the East. There are people who mix Christianity with new age philosophies and occultism. This is very dangerous and can lead people to isolation and unbalanced behavior. If you want to be a Christian, be real and stay away from the patterns of this world.

The Circle of Sin

We can summarize the entire book of Judges in chapter 2. God raises a judge whenever Israel falls into sin. Their duty is to save the Israelites from the hands of their enemies. Let us analyze this chapter and relate it with the entire book of Judges.

Forgetting the Lord Leads to Sin

The new generation forgot God's love and faithfulness. There came the next generation who knew neither the Lord nor what He had done for Israel (2:10). One of the greatest problems in our society today is that there is a gap between the new generation and the old generation. The new generation has no sense of history. For example, the average European teenager is not knowledgeable about the history of the Second World War and the events that took place in this dark period which caused the deaths of millions of people. They are not interested and do not even want to hear about the cold winters during the war and the tragedies of the people around the world. When a society forgets His roots, it is heading towards destruction and chaos. When the youth loses their visions everyone will perish. I believe it is the responsibility of the parents to pass on what they have seen to their children.

The same thing is happening in our Christian families today; the children are not on fire for the Lord Jesus as their parents once were. The anointing does not flow to their children. I believe it is not only the fault of the children, it is also the fault of the parents.

Some parents are so busy with their own things and are so engaged in church ministry that they do not give proper attention to their children. So after awhile the children will no longer be interested in Christianity and they go out to enjoy the pleasures of the world. The parents must talk to their kids and pass on to them God's grace, mercy, and the miracles they received in their lives. Our faith is a three-generation faith. Our God is the God of Abraham, Isaac and Jacob. Our children should do the same things we are doing in the Lord and continue to do so when we die. The Israelites forgot God. Therefore, their society headed for chaos and God's anger. They began to sin and worship the Baals and other gods. This happened for twelve generations.

Times of Distress

> *Because they have forsaken Him, the Lord in His anger against Israel handed them over to raiders who plundered them. He sold them out to their enemies all around, to whom they can no longer resist. Whenever Israel went out to fight, the hand of the Lord was against them, just as He had sworn to them. They were in great distress.*
>
> (Judges 2:13-15)

When societies forget the Lord and sin against Him, they will receive distress and disaster. That is why Ephesians 6 teaches us to put on the armor of God.

> *Put on the full armor of God so that you can take your stand against the devil's schemes.*
>
> (Ephesians 6:11)

In Ephesians 6:13-18 the apostle Paul teaches us what these pieces of the armor are:

a-belt of truth
b-breastplate of righteousness
c-shield of faith

d-helmet of salvation
e-sword of the spirit
f-prayers
An inability to use the armor leads nations and individuals to perish. When we lose the armor we are sold to our enemies. God hates sin. That is why He sent His Son Jesus Christ so that those who believe in Him will not perish but have eternal life. Full obedience to God brings blessings in our lives, but to live in sin leads to distress. (read Eph. 6:12-20.)

The Judges as God's Call

In times of sin and adultery, God always chooses certain men or women to be His voice. They call in the wilderness and ask the people to repent. In those days Israel had no king yet, but God chose judges to save them from the hands of their enemies. God was always with the judges and He saved the Israelites through them. However, every time a chosen judge died, the Israelites would fall in sin again and live worse lives than their fathers. They were in great distress, but when they repented, God sent another judge to save them. They lived in circles of sins that lasted for twelve generations. God chose one judge to save the people of Israel. In total, the book of Judges counts for twelve judges through twelve generations.

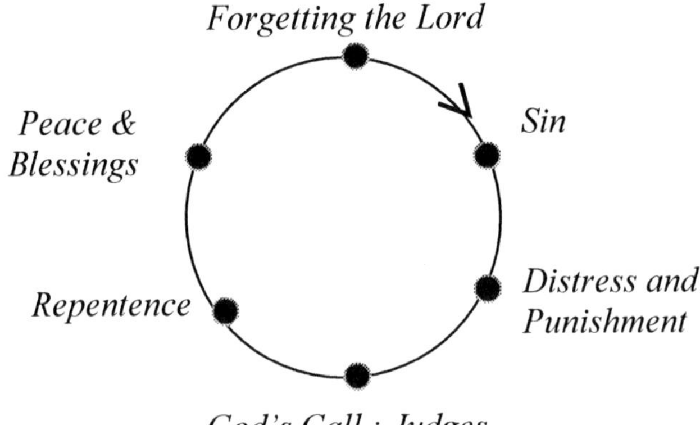

Today you and I are the judges of the world. We are the ambassadors of Christ Jesus here on earth. The earth and its inhabitants need to be set free from the bondage of the enemy and it is our duty to do so.

> *The creation waits in eager expectation for the sons of God to be revealed. For the creation was subjected to frustration, not by his own choice, but by the will of the one who subjected it, in hope that the creation itself will be liberated from its bondage to decay and brought into the glorious freedom of the children of God.*
>
> (Romans 8:19-20)

We are the chosen voices of this generation. May your children and mine be the chosen voices of tomorrow's people. We are the heroes of Christ.

Here are the names of the twelve Judges of Israel mentioned in the book of Judges:

Onthiel 3:7-11
Ehud 3:12-30
Shamgar 3:31
Deborah/Barak 4:1–5:31
Gideon 6:1–8:35
Tola 10:1-2
Jair 10:3-5
Jephthah 10:6–12:7
Ibzan 12:8-10
Elon 12:13-15
Abdon 12:13-15
Samson 13:1–16:31

(It will be too complicated if we study all these judges in one lesson. Therefore, read the above-mentioned Scriptures and get to know these men and women of God yourself.)

Repentance Leads to Peace

Every time the Israelites repented God heard their cries and forgave them. There were short periods of peace in Israel until they sinned again! Repentance leads to peace and God's love. If you live in sin today, or if you are carrying a burden of sin in your life, it is time for you to repent. Only then will God's blessings be restored unto you. Jesus Christ died for our sins. If we confess our sins to Him, He will hear us and forgive us from all our infirmities.

SUMMARY

The history of Israel in the book of Judges is a great lesson to all those who will read it and to all who call themselves Christians. Take note of the following: Forgetting the Lord, or putting Him aside to worship other gods and idols, will carry us away from Him. Christians should never forget their past and the roots of their faith. A Christian, while reading the Bible, should feel that he himself is living in those times and he should even praise God for all those miracles God did in the Old and New Testaments. A Christian parent should have time with their children and pass to them their family history with the Lord. A child must know how his or her parents became Christians!

MAIN SCRIPTURES
Judges (all chapters)

REFERENCE SCRIPTURES
Romans 12:2
Romans 8:19-20
Ephesians 6:11-20

TO MEMORIZE AND MEDITATE UPON
ROMANS 12:2

DO NOT CONFORM ANY LONGER TO THE PATTERNS OF THIS WORLD, BUT BE TRANSFORMED BY THE RENEWING OF YOUR MIND. THEN YOU WILL BE ABLE TO TEST AND APPROVE WHAT GOD'S WILL IS-HIS GOOD, PLEASING AND PERFECT WILL.

QUESTIONS:

1. Read the life of Samson and mention his good and bad characteristics.

2. Explain one of the mistakes Gideon made in his lifetime.

3. What does the "circle of sin" mean?

NOTES:

LESSON 17
Ruth

Ruth (all chapters)

INTRODUCTION TO THE BOOK OF RUTH

The book of Ruth is named after its main character, Ruth, a young lady from Moab. The book of Ruth, together with the book of Esther, are the only the books in the Bible that are named after a woman. The story took place in the time of Judges, a period of religious and moral deprivation (read last lesson). However, in the story, there is a temporary peace between Israel and Moab.

In this book we find the story about the Moabite woman, Ruth, who was married to an Israelite. After the death of her husband, her mother-in-law, Naomi, requested that she return to her homeland. But Ruth opposed it. She loved her mother-in-law as her own mother. She followed her and travelled with her to Bethlehem where she was a total stranger.

This book is a book of faithfulness and love. We will be studying this book from the New Testament's point of view, and we will connect it to our own personal lives today.

The author of this book is unknown, but Jewish traditions points to Samuel. The book of Ruth can be divided into four major areas with each chapter representing these areas:

Ruth's Faithfulness & Conversion (chapter 1)
Ruth Finds Mercy and Grace (chapter 2)

Ruth Claims Her Rights (chapter 3)
Ruth is Rewarded (chapter 4)

TODAY'S JOURNEY

In the days when the Judges ruled, there was famine in the land and a man from Bethlehem in Judah, together with his wife Naomi and their sons, went to live for a while in the country of Moab. In Moab the man died and her two sons married Moabite women, Orpah and Ruth. After a while, the sons also died and poor Naomi remained alone with her two daughter-in-laws from Moab. Both daughter-in-laws were young and childless. Thus, there was no hope for Naomi's genealogy to be continued.

Ruth's Faithfulness and Conversion

Naomi was disappointed and totally broken. She decided to go back to Bethlehem. She called her daughter-in-laws and told them to go back to their homes. But Ruth resisted. Ruth replied, "Don't urge me to leave you or to turn back from you. Where you go I will go, and where you stay I will stay. Your people will be my people and your God will be my God. Where you die, I die and there I will be buried. May the Lord deal with me, be it ever so severely."

Ruth was a foreigner to the Israelites. She knew that there was a possibility to be discriminated against by the Jews in Bethlehem. But still she wanted to go. Her faithfulness to her mother-in-law is a great lesson for us today.

The first thing Ruth did was to choose for Jehovah, the Almighty God. She decided to leave her own religion, tradition, and her own gods to follow the true living God.

Life is a matter of making a choice of whom to worship whether it's Jehovah God or others. No matter who you are, whether you are a Jew or not, God is God and there is only one way to belong to God's family and that is by believing and accepting Jesus Christ as your Lord and Savior. Ruth not only chose to believe in the God of Abraham, Isaac, and Jacob, but she also showed her faithfulness and trust in God when she decided to follow Naomi no matter what the cost. Ruth followed Naomi everywhere even to the end.

To believe in Christ is not sufficient for us Christians. We must go along with Jesus and follow Him to the end. Jesus needs you here on earth. He has a mission for you and that is why you were created. God wants you to fulfil that mission no matter how hard it may be. WE MUST TAKE OUR CROSS AND FOLLOW HIM.

Ruth Finds Mercy and Grace (chapter 2)

When Ruth and Naomi arrived in Bethlehem, they started to build their lives. They had nothing. They were poor. Because Naomi was an old woman, Ruth took good care of her and decided to work and support Naomi. This was not easy for Ruth because she came from Moab, one of the enemies of Israel.

In chapter 2, we read that Ruth went to the fields of Boaz and gathered the left-over grain on the ground. Boaz noticed her and allowed her to work in his field and to take as much as she wanted. She found grace from Boaz.

There's a lesson here that we can apply in our lives. When we make the choice to follow Jesus and remain faithful in our love and faith to the Lord, He will notice us and His grace and mercy will be given to us. God will never leave His children unnoticed. He only wants us to obey Him and everything else will be given unto us.

Ruth Claims Her Rights and Ruth is Rewarded (chapter 3)

With the Jewish custom, if a woman loses her husband because of death, she has the right to marry the closest male relative from her husband's side. Ruth, even though she was not a Jew, was accepted into the family. Naomi wanted Ruth to build her life again and find a husband. No one was better than Boaz. However, according to the Law, Boaz was not the closest male relative of Ruth's ex-husband.

Therefore, Naomi had a plan for Ruth. Ruth was to clean and put perfume on herself and go to the threshing floor. But she must be unrecognized because, according to the tradition, women were not allowed to go there. In that evening, Boaz noticed Ruth and accepted her as a wife. But they needed to wait for the nearest male relative. If he did not claim Ruth, then she could marry Boaz. In the end, nobody came to claim Ruth and she married Boaz.

The story of Christianity looks like Ruth's story. Once, God chose the Jews as His nation, but through the coming of Jesus Christ, we as Gentiles received the same rights and love from God. We can compare ourselves with Ruth. Through Jesus Christ we have received the same rights and the same love that were meant for the Jews.

The apostle Paul said:

> *I am not ashamed of the gospel, because it is the power of God for salvation of everyone who believes; first for the Jews, then for the Gentiles.*
>
> *(Romans 1:16)*

Read also Romans 2.

Lastly, because of Ruth's faithfulness, God awarded her in a very special way. Ruth became the ascendant of David and our Lord Jesus Christ. So what about you today? By believing in Jesus Christ you have become the mothers and brothers and sisters of Jesus Christ.

Jesus said:

> *My mother and brothers are those who hear God's word and put it into practice.*
>
> *(Luke 8:21)*

SUMMARY

Faithfulness always leads us to God. Ruth was faithful to her mother-in-law and faithful to God. She was blessed so much that our Lord Jesus Christ descended from her.

MAIN SCRIPTURES
Ruth (all chapters)

REFERENCE SCRIPTURES
Romans 1:16
Romans 2
Luke 8:21

TO MEMORIZE AND MEDITATE UPON
ROMANS 1:16

I AM NOT ASHAMED OF THE GOSPEL, BECAUSE IT IS THE POWER OF GOD FOR SALVATION TO EVERYONE WHO BELIEVES: FIRST FOR THE JEWS, THEN FOR THE GENTILES.

QUESTIONS:

1. What can you learn from the story of Ruth?

2. What were the names of the two sons of Naomi?

NOTES:

NOTES:

LESSON 18

Samuel

1 and 2 Samuel (all chapters)

INTRODUCTION TO THE BOOKS OF 1 AND 2 SAMUEL

The books of Samuel are named after a great man, a great prophet, and the last judge of Israel—Samuel. Originally, the books of Samuel were one book, but because of the Greek translation, the book was divided into two books: 1 Samuel and 2 Samuel. However, the author of these books is unknown. Some scholars argue that Zabud, the son of the prophet Nathan, and the personal advisor of King Solomon, wrote it. The books were probably written after Solomon's death (930 B.C.).

The books of Samuel are the written history of the formation of the Kingdom of Israel and the establishment of the monarchy in Israel. In the books of Samuel three men are very important:

Samuel (the Last Judge of Israel)
Saul (the First King of the United Kingdom of Israel)
David (the Successor of King Saul and the Ascendant of Christ Jesus)

First Samuel can be divided into the following parts:

The Birth of Samuel and his ministry as the last judge of Israel (chapters1–7)

The Beginning of Kingship and the reign of the first King of Israel (chapters8–31)
Saul's rebellion against God (8–15)
David chosen as the future king and Saul's persecutions against him (16–31)

The books of Samuel describe one of the darkest eras in the history of Israel. One can call this period the dark-ages of Israel.
The second book of Samuel can be divided into the following parts:

David becomes King (chapters 1–6)
David's glory and victories: flourishing era (chapters 7–10)
David's disobedience and the weakening of his kingdom (chapters 11–24)

TODAY'S JOURNEY

Samuel, Answer from God

Samuel is the answer of God to a crying woman, Hannah, who was barren. Because of her situation, she was ridiculed and discriminated against by the other wife of her husband (1 Samuel 1:6-7). But Hannah kept on praying and weeping until the Lord answered her and gave her a son. They called him Samuel which means, "heard of God" or "God has answered." Hannah promised the Lord that she would dedicate the boy to Him. She brought him to Eli to be raised. Eli had a high position in the temple. She said to Eli:

> *As surely as you live, my Lord, I am the woman who stood here beside you praying to the Lord. I prayed for this child, and the Lord has granted me what I asked from him. So now I give him to the Lord. For his whole life he will be given over to the Lord.*
>
> *(1 Samuel 1:26-28)*

Hannah is an example of a godly woman. She was desperate to receive an answer to her prayers, but when she received it she did not forget the Lord her God and she dedicated her child totally to the Lord.

What about you today? What are you asking from God? Is He answering you? These days there are many people who receive their answers from God, but then they simply forget Him and break His heart. They go to church simply to ask for things. Our prayers must have roots of dedication in the Lord, just like Hannah's did.

Samuel grew under Eli in the temple. While the sons of Eli were busy with their sinful acts of lust and idolatry, Samuel was growing under God's control and God's discipline, until one day, Samuel, as a young boy, was called by God. God chose him to be the future judge of Israel (1 Sam. 3). All his life, Samuel served the Lord and His people with honesty, righteousness, and loyalty (1 Sam. 12).

The Ark of the Lord Was Captured

In those days, around one thousand years before Christ, Israel was constantly in conflict with the Philistines. In chapter 4 we read that in the battle against the Philistines, the Israelites thought that if they brought the Ark with them they would automatically win the battle. In the past, bringing the Ark always gave the Israelites the victory over their enemies, but not this time. This was an act of manipulating God's power and God's symbol. God never asked them to bring the Ark to that particular battle, yet the Israelites followed the tradition of the past without asking God Himself. That is why in that battle the Lord was not with them. Though the Ark of the Lord was with them they lost the battle and the Ark of God was captured by the Philistines (1 Sam. 4).

Many people today are putting their hope and trust in symbols rather than in the power of God Himself. For example, there are people who wear necklaces with the cross pendant believing that it will protect them from any harm. Some have idols of different saints and the Virgin Mary at home believing that these will protect them. Some people even kiss the Holy Bible but they never read it. They put these Bibles in their homes only for display. These acts are signs of religiosity. God does not like religion that is why such acts declare the enemy's victory over the person doing these things.

In place of hanging the cross on the neck, it is better to believe in the real cross, the cross of Jesus Christ that brought forgiveness and love to us so that we can carry our own spiritual cross and follow Jesus.

The Israelites lost the battle simply because they did not have the anointing and God's presence among them. We Christians must focus on God's anointing power and His presence among us. We must focus on God's anointing power and God's blessing by obeying His commands rather than putting our trust in wood or metal symbols. Is God in your heart? That is the question.

The Lord's Ark Returned to Israel (1 Samuel 5 and 6)

In chapter 5 we read that the Philistines took the Ark of the Lord and brought it to the temple where their god, Dagon, was placed. Early on the next day they visited Dagon's temple and saw that Dagon was fallen on his face on the ground before the Ark of the Lord. They put Dagon back to his place and the next day Dagon was again found fallen on his face with his hands and head broken. God punished the Philistines with tumors until they decided to bring the Ark back to Israel. After seven months the ark returned to Israel.

The Philistines believed in many gods. Thus, they were a polytheistic society. They considered the Ark of the Lord as an idol just like all the other gods of the Philistines. Because of this act, God punished them and proved to them that He was the only Lord and the only God.

In our time, many people believe like the Philistines believed. They believe in many gods or many sources of gods. The New Age Movement is also an example of this type of belief. God is against these types of beliefs because He sent His only Son Jesus Christ. He is not *one* of the gods, but He is *the* God Himself; He is the only Way, the Truth, and the Life. God is one and that is the Triune God: God the Father, God the Son, and God the Holy Spirit. Sooner or later all these man-made gods will be destroyed by God's power. They will fall under God's feet like Dagon the god of the Philistines fell.

Israel Chose a King (1 Samuel 8)

One of the most tragic events in Israel's history happened when the people decided to choose a king and be the same as the surrounding countries (1 Sam. 8). Until Samuel, Israel was governed by judges and priests. There was no such thing as kings in Israel, unlike the situation in the neighboring countries. Israel was a theocratic country which means that God Himself was Israel's King. As King, God used the prophets and judges to guide Israel and to instruct them.

Samuel was the last official judge of Israel. It was in his time that the Israelites rejected theocratic government and chose a monarchy instead. This broke the heart of God because the Israelites, the chosen nation of the Lord, wanted to be the same as the other countries. It broke God's heart because they replaced God's position with a human king who was limited and corrupt. God promised them a human king, but He also explained the consequences that would come with having a human king. Their sons would be taken away to war and their daughters would be taken as wives of the king.

Once again we can see the choice for rules, regulations, and traditions. Israel wanted a king, because all the other countries had a king. It was the custom and tradition for every nation to have a human king, therefore, Israel wanted the same.

I believe the same mistake took place after the birth of the church. When the Body of Christ was born, the church had a different meaning. "Church" (*ekklesia*) refers to the "called out ones." When Christians gather together, they break the bread and drink the wine in remembrance of the Last Supper. They sing hymns and read the Holy Scriptures. All these things take place under the leadership of the apostles and prophets, evangelists, pastors and teachers, or what is better referred to as the five-fold ministry.

However, there was a certain period in church history when the Church of Jesus Christ turned into rules and regulations. It embraced leadership politics and emphasized an approach that did not know much about the living God. The Middle Ages was a good example. During these dark periods, many people were killed in the name of Christ. The Holy Spirit was no longer the King, the Teacher, and the True Guide. In the Middle Ages, the Holy Spirit left the Catholic Church and their man-made religious kingdom. Nevertheless, God still raised Spirit-filled and anointed Christian movements to demonstrate the power of the Living God. But the moment they begin to control the Holy Spirit and make their own rules and regulations, God will depart from them as well!

Saul, the First King of Israel

The Holy Spirit changed Saul (1 Samuel 10:1-8).

After the people's choice for a king, God appointed Saul, the son of Kish the Benjamite. Samuel anointed Saul as king over all twelve tribes of Israel. And so Israel became the United Kingdom of Israel. The coming of the Holy Spirit upon Saul (1 Sam. 10:1-8) changed him from an ordinary farmer boy into the national king of Israel.

Every Christian needs the Holy Spirit in his life. Without the Holy Spirit there will be no change in a person's life. Even Jesus Christ received the Holy Spirit before He started His ministry (Luke 3:21-22). The Holy Spirit is the Spirit of Truth, and only by being filled with His anointing can a person's life be changed. For we have received the Holy Spirit through Jesus Christ, and through His Holy Spirit we have become kings and priests. We were changed and became a new creation. What about you? Are you filled with the Holy Spirit? Are you allowing Him to baptize you in His Holy Spirit? (Read John 16).

Saul's Disobedience and Samuel Leaves Saul (1 Samuel 15)

In the early years of Saul's reign Saul was known for his generosity and courage, but Saul slowly lost God's favor by disobeying God at crucial points in his life. Because of Saul's disobedience to God and His prophet Samuel, God's favor departed from him. God chose a young man named David to be his successor. He was now the anointed one, the next king of Israel. In 1 Samuel 15 we read Samuel's argument with Saul that resulted after Saul disobeyed the commands of the Lord in the battle against the Amalekites.

Saul took the best cattle when they should have been slaughtered. He clearly disobeyed God on this. This was the historical turning point of King Saul. The Lord rejected Saul's kingship and chose another man, David, to be the king. Since that time Samuel left Saul and they never saw each other again.

> *Until the day Samuel died, he did not go to see Saul again, though Samuel mourned for him. And the Lord was grieved that he had made Saul King over Israel.*
>
> *(1 Samuel 15:35)*

From that time the Spirit of the Lord departed from Saul and disasters and calamities began to happen in his life. He became a loser, a man without victory. Samuel left Saul alone. We can compare the account of Samuel with the Holy Spirit of God. If we ignore the Spirit and never allow Him to work in our lives, He will depart from us and never visit us again if we do not repent and ask Him to come back. He will depart from us and He will grieve constantly for us. That is why the Bible teaches us not to grieve the Holy Spirit of God (Eph. 4:30).

DAVID, THE NEW KING

(1 Samuel 16–30 and 2 Samuel)

David's Anointing

Immediately when God rejected Saul as a king, He chose David as the anointed king (1 Sam. 16). David was the youngest son of Jesse from Bethlehem. Jesse had many sons but God chose David because he had spiritual capacity. David was a shepherd and a skilful musician. Samuel took the oil and anointed David, and from that day onward, the Spirit of the Lord was upon him (1 Sam. 16:13).

God anointed David with a kingly anointing, but the Lord did not allow him to immediately become king over Israel. God wanted to build David up first. He also wanted to test David. Therefore, God hardened the heart of Saul by persecuting David. After David's anointing, Saul's persecutions against David started. David wandered around caves and mountains. He suffered for many years (1 Sam. 16–30). Amidst all these persecutions, David always loved and respected Saul as the King of Israel. There was even a time when Saul was sleeping, that David could have killed Saul, but he spared his life (1 Sam. 24).

What about you today? Maybe God has promised you something or has anointed you for a work or a ministry, but it is somewhat delayed. Remember, God never forgets His promises. Before He fulfils His promises, He will test you through hardship. He will build you up so that you will be strong enough to handle the work or the ministry He has anointed you for.

David's victory over Goliath was the starting point for David's popularity and Saul's jealousy towards him. Saul's plan was to make his son Jonathan the next king of Israel, not David. However, the friendship between Jonathan and David grew and this provoked Saul's anger even against his own son.

Saul continued to chase David in the wilderness and even tried to kill him, but his efforts were never successful for God decided that David would be the next king of Israel. Saul's life came to an end during a battle with Philistines at Mount Gilboa. He was wounded in the war and took his own life rather than be captured by the enemy (1 Sam. 31).

David Became King

After Saul's death, there was great confusion in Israel. David was declared king in Hebron for the tribe of Judah, but he was not yet viewed as king over all Israel. One of the sons of Saul, Ish-bosheth, was declared king over the rest of Israel (except Judah). He ruled Israel for two years. After two years of conflict, the followers of David captured the enemy. David executed the murderers of Saul's son to show that he had no intention of gaining Saul's throne by murder (2 Sam. 3).

Since then David became the ruler of all Israel and he ruled Israel from Hebron for five years. Later he changed his capital city to Jerusalem which was a strategic place. In those days, Jerusalem belonged to the tribe of Israel but it was under the control of the enemy. He made Jerusalem the capital city for the religious and political activities of Israel. David brought the Ark, which was ignored in the time of Saul, to Jerusalem. In Psalms 8 and 103 we can read David's thankfulness to God.

David's Desire to Build God's Permanent House (Temple) (2 Samuel 7)

David had a great desire to build a permanent house for the Ark of the Lord since David himself had a wonderful palace. The Prophet Nathan agreed with David. The Lord answered David through Nathan. God had a greater plan than David. For out of David's family, He would bring forth the Messiah, the King of Kings and the Lord of Lords, the Savior of all mankind—Jesus Christ. Through Him, a permanent and everlasting house would be established (2 Sam. 7). David had a worldly and materialistic plan, but God had a spiritual and everlasting plan. Nevertheless, God blessed David with his worldly plan. In the time of David, Israel turned into one of the most powerful nations in the world. He captured the neighboring countries from the Nile River and the Red Sea in the South to the Euphrates River in the North (2 Sam. 8).

David's Disobedience (2 Samuel 11)

Even though David is called God's beloved one, he committed sins. Pride and arrogance took hold of him. At the high point of his power David committed a series of deliberate sins that influenced God's will in his life.

He had sexual desires for Bathsheba and killed her husband in order to have her (2 Sam. 11). This stirred God's anger against him. God assured David that his family would be torn apart through adultery and murder (2 Sam. 12:7-12).

However, David deeply confessed his sins. God forgave him (2 Sam. 12:13-14; Psalm 51), but God never removed the sufferings from David and his family. After this terrible sin, peace never returned to Israel. David's sons rebelled against him, especially Absalom. David was forced to flee Jerusalem and Absalom seized his throne. In the battle that followed, Absalom was killed, and due to the people's request, David came back to Jerusalem and became king over Israel again (2 Sam. 14–20). The last days of David's life were engaged with conflicts concerning which son would be his successor. David chose Solomon and God blessed him. Solomon was the child of Bathsheba. Solomon was actually the result of a sinful act, but yet God still chose him. This shows that our God is a God of mercy and love. He can change the most horrible situation into a good and pleasant plan. God has mercy for sinners. He never wants them to perish. He wants them to repent so He can forgive them.

Through all of David's disobedience, why did God delight in him and love him? I believe David was a man filled with passion towards God. He loved God even though he sinned. He was an artist, a musician, and a songwriter. God delights to be worshipped, and I believe David had the heart that God was looking for.

David did not care what people thought about him. For example, when the ark was brought to Jerusalem, he danced for the Lord like a child. Also, David was a forgiving man. He forgave Saul and spared his life many times. For this reason, God also forgave David for his sinful acts. Even though David was king unto the people, he was a child unto God. In the Psalms we can read many reflections of David's life. David wrote 73 of the 150 psalms in the book of Psalms.

SUMMARY

In this lesson we have learned about the three important men in Israel: Samuel, the last judge over Israel; Saul the first king of Israel; and David, the Beloved One of God, the ascendant of Jesus Christ the Lord. Here follows a short chronology of the times from Samuel to David:

1105 B.C.	*Birth of Samuel*
1080 B.C.	*Saul anointed to be king*
1025 B.C.	*David anointed to be the successor of Saul*
1010 B.C.	*Death of Saul and the start of David's kingship over Judah*
1003 B.C. to 970 B.C.	*The beginning and the end of David's reign over all Israel.*

In this lesson we learned that God does not delight in symbols, but He rejoices in obedience. God loves passion and wants us to be like a child to Him. God wants to be your only God and we must not be involved with other types of religions and gods. We can only worship God through His everlasting covenant with the House of David. God will send the Messiah, the Lord Jesus Christ, to save mankind.

Only through Jesus Christ can we be saved, for this was God's promise to David. Rejecting Jesus Christ means rejecting God's covenant with David and the entire Old Testament.

MAIN SCRIPTURES
1 Samuel (all chapters) and 2 Samuel (all chapters)

REFERENCES SCRIPTURES
Psalms 8 and 103
Luke 3:21-22
John 16
Ephesians 4:30

TO MEMORIZE AND MEDITATE UPON
1 SAMUEL 22

DOES THE LORD DELIGHT IN BURNT OFFERINGS AND SACRIFICES AS MUCH AS IN OBEYING THE VOICE OF THE LORD? TO OBEY IS BETTER THAN SACRIFICE, AND TO HEED IS BETTER THAN THE FAT OF RAMS.

QUESTIONS:

1. Read 1 Samuel 12, the farewell speech of Samuel. Find out the characteristics of Samuel. What kind of man was he?
2. What are the differences between Saul and David?
3. Why did God reject Saul as king? Mention the exact reason.
4. Explain one of the sins David committed.
5. Why did David chose Solomon to be his successor?

NOTES:

LESSON 19

1 & 2 Kings and 1 & 2 Chronicles

(all chapters)

INTRODUCTION TO THE BOOKS OF KINGS AND CHRONICLES

The books of Kings and Chronicles are very essential books in understanding the prophetic books of the Old Testament. The books are actually the historical and geographical settings of the prophetic books (Isaiah–Malachi). If someone wants to understand the prophetic books he needs to know Israel's history. This is the reason why God allowed the books of Kings and Chronicles to be a part of the Holy Bible. These books were written in different times and by different authors. The books of Chronicles are a review of the books of Kings but from a different perspective. In this lesson I have chosen to give brief studies concerning all four books: 1 and 2 Kings, and 1 and 2 Chronicles.

KINGS

The books of Kings are named after the various kings of Israel and Judah. In these books, prophets like Elijah and Elisha were the focus of attention. One can call the books of Kings the books of Miracles. In these periods of Israel's and Judah's history, God did great miracles through His prophets. Some scholars speak about three major eras in Israel's history in which God's miracles were highly concentrated. The first period was the Exodus period; the second period was the period of Kings; and the third was the period of Jesus Christ. However, I would like to add one more period and that is the period of the Holy Spirit which began in the book of Acts. We have no information about the author of the book of Kings.

The books of Kings can be divided into the following parts:

1 Kings:
Solomon's Kingdom (chapters 1–11)
The Various Kings of the Divided Kingdoms (chapters 12–22)

2 Kings:
The continuation of Kings to Israel's captivity (chapters 1–17)
The weakening of Kingdom of Judah and its fall (chapters 18–25)

CHRONICLES

The original name of these books in the Hebrew was "journals" or "accounts" of the day. These books were written after the books of Kings and probably during the time of the Babylonian captivity. According to tradition, their authorship is ascribed to Ezra or Nehemiah!

The division in the books of Chronicles are as follows:

1 Chronicles:

Genealogies (chapters 1–9)
David's reign (chapters 10–29) (parallel 2 Samuel)

2 Chronicles:

Solomon's Kingdom (chapters 1–9) (parallel to 1 Kings 1–11)
Kings of Judah to Babylonian Captivity (chapters 10–36)(parallel to 2 Kings 18–25)

TODAY'S JOURNEY

Last lesson we learned about the United Kingdom of Israel. Saul was its first king, followed by David who made Jerusalem the capital city. We also learned that Israel was the only theocratic country among the nations until they chose a human king to rule over them. The book of 1 Kings began with Solomon as the successor of King David.

Solomon was the last king of the United Israel. After Solomon, Israel was divided into two kingdoms (930 B.C.). The Northern Kingdom, also known as the Kingdom of Israel; and the Southern Kingdom, also known as the Kingdom of Judah, which consisted of the tribes of Judah and Benjamin. The rest of the tribes belonged to the Kingdom of Israel. The books of Kings and Chronicles describe the various kings of these kingdoms and their works. None of the nineteen kings of Israel were good. They led Israel into sin and spiritual adultery. Out of the twenty kings of Judah, only eight kings were good and godly; the rest were corrupt. The Kingdom of Israel lasted until 722 B.C. when it fell to the Assyrians. The Kingdom of Judah lasted longer and ended in 586 B.C. when the Babylonians captured Jerusalem.

Solomon

Solomon, the son of Bathsheba, was chosen by David because Adonijah rebelled against him. Solomon became king of the United Israel (1 Kings 1; 2 Chron. 1). Due to David's sins and disobedience towards God, he could not fulfil his oath to build a permanent

temple for God. This task was carried out by his son, Solomon. The idea of building a permanent house for God was David's own idea. It was a man-made idea that God honored. God, though, had a greater plan than David's. Out of David's offspring, the King of Kings, Jesus Christ the Messiah, would come to save mankind. That is why God kept His promise even though David had sinned.
God never changes His plans for you. He will fulfil every promise He gave you, but sometimes He disciplines you by keeping your worldly projects unsettled.

In the beginning of his reign, Solomon showed his love for the Lord by walking according to the statues of his father David. Once in Gibeon, the Lord appeared to him during the night in a dream. He asked Solomon what he wanted and Solomon chose wisdom because he was a young and inexperienced man. Solomon chose for a discerning heart to govern God's people and for the ability to distinguish between right and wrong. For this reason God gave him so much extraordinary wisdom that even people from far away kingdoms came and visited him. Most of the proverbs in the Old Testament were written by King Solomon, and some of them were gathered after his death. According to 1 Kings 4:32, Solomon wrote at least three thousand proverbs. The book Songs of Songs and probably the book of Ecclesiastes were also written by Solomon.

Because Solomon asked for wisdom and humbled himself before the Lord, God gave him all the riches of the world. During the time of Solomon, Israel flourished and became rich (1 Kings 3 or 2 Chron. 1:2-13). Some people call this period 'the golden age of Israel.' What do you ask from God?

God is pleased with praying people who do not seek the things of the world. God answers those who seek His kingdom first, and all the things of the world will automatically be given to them. Further, we read that Solomon asked for wisdom concerning other people. He did not hate his enemies in his prayers nor did he ask God to punish them. Rather, he asked wisdom to honestly rule over them. If you want God to bless you, ask God's wisdom and pray that God will give you a loving heart to treat those around you according to the love of Christ.

Solomon Builds the Temple

In the four hundred and eightieth year after the Israelites came out of Egypt, in the fourth year of Solomon's reign, Solomon began to build the temple which his father David promised. (1 Kings 6; 2 Chron. 3:1-14). You can read in 1 Kings 6 the description of the temple. The Lord's temple was beautifully made and expensively designed, and God was pleased with that. When the temple was finished, Solomon prayed and dedicated the temple to the Lord (1 Kings 8:22-53; 2 Chron. 6:12-40). After his prayer, the Lord answered him and sent fire down and consumed the burnt offering and sacrifices. The glory of the Lord filled the temple in such a way that the priest could not enter the temple to minister.

There is one greater than Solomon: Jesus Christ—the fulfilment of God's promise to David. The establishment of the Messianic Kingdom would come through Him. This is the Spiritual Temple. For this reason, on the Day of Pentecost, God sent His Holy Spirit and officially, the Body of Christ, the everlasting temple, was established. Tongues of fire came upon the disciples and that was the beginning of the church (Acts 2:1-14). Once more we can clearly see that the New Testament is the spiritual fulfilment of the Old Testament.

Solomon's Fall and Divided Kingdoms

Solomon's kingdom flourished, but gradually his spiritual life declined to almost zero. He rejected the commands of God and married ladies from other nations. These ladies brought with them their own native and man-made gods, and Solomon built altars and bowed before them. The Bible tells us that as Solomon grew older, his wives turned his heart after their gods and his heart was not fully devoted to the Lord. Solomon did evil in the eyes of God. For example, he built a high place for Chemosh, the detestable god of Moab, and for Molech, the detestable god of the Ammonites, on a hill east of Jerusalem.

As Solomon grew older he became tolerant of other gods and this provoked God's anger. Toleration to other gods or religions is a phenomenon of modern false Christianity today. As Christians we must only bow before Jesus Christ and obey the Holy Spirit and the Holy Bible. Not more and not less. By doing this we will be pleasing to the Father.

Solomon's sins made God angry and God caused uprising and rebellion against Solomon. Jeroboam, the son of Nebat, rebelled against him. Jeroboam was an Ephramite, one of the officials of Solomon. God promised to Jeroboam that after Solomon's death, He would divide the United Kingdom of Israel, and Jeroboam would be the king over the Northern Kingdom. Jeroboam fled to Egypt and stayed there until Solomon died. God, however, gave the Southern Kingdom of Judah to Solomon's descendants because He was merciful to David's line. David was the beloved one of God (1 Kings 11:26-43).

Divided Kingdoms

After Solomon died, his son, Rehoboam, became king over the United Israel. When Jeroboam heard this he returned to Israel and proposed to Rehoboam that they be under his authority, but Rehoboam's heart was hardened against Jeroboam. So the northern part of Israel rebelled against Jeroboam, and they separated themselves from Rehoboam and established the Northern Kingdom of Israel. Jeroboam became their king. The remaining parts in the south, the regions of Benjamin and Judah, became the Southern Kingdom and Rehoboam became their king. This event happened about 930 B.C. As I mentioned before, each kingdom had twenty kings. All the kings of the Northern Kingdom were ungodly men. Also the eleven kings of Judah were bad kings.

The books of Kings and Chronicles describe the regions of all these kings and their good and bad deeds. If someone wants to understand the prophetic books, he or she needs knowledge about these kings. God brought forth prophets against all these wicked kings from both kingdoms to correct them. From those times, the prophets began to have more important roles. Examples were Elijah and Elisha. God did wonderful miracles through them. Elijah was a prophet whom God raised against King Ahab of Israel and his wicked wife, Jezebel. First Kings 17–22 describes all the miracles and victories achieved by the prophet Elijah until he was taken away by God. Elisha, followed his works. The second half of 1 Kings and the first chapters of 2 Kings give detailed information about the various miracles God did through them.

In short, one can summarize the books of Kings as the battle between good and evil, the battle between the worldly king and the heavenly true King, God.

Thank God that Judah knew some good kings like Asa, Jehoshaphat, Joash, Amaziah, Uzziah, Jotham, Hezekiah, and Josiah who destroyed the altars of the enemy and their idols. These kings reigned longer than the other kings and God was with them and for them in times of war and need.

The Northern Kingdom ended in 722 B.C. when king Hoshea and Israel were exiled because of their sins. God gave them over to the Assyrian Kingdom (2 Kings 17).

Assyria was centered on the Tigris River. The Assyrians were the descendants of Asshur (son of Shem, son of Noah). Assyria became a great nation around 900 B.C. and it became the superpower in the region. On one occasion, God sent the prophet Jonah to preach in Assyria and to call the Assyrians to repent (Jonah 3:1-10). The captivity of the Northern Kingdom lasted for seventy years, approximately from 722 B.C. to 625 B.C.

In a similar way, the Kingdom of Judah ended in 586 B.C. King Zedekiah was its last King (2 Kings 24:17). Because of its sins, God gave Judah over to the Babylonian Empire, and that started Judah's captivity. Second Kings 25 describes the terrible fall of Jerusalem by king Nebuchadnezzar of Babylon.
Later, the Babylonian Empire was defeated by the Persians and the Jews lived in captivity under the Persians. But this exile came to an end after Persia's conquest of Babylon. In 539 B.C., King Cyrus of Persia allowed the captive Jews to return to their land. The book of 2 Chronicles ends with a declaration of King Cyrus to build God's temple. The captivity of Judah lasted almost fifty years, from 586 to 539 B.C.

The prophetic books such as Daniel, Zephaniah, Haggai and Malachi were written in the period of the Persian kings. For instance, in the book of Isaiah, God already prophesied that He would bring Judah into captivity by Babylon. He also prophesied that He would raise a redeemer to set them free from the Babylonians. This was fulfilled with Cyrus, King of Persia (Isa. 42; 48). But notice that Isaiah did not live in the period of captivity.

The Persian Empire came to an end when Alexander the Great from Greece defeated the King of Persia, Darius II. He conquered a great part of Asia. Once again Israel came under the rulership of another nation, and this time it was Greece. This happened almost three hundred years before the coming of Christ. It was prophesied through Daniel (Dan. 8:8-22). This captivity did not allow religious freedom for the Jews. Even the temple of Solomon was destroyed by Alexander the Great. But the Jewish priests rebelled and gained this freedom by force around 165 B.C. Later, the Roman Empire ruled Israel, but the Greek language was still widely common and it became the international language of that time. Jesus Christ our Lord carried out his ministry during the Roman Empire.

Here are the empires that ruled Israel until New Testament times:

Assyrians ruled Northern Kingdom: Israel

Babylonians ruled Southern Kingdom: Judah
Persians: Gave freedom to the Jews and called them to return to their land
Greek Empire
Roman Empire

The following chart gives us a short summary of every king in Judah and the prophets of those times.

Kings of Judah	Good or Bad	Prophets
Rehoboam (1Kings 12:1)	Bad	
Abijah (1Kings 15:1)	Bad	
Asa (1Kings 15:9)	Good	
Jehosaphat (1KINGS 22:41)	Good	
Jehoram (1Kings 22:50)	Bad	Obadiah
Ahaziah (2Kings 8:24)	Bad	
Athaliah (1Kings 11:1)		
Joash (1Kings 11:4)	Good	Joel
Amaziah (1Kings 14:1)	Good	Amos/Jonah?
Uzziah (2Kings 15:1)	Good	Amos/Hosea
Jotham (2Kings 15:32)	Good	Isaiah/Hosea/Micah
Ahaz (2Kings 15:38)	Bad	Isaiah/Hosea/Micah
Hezekiah (2Kings 18:1)	Good	Isaiah/Hosea/Micah?
Manasseh (2Kings 21:1)	Bad	Nahum
Amon (2Kings 21:19)	Bad	Nahum
Josiah (2Kings 22:1)	Good	Zephaniah
Johoahaz (2Kings 23:31)	Bad	Habakkuk
Jehoiakim (2Kings 23:36)	Bad	Jeremiah
Jehoiachim (2Kings 24:6)	Bad	Jeremiah
Zedekiah (2Kings 24:17)	Bad	Jeremiah
BABYLONIAN CAPTIVITY Nebuchadnezzar (2 Kings 25:1)	586 B.C.	Ezekiel/Daniel
PERSIAN EMPIRE OVER BABYLON		Ezekiel

The following chart shows the ministry of the prophets during the Persian captivity.

Persian Kings	Prophets	Other famous men
Cyrus the Great	Daniel	
Cambyses	Daniel	
Darius I	Daniel/Zechariah/Haggai	
Xerxes	Zechariah/Haggai	Esther
Artaxerxes		Ezra/Nehemiah
Darius II	Malachi	
The Greek Captivity, Alexander the Great		

If someone wants to have a better understanding of the prophetic books, it is better to compare the name of the prophet and read about the involved king(s) in the books of Kings and Chronicles. The chart above can help you do this.

SUMMARY

In this lesson we reviewed a short history of Israel as a nation and its divisions. We also learned about Solomon including his rise and fall. Shortly said, the books of Kings and Chronicles are the bones of the prophetic books. In this lesson, we also learned God's historical plan for the Jewish nation until the coming of Jesus Christ. All these events took place for one purpose—the coming of Jesus Christ.

> *But when the time had fully come, God sent his Son, born of a woman, born under law, to redeem those under law, that we might receive the full rights of sons.*
>
> *(Galatians 4:4)*

The books of Kings and Chronicles are the historical battle field between good and bad, between God's prophets and the devil's kings. I hope that this lesson will make the coming lessons more clear and understandable for you.

MAIN SCRIPTURES
1 and 2 Kings (all chapters)
1 and 2 Chronicles (all chapters)

REFERENCE SCRIPTURES
Isaiah 42 and 48
Daniel 8:8-22
Acts 2:1-13
Galatians 4:4

TO MEMORIZE AND MEDITATE UPON
GALATIANS 4:4-5

BUT WHEN THE TIME HAD FULLY COME, GOD SENT HIS SON, BORN OF A WOMAN, BORN UNDER LAW, TO REDEEM THOSE UNDER LAW, THAT WE MIGHT RECEIVE THE FULL RIGHTS OF SONS.

QUESTIONS:

1. Read the books of Kings and try to make your own chart for the names of the Kings of the Northern Kingdom: Israel. See the chart in this lesson.

2. What does this mean: "When the time had fully come. . . ."? (Galatians 4:4)

3. Read Isaiah 42. The prophecy of Isaiah was about a king. Who was this king?

NOTES:

NOTES:

LESSON 20

A New Beginning

Ezra and Nehemiah (all chapters)

INTRODUCTION TO THE BOOKS OF EZRA AND NEHEMIAH

The book of Ezra begins where the last chapter of 2 Chronicles ends. In the last chapter of 2 Chronicles, we read that the Jews were liberated from the hands of the Babylonians by the Persian king, Cyrus the Great. Chronicles ends with the King's decree that the Jews were free and the temple of the Lord must be rebuilt again. The book of Ezra begins with this historical moment. The book of Ezra describes the two returns of the Jews to build the temple, the first under the leadership of Zerubabel and the second return under the leadership of Ezra. Later, there was a third return of the Jews that took place under the leadership of Nehemiah. We can read about this third return in the book of Nehemiah. The books of Ezra and Nehemiah were originally considered one book, even though they had different writers. The book of Ezra was written by Ezra and the book of Nehemiah was written by Nehemiah.

In this lesson we will be studying both Ezra and Nehemiah because they will give us a clear understanding of Israel after its captivity.

The book of Ezra can be divided into two major parts:

First return under Zerubbabel (chapters 1–6)
Second return under Ezra (chapters 7–10)

The book of Nehemiah can be divided into three parts:

Rebuilding the walls of Jerusalem (chapters 1–7)
Confessions, Review of Israel's history, revival (chapters 8–10)
Rebuilding Jerusalem (chapters 11–13)

While you are reading the books of Ezra and Nehemiah do not forget that there were other great prophets at the same time supporting the restoration of Jerusalem and God's temple. Daniel and Haggai were also ministering then.

The prophetic book of Haggai was actually written at the same time the events of Ezra and Nehemiah were taking place. The prayer of Daniel 9 is another example.

TODAY'S JOURNEY

Last lesson we learned about the division of Israel into two parts: the Northern Kingdom of Israel and the Southern Kingdom of Judah. We also learned that the Jews sinned against God's command and Jehovah punished them by sending them into the captivity of the Assyrians and the Babylonians. Sin leads to captivity, for the wages of sin is death.

Actually, this event is not a new happening in the Bible. The first time the brothers of Joseph sinned against God and Joseph, God sent them to Egypt. After some time, their children became slaves of the Egyptians and they suffered under Pharaoh's dictatorship. Later, God sent them a redeemer, Moses, who saved them from their captivity. They were saved and promised a land of milk and honey. Because they sinned and rebelled against God, He punished them for forty years. They wandered in the desert and none of them saw the Promised Land except Joshua and Caleb and the new generation of Jews at that time.

God gave them victory after victory. They got their Promised Land and God was their King until they asked for a worldly king. They got Saul. After that David and Solomon were the last kings of a United Israel. After Solomon, Israel was divided into two parts: North and South. These two kingdoms each had their own kings. But the kings and the nations sinned against God and God gave them over to captivity again. The Persian King Cyrus declared freedom to the Jews. In this historical moment of the Jewish nation the book of Ezra began.

The First Return under Zerubbabel: Rebuilding the Temple

The Jews were taken away from their land and were brought to exile in the time of the Assyrian king and later the Babylonian king. In those days, and later in the days of the Persian Empire, the Jews were already settled. They had their own businesses even though they were in exile in the Babylonian and Persian eras. They were well-treated and they were rich. But they still missed their homeland. They were always remembering the good times in their own land which was now deserted and destroyed. While they were living their good lives, Jerusalem was isolated, destroyed, and forgotten. God's temple, which they built, was now ruined.

They were longing to go back again to Jerusalem and rebuild the land again. In Lamentations, which was written in Babylon by Jeremiah the prophet, we see the desire and longing of the Jews for their homeland (read Lam. 1 and 5). The Jews were sorry and they regretted all those things they did and their forefathers did a generation ago. God heard their cries and touched the heart of the pagan king, Cyrus. Cyrus was a Persian; he was not a believer of Jehovah alone. He believed that gods were territorially appointed and he thought that the God of Israel was called the God of Heaven, which, according to him, was a god for the region of Israel. However, Cyrus was the first man in history who gave the declaration of freedom of religion. The Persians were the first nation in the world who gave freedom of religion. Persia was also the first nation that introduced organized news systems. Within a few days of an event, the king became aware of the news. That is why today, another word for news and communications is called Pers & Media. These names come from Persians and the Medes which are considered one nation.

So Cyrus the king chose Zerubbabel to lead the Jews to Jerusalem to build the temple of God. Zerubbabel (descendant of David's royal line) and Joshua the high priest arrived in Jerusalem with almost 45,000 Jews to rebuild God's temple. The people started to lay the foundation of the temple (Ezra 3:10), but the rebuilding was stopped because of opposition of those pagan nations who were living there. After the king of Assyria captured Israel, he appointed different nations to go and live in the Promised Land. Those people took over the Promised Land. Because they thought that Jehovah was the territorial god of those regions, they also worshipped Him. They did not worship Him, though, because He was the only God. They mixed the worship of the true God with the worship of other gods.

When the Jews returned under Zerubbabel the pagans also wanted to rebuild the temple together with the Jews, but Zerubbabel did not allow them to do this. This provoked their anger and jealousy against the Jews. Then the pagans set out to discourage the people of Judah and make them afraid to go on building. They hired counselors to work against them and frustrate their plans. So rebuilding the temple was delayed until the time of King Darius I (Ezra 4:4-5).

However, the Jews remained in the Promised Land, but they did not continue rebuilding the temple and Jerusalem. They were waiting for the right time to continue building the temple. So in the right time, the prophet Haggai recalled Judah to the task of building the temple. So Haggai convinced the Jews that it was time to build the temple (Haggai 1 and 2). Haggai called again to Zerubbabel to finish the temple. So after this the temple was rebuilt and restored (Ezra 6:13-18).

The Second Return: Under Ezra (The Law Was Rebuilt)

After delaying the Jews to build the city of Jerusalem, King Artaxerxes changed his mind and gave a new decree that the remaining Jews in Persia and Babylon were free to return. So the king appointed Ezra to lead the people back to their land. He also gave him all the authority and money, silver and gold. This was now the second biblical record of the return of the Jews to Jerusalem during the Persian era. This took place fifty seven years after the rebuilding of God's temple.

Ezra was a man of knowledge and he was a teacher of the Law. He was a man who studied the Law carefully and tried to bring the people back, not only to the Promised Land, but also to the Spiritual laws of Moses (Ezra 7:10). Ezra taught the people the Law and he led them to a spiritual return to God. Ezra was a spiritual reformer.

When Ezra arrived in Jerusalem he saw that the Jews from the first return disobeyed God and forgot His commands to not inter-marry with other nations. When he heard this news he tore his garment and cried bitterly; he prayed to God, begging Him for grace (Ezra 9).

People heard Ezra's prayer and they confessed their sins, and they promised God with a covenant that they would never inter-marry with pagans again. Ezra told the Jews to separate from their foreign wives and the people around them (Ezra 10:11). The book of Ezra ends up with the names of those who were guilty of inter-marriage. However, the city of Jerusalem was not totally rebuilt and it was still under ruins and dust.

THE BOOK OF NEHEMIAH

The book of Nehemiah begins with Nehemiah's prayer to the Lord, for he heard about the desolation and ruins of Jerusalem. He begged the Lord for Jerusalem's restoration (Neh. 1). Nehemiah, who was the wine taster of the Persian King, Artaxerxes, asked permission from the king to go back to Jerusalem to rebuild the city and its walls. Twelve years after Ezra's return to Jerusalem, Nehemiah arrived with the hope to rebuild the city.

Rebuilding the Walls

After examining the city of Jerusalem, Nehemiah saw that the city walls were destroyed and it lay unprotected and naked to the surrounding enemies. He started first to build the walls (Neh. 3–6).

During the rebuilding of the walls, various oppositions rose from the pagans, especially the Amorites, the Arabs, and others. They ridiculed and mocked Nehemiah; they even threatened Nehemiah's people with fighting. But the Jews did not give up. They continued building the walls and God confused their enemies and protected the Jews. In twenty two days the walls of Jerusalem were completely finished. Now Jerusalem was a city protected by its walls.

After the wall's completion, the Israelites were rejoicing and feasting, for the joy of the Lord was with them. For various days in a row the Israelites celebrated in a way never seen before (Neh. 8).

Rebuilding Jerusalem

After rebuilding the walls of Jerusalem it was time to rebuild the city itself. Now the city was protected so it was ready for prosperity and a flourishing future. In Nehemiah 11, we read about the new residents of Jerusalem. They cast lots to bring one out of ten people to live in Jerusalem, the holy city, while the remaining nine were to stay in their towns (Neh. 11:1-2).

The book of Nehemiah ends with a very interesting story in which Nehemiah rebuked those who were inter-marrying with foreigners. He even beat some of the men and pulled out their hair. He said to them: "Was it not because of marriages like these that Solomon King of Israel sinned? Among many nations there was no king like him, Even he was led into sin by foreign woman . . . ." (Neh. 13:23-30).

This is a very proper end for this chapter in the history of Israel, and Nehemiah warned them again that disobeying the Lord would cause every one, even King Solomon, to fall.

SOLOMON'S TEMPLE

 SUMMARY

A Great Lesson

The history we just learned about is not only about the Jews, the chosen nation. It is also the history of fallen man. God created Adam to rule over the world, but through Eve, his wife (a woman), he sinned. Eve led Adam to sin the same way those pagan women led Israelites to sin. God threw both Adam and Eve to exile: to this world (Gen. 3). Because they had disobeyed Him, He dealt with the Israelites by giving them over to the Babylonians and the Assyrians.

Gradually, those Jews in Babylon and Persia adapted to the society. In exile, we learned that they were treated well and they had everything they needed. They were rich, but they still were longing for the old times in their own land.

The same thing happened with the human race of course. God blessed them and they even prospered. Today when you look at our world, we see all the possible technologies, riches, science and the like. But still mankind is not satisfied. There is a great need and desire for joy and happiness deep in the heart of man. These desires are rooted deep in the history of creation when there was no separation between man and God. They are rooted in those times of absolute peace, joy, and prosperity in the Garden of Eden.

Return to God and Rebuilding the Temple

In this lesson, we learned that the Jews longed to return to Jerusalem. God chose Zerubbabel to lead the return. The first thing the Jews did was long to return and rebuild the temple of God.

Are you longing to return? Is the world longing to return? God is calling the world today to come back to Him and rebuild His temple. Not only does God want us to come to Him, but He actually came to us by becoming a human being, Jesus Christ. By coming to

Jesus Christ and believing in Him as Lord and Saviour, our lives will be changed and the temple of God (you) will be restored again, for we are the temple of the living God. He will live in you forever through His Holy Spirit.

> *For we are the temple of the living God. As God has said: "I will live among them and walk among them, and I will be their God and they will be my people."*
>
> *(2 Corinthians 6:16)*

Obeying the Word

After the Jews rebuilt the temple, some sinned again by marrying foreign women. God sent Ezra the priest to them to call the Jews back to the Law of Moses and to teach them again what the Lord had commanded them.

These days many people call themselves the temple of the Lord, but they are not. They mix their faith with other religions and gods. How can we know the truth? We can only know the truth that we are God's rebuilt temples if we fully accept the Holy Bible as the only book for life and obey its words. Believing in Jesus Christ is not enough to be called a Christian; we should live according to God's Word and teachings by obeying them. A Liar is a man who calls himself God's temple but continues to sin.

> *The man who says, "I know him (Jesus)" but does not do what He commands is a liar, and the truth is not in him.*
>
> *(1 John 2:4)*

Build the Wall

Nehemiah rebuilt the wall around Jerusalem. This wall separated Jerusalem from the rest of the pagan people. So Jerusalem was protected from foreign gods and foreign marriages.

In the same way we must build a wall around ourselves to separate ourselves from the sinful activities of the world. By making these walls we must say NO to the world and YES to God. We are not ordinary people anymore. Certain things we will do no more; certain people we must not see anymore. This will be our wall, to separate ourselves from the sinful world. This wall is called: HOLINESS. We have learned before that the word Holy means "separated ones." Today we are a Holy Nation by believing and obeying the Word of God, Jesus Christ.

> *Therefore, come out from them (worldly people and things) and be separate (be Holy), touch not the unclean things and I will receive you*
>
> *(2 Corinthians 6:17)*

A New Life

After the walls of Jerusalem were built and Jerusalem was separated from the world, a time of prosperity and joy began in Jerusalem's history. Jerusalem began to prosper. Today if you hear His voice and come to Him with all your heart and mind and separate your life by choosing Him, a great award and restoration is waiting for you. He will change your life and heal you from the ruins of your life and He will give you a new birth. Jesus is alive for you today. Praise be to the God and the Father of our Lord Jesus Christ! In His great mercy He has given us a new birth into a living hope through the resurrection of Jesus Christ from the dead, and into an inheritance that can never perish, spoil, or fade, kept in heaven for you, who through faith, are shielded by God's power until the coming of the salvation that is ready to revealed in the last time (1 Pet. 1:4-5).

MAIN SCRIPTURES
Ezra (all chapters)
Nehemiah (all chapters)

REFERENCE SCRIPTURES
Daniel 9
Haggai (all chapters)
2 Corinthians 6:16-17
1 Peter 1:4-5
1 John 2:4

TO MEMORIZE AND MEDITATE UPON
2 CORINTHIANS 6:16

FOR WE ARE THE TEMPLE OF THE LIVING GOD. AS GOD HAS SAID: "I WILL LIVE WITH THEM AND WALK AMONG THEM, AND I WILL BE THEIR GOD, AND THEY WILL BE MY PEOPLE."

QUESTIONS:

1. Read the book of Haggai (all chapters) and try to relate it to this lesson.

2. Why did Nehemiah build the walls?

3. Why did God not want the Jews to marry foreign women?

4. Compare Ezra's character and task to that of Jesus Christ. What kind of similarities can you find?

NOTES:

LESSON 21

A New Decree

Esther (all chapters)

INTRODUCTION TO THE BOOK OF ESTHER

The book of Esther is named after its main character, Esther. However, the book's authorship is not attributed to her. The books Esther and Ruth are the only books in the Bible named after a woman. The book of Esther describes the events that took place during the time of Ezra and the King of Persia, Xerxes. The story in the book of Esther is a fascinating one because once again God showed His power to save the Jews. This event concerns those Jews who did not return with Zerubbabel or Ezra. In those days the remaining Jews in the Persian Empire had scattered themselves throughout all the 127 provinces of Persia, from India to Egypt. In those days the Jews lived a peaceful life. They were treated well and were in some degrees respected. But Persia in those times was made of different races and nations. The enemies of Israel, like the Amalekites or Amorites, were also living in Persia together with the Jews. There were always tensions between the Jews and the enemies of Israel within the Persian Empire.

The book of Esther can be outlined as follows:

Esther became queen (Esther 1–2)
Haman's plan to massacre the Jews (Esther 3– 6)
God's victory and redemption of the Jews and Mordecai's promotion (Esther 7–10)

TODAY'S JOURNEY

The book of Esther begins with the description of King Xerxes' kingdom. He reigned from his throne in Susa, the capital city of Persia. Once, King Xerxes gave a great feast that lasted for seven days. All the people from poor to rich in Susa were invited. On the seventh day the king invited his queen to visit him and display her beauty to the people and to the nobles. She was lovely. However, Queen Vashti rejected the king's invitation. This made King Xerxes very angry and disappointed. The king made a decree that Queen Vashti would never again be allowed to enter King Xerxes' presence. The king took away her royal position and gave it to someone else.

Rejecting the Invitation

The above story reminds us of a parable Jesus gave about a king who invited many people to the wedding banquet of his son. No one came and he was extremely disappointed. He said to his servants, "Those who were invited do not deserve this banquet, go out to the street corners and invite anyone you find. . . . (Matt. 22:8-9).

In the same way, King Xerxes invited his queen to come because she was beautiful. He wanted to show her beauty to the people and his nobles. To come to the banquet of a king is a choice. Does one reject or accept?

Today, God is calling His people to His banquet. He is inviting the world to participate in a feast by becoming His queen because He is proud of His people's beauty. He is proud of your beauty. God is always proud of His creations. He is proud of you and He invites you to be His queen, His bride.

For this reason God sent His Son Jesus Christ. Jesus is the bridegroom and those who believe in Him are the bride. God asks us to come and appear in His presence by accepting Jesus Christ the Messiah as Lord and Savior. But if we reject Him, He will reject us. The same way King Xerxes rejected Queen Vashti. Queen Vashti was a queen; she belonged to the royal family, but King Xerxes abandoned her because she rejected him. Just as the Jews belonged to the royal family of God, Israel was a queen for God. The Jews were the only chosen nation of the world, but because some of them rejected Jesus Christ as Lord and Savior, God took away this privilege and gave it to all the nations who wanted to believe in Jesus and accept Him as Lord and Savior. Even today, there are some Christians who are stuck in religious theology and traditions that deny and strongly oppose God's revival. We need to accept God's invitations in our lives no matter when and how this invitation comes. We cannot put God in a little box. There are so many people in the Body of Christ who are rejecting the revival of signs and wonders. If these people do not accept these revivals, though, God will give them to someone who will.

Esther Was Chosen

King Xerxes gave the order to look for a new queen. The servants searched throughout the land and throughout the city of Susa. Many girls were brought to the king, but only one pleased him—ESTHER. She was a beautiful woman and she pleased the king. However, Esther was a suffering Jewish girl who had lost both her mother and father. Her uncle's son, Mordecai, took care of her and treated her as his own daughter. When she was brought up to the king's palace she did not mention her nationality and family background. Mordecai suggested that she not reveal these matters to the king.

But before she appeared before the king, she needed to go through beauty treatments for twelve months; six months of which were for oil and myrrh treatment and the other six months for perfume and cosmetics treatment. When the king saw Esther he took her as his queen. Esther, a suffering, ordinary second-class Jewish citizen of

Persia, received the beauty of purification treatments and was made the Queen of Persia. The king gave a great feast and called it the Banquet of Esther.

Today, through Jesus Christ, God is inviting everyone who wants to believe in Him like a bridegroom. Esther, a rejected girl without mom and dad, became the choice of the king. God is always looking for suffering people, rejected stones, the ones who never had the chance to be someone. God chooses the most foolish things to shame the wise. Today there is hope for the world that is rejected by the society and people. He has great plans for you. By becoming the Queen of Persia, Esther received treatments of perfumes and oils of beauty. Yes even today, when we receive Jesus Christ as our Lord and Saviour, He will give us treatments of beauty through His Holy Spirit. As you probably know, oil is a symbol of the Holy Spirit. He will anoint you with His oil. Your life will be changed just like how Esther's life was changed. For everyone who believes in Him will be a new creation, born again into a new life. He will change you from glory to glory before you appear before God's throne.

Esther, the Hope for the Jews

In Esther 3, we read that King Xerxes chose a man called Haman the Agagite (descendant from Amalekite) to be the chief of all governmental affairs of Persia. You can compare this post to that of a Prime Minister. Because of Haman's high position, everyone bowed before him and honored him. In those days, the cousin of Esther, Mordecai, was also working in the royal palace but he never bowed before him.

God prohibited the Jews from bowing before any image or mortal man. Because of this, Haman not only decided to kill Mordecai, he also decided to kill all people having Mordecai's faith—the Jews. He made up his mind to uproot all Jews throughout the 127 provinces of Persia, from India to Egypt.

Haman informed King Xerxes that there were some rebellious groups in their country. These people would not bow before the king and worship him. However, he did not mention the name of this nation (the Jews) to the king. He kept the name of that nation a secret. The king gave Haman his ring and told him he could do whatever he wanted to do with those people. He wrote a letter to all the governors of the 127 regions and sealed it with the king's ring. Once the letter was sealed with the king's personal ring, it would be impossible to change the decree.

Haman gathered his people and cast lots (PUR) to choose the day he would kill all the Jews in Persia. The lot fell on the thirteenth day of the twelfth month. There were eleven months left to fulfil the plan because they cast the lot (PUR) on the first month of the year. Of course, this was God's will so He could prepare the Jews. Haman wrote the letter to all the governors and told them that on the thirteenth day of the twelfth month all the Jews must be killed. He signed it with ring of the king. Now all the Jews in Persia were disturbed and they wept and cried. They were terrified by the decree given by Haman in the name of the king himself. Mordecai was terrified and tore his garment and threw dust on his head. But suddenly he realized that Queen Esther could save the Jews. She was their only hope, yet the king never knew that Esther was a Jew and that those Haman wanted to be killed were the Jews (Esther 5).

The king saw Esther disturbed so he asked her what she wanted. He said he would give half of his kingdom to her. Esther planned a banquet and invited only the king and Haman. The banquet was held for two days. On the first day, Esther said nothing and Haman went home feeling so proud. But when he saw Mordecai in the palace his joy left him. He decided to kill Mordecai the next morning. He prepared the gallows to hang Mordecai (Esther 5).

In the night the king couldn't sleep so he called his servants to read for him the history of his kingdom. When they read for him how Mordecai saved the king's life from a plot, he asked the servants how Mordecai had been rewarded. They said he received no award at all. So the king was disturbed and gave a command to honor him.

When Haman was on his way to ask permission for hanging Mordecai, he was so surprised when the king told him that he wanted to honor someone without mentioning Mordecai's name. The king asked Haman's opinion what must be done in order to honor the man. Haman suggested that servants put a royal robe on the man and let him ride on the kingly horse with the royal crest placed on his head. Then a servant should bring him into the streets and proclaim to the people, "This is what is done for the man whom the king delights to honour." To Haman's surprise, the king commanded Haman to put the royal robe on Mordecai and do all that Haman suggested. Remember, Haman was the man who planned to kill Mordecai, now he had to honor Mordecai.

In this story, we learn that there are two types of plans in the world for every man. The first is the plan of Satan; he wants to kill us and destroy our lives. From the other side, we have a kingly plan and that is the plan of God, through Jesus Christ His Son. The funny thing is that God always shames Satan, just like Xerxes shamed Haman. God always lets the devil clean up his own dirt. The enemy will come to us in one but he will be scattered in seven parts, for we believe and obey God's commands.

One night, when Esther held the second banquet, she told the king that there was a man who wanted to kill her people (she still did not mention that these were the Jews). She said that she was tremendously disturbed. The king guaranteed her that he would execute the one who planned to kill her people. He asked her who the man was while Haman was sitting there. Esther looked at Haman and replied to the king "This man!" Haman was so disturbed that he begged Queen Esther for mercy. The king got mad and commanded that Haman be executed. Haman was hanged on the same gallows he had built for Mordecai (Esther 7).

This is the irony of God: He takes Satan and throws him into the same pit he dug for you. We are more than conquerors. If you are sick, God will heal you when you come to Jesus Christ. The sickness will return to the devil himself. Our God is a great God. He changes all the things for the good of His people.

If you are sick, it means the devil is doomed to eternal sickness; if you are suffering, it means the devil is doomed for eternal suffering; if you are poor, it means the devil is doomed to eternal poverty!

A New Decree

After that, Esther begged the king to eliminate the decree against the Jews. But the king told Esther that this was not possible because of the Law of the Persia and Mede. When the king had signed a decree with his ring, the decree must come to pass. But the Lord made Mordecai the successor of Haman as the Prime Minister. The king gave his ring to Mordecai and told him to write another decree under the king's name and the king would sign it.

Mordecai then wrote a contra decree against the decree of Haman. He wrote that all the Jews were allowed to kill and destroy their enemies, and this decree was distributed to all 127 governors throughout the area. Everyone was terrified because of the Jews and even the governors of the provinces helped Mordecai because of fear. On the appointed day, the Jews killed all their enemies and even killed the ten sons of Haman. They got the victory, and Mordecai gave a decree to all the Jews that the fourteenth and fifteenth days of the twelfth month must always be remembered and celebrated. Even today, in Israel they celebrate these days. The Jews call this the Feast of Purim because the enemies of the Jews cast lots (PUR) to destroy the Jews, but the tables were turned. It was the Jews who destroyed their enemies.

In this story we read that both decrees were signed by the king, for the king's decree could never change. When God made man, man sinned against Him. God cursed the man and after that God gave the Law of Moses which brought condemnation and death. Disobeying the Law brought death to the sinner. God could never change His decree, the Law. This was His word; this was His command. But He saw the sufferings of the world and He sent someone to fulfil the Law by bringing life to the people. This is through His Son, Jesus Christ. This is related to the New Testament.

This is exactly related with the new and old decrees of the king. In the first decree, the king signed a decree to kill the Jews even though he did not want this to happen. In the same way, our Father in heaven never wants His people to die because of sin, but He must give the decree of law. Of course, we cannot compare God with a gentile king who is mortal. But in a certain way we can learn a lot from this story.

The second decree which came through Mordecai gave life and power to the Jews and allowed them to live. There is a parallel here with Adam and Jesus. When Adam sinned and brought the law of death to the people, the Gospel of Jesus Christ came as a new decree which gives life and power to those who believe. They will have eternal life (read Rom. 5:12-21).

SUMMARY

Once again we read in the Bible how God rewards faithfulness. When you choose for God, God will choose for you. Come near to God and he will come near to you (James 4:8). We also read that God can turn a negative situation into something positive for the benefit of His people.

> *And we all know that in all things God works for the good of those who love Him, who have been called according to His purpose.*
>
> *(Romans 8:28)*

Esther kept her true identity as a Jew, but at the right time she revealed it and saved her people, for that was the plan of God.

As you are reading this book, the only step you must take is to love the Lord God, through Jesus Christ, and then God will turn your negative situations into blessings according to His purposes.

This lesson is the closing of the historical books in the Bible. I hope that the previous lessons gave you foundational teachings and brought you to higher revelations concerning our Lord Jesus Christ.

MAIN SCRIPTURES
Esther (all chapters)

REFERENCE SCRIPTURES
Matthew 22:1-14
Romans 5:12-21; 8:28
James 4:8

TO MEMORIZE AND MEDITATE UPON
ROMANS 8:28

AND WE KNOW THAT IN ALL THINGS GOD WORKS FOR THE GOOD OF THOSE WHO LOVE HIM, WHO HAVE BEEN CALLED ACCORDING TO HIS PURPOSE.

QUESTIONS:

1. Explain some other events in the book of Esther that relate to Romans 8:28.

2. What can you learn from the book of Esther?

NOTES:

NOTES:

. PART III .

Journey With Wisdom

LESSON 22

Rhema

Job (all chapters)

INTRODUCTION TO THE BOOK OF JOB

The book of Job is one of the poetical and wisdom books of the Bible. It is named after the main person in the story, Job. No one knows the writer of the book, but some believe that it was written by Moses. Some suggest that it was Solomon who wrote the book. Some say that one of the writers of Proverbs wrote it. From the lifestyle of the people described in the book, we can approximate that the story of Job took place somewhere between 2000 B.C. and 1800 B.C.

The book of Job is about suffering. Why do Christians suffer? How can we deal with suffering? We learn from Job that suffering and pain are universal. Everybody must face it.

The Book of Job can be divided into the following parts:

Prologue (behind the scenes in Heaven) (chapters1–2)
Job's verbal controversies with his friends (chapters 3–41)
The Lord speaks (chapter 42)

TODAY'S JOURNEY

God declared Job to be a righteous and blameless man. Job lived in the land of Uz and he had seven sons and three daughters. He was a rich man for God had blessed him in this way. He also feared God. He sacrificed regular burnt offerings to the Lord because his children sinned and cursed God in their hearts while they were having feasts (Job 1:1-7).

Further, we read in chapter 1 that this righteousness of Job and his fear for God stirred up Satan's anger and jealousy towards him. So Satan appeared before God the Father and challenged the Lord to test Job. Yes, even today, Satan doesn't like people being upright and fearful to God. He hates seeing people worship God.

Do Not Touch the Man

Satan appeared before God and said: "Does Job fear God for nothing? Have you not put a hedge around him, his household and everything he has?"
"Stretch out your hand and strike everything he has, and he will surely curse you to your face." This was the challenge of Satan. God accepted Satan's proposal because God knew for certain that Job would never curse Him. Even today if you are being tested or you are in a certain difficult situation, fear not because God never tests you beyond your ability.

God replied to Satan: "Very well everything he (Job) has is in your hands, but on the man himself do not lay a finger."

From that moment everything Job had belonged to Satan. Satan struck his hands to Job. Instantly, Job lost all his properties and his children. They all died! He lost everything in one day. But Satan was not allowed to touch Job's body because God commanded him not to.

At this, Job got up, tore his robe, and shaved his head. Then he fell to the ground in worship and said:

> *"Naked I came from my mother's womb, and naked I will depart.*
> *The Lord gave and the Lord has taken away;*
> *May the name of the Lord be praised." In all this, Job did not sin by charging God with wrong doing.*
>
> *(Job 1:21-23)*

Cursing God is one of the greatest goals of Satan in this world. Today, there are many people cursing the name of God. They curse God in the movies and in music.

Yet amidst of all these disasters that happened to Job, he did not curse God.

You have noticed that God commanded Satan not to touch Job's body. But after Satan destroyed his property and killed his children, Job still did not curse God. For the second time Satan appeared in the presence of Almighty God. He challenged God to touch Job's body with physical sickness. Then Job would curse God, Satan claimed (Job 2). Again, God knew with 100% certainty that Job would never curse Him even if Satan touched his health. So God told Satan he could make Job sick, but he was not allowed to take Job's life.

In the challenges of Satan and the tests of Job, there are three major things: (1) property, (2) health, and (3) life. Property is less important than health, and health is less important than life. So life is the most important of all; that is why God is fighting for the world to give life, everlasting life. God is there to tell Satan that he cannot touch the lives of His people. That is why He sent Jesus Christ to give us everlasting life. Money, properties, cars, houses, and huge bank accounts are useless and are not comparable to having Jesus in our hearts. These material things cannot buy the everlasting life that comes through believing in the Lord.

Jesus Christ said:

> *I am the resurrection and the life, whoever believes in Me even if he is dead he will live.*
>
> *(John 11:25)*

Curse God and Die

So Satan afflicted Job with painful sores from the soles of his feet to the top of his head. Then Job took a piece of broken pottery and scraped himself with it and sat among the ashes. His wife said to him "Are you still holding on to your integrity? Curse God and die!" (Job 2:8-9).

The story of Job reminds me of the story in the Garden of Eden. Eve, the wife of Adam, was the cause of Adam's sin. However, here, the same spirit is working through Job's wife. The only difference is that Job did not sin, and he did not curse God. However, the story of Job is exactly the opposite of the Garden of Eden. Here, Adam and Eve had everything. Adam was the head of all creation. He was allowed to do everything he wanted except eat from the fruit of knowledge. In Job's story, Job was in the middle of a miserable situation. He lost his family, he lost his properties. He was afflicted in awful ways but he did not curse God. Today, there are also two types of people. There are those who have everything and those who have nothing and are afflicted. In both categories there are people who curse God: the rich by their riches and the afflicted because of their afflictions. However, there are also people like Job, who in every situation, try to do their best and do not deny Him.

The Friends of Job

After Job's affliction, his three friends, Eliphaz the Temanite, Bildad, and Zophar came to visit him and sympathize with him.

When they saw Job's suffering and affliction they wept out loud, tore their robes, and sprinkled dust on their heads. They sat on Job's side for seven days and did not open their mouths.

However, after seven days Job opened his mouth and cursed the day of his birth. Then his friends, one by one, opened their mouths with hypocrisy. They claimed that Job and his children sinned and that was why he was suffering and why God was punishing him. Eliphaz said Job supported those who stumbled with words and strengthened those with tumbling knees. But why was he suffering? (see Job 4).

In the speeches of Job's friends (Job 4–36), they said a lot of things that were mostly true about God and His character. But what they said was hurtful to Job. He wished that they hadn't said anything at all. The intention of the friends was good. They wanted to sympathize but they spoke unprofitable words.

That is why the apostle Paul advised Titus of the following:

> *But avoid foolish controversies and genealogies and arguments and quarrels, about the law, because these are unprofitable and useless.*
>
> *(Titus 3:9)*

Likewise, the words of Job's friends were useless. If you have a friend who is suffering, you don't need to give him the reason of suffering all the time. Sometimes there are no immediate answers to our questions like Why? and How?

Hypocrisy is an extra wound in the heart of a suffering man. In place of talking, it is better to pray for the afflicted ones. That is why God sent His Son Jesus Christ. He did not talk when He healed people, He just healed them. He just gave freedom. He just had compassion with them, and through His prayers, they were set free.

At the end, another personality comes on the scene, a young man called Elihu. He also added to Job's wounds (Job 36).

God Speaks

After Job's friends were finished talking Job also stopped arguing with them. Another personality jumped into the conversation: God the Father. Job 36–41 is actually words that God spoke directly to Job. However, God never gave the answer why Job was suffering. He totally talked about other things: about creation, about oceans, and about animals. In these chapters, God shared with Job and us a glimpse of His glory and the wisdom behind His creations. In the end, God said that He was angry with the friends of Job because they did not speak right about God (Job 42:7).

After God spoke to Job, and after Job prayed for his friends according to what God commanded, they sacrificed seven bulls and rams. God restored Job from his affliction. And God gave back to Job twice as much as he had before Satan took it. Job lived as a righteous man for 140 years (Job 42).

The Touch of God

Job in his affliction did not need sympathy from his friends. He did not need words of knowledge and theology. The words of his friends did not heal Job even though they had some elements of truth in them. The only thing that helped Job rise from his ashes was the touch of God. Job had a supernatural encounter with God. God talked to him directly from His throne. God touched Job with His Words: Rhema. It means the spoken word that comes out from the mouth of God.

It is only by God's spoken word and the supernatural manifestation of God's power that someone's life can change. We do not need empty words; we do not need empty theology. Someone who is dying, crying, and suffering does not need hypocrisy. What he needs is the Rhema—God's Word being manifested in power and authority.

Once again Paul said:

> *My message and my preaching were not with persuasive words, but with a demonstration of the Spirit's power.*
> *(1 Corinthians 2:4)*

It's only God's Word and Spirit that can set the captives free. That is why God's Word manifested Himself in Jesus Christ. He is the Word of the Living God:

> *In the beginning was the word, and the word was with God and the word was God. He was with God in the beginning.*
> *(John 1:1-2)*

Two things that can change a person's life—the Word and the Spirit (God's breath). Word alone cannot change a person's life; word alone is empty. But the moment the same word is loaded with the breath of the Spirit of God, it will become Rhema. That is why Jesus sent His Holy Spirit to us. Through the Holy Spirit we became born again. But to receive the Holy Spirit, we need Jesus Christ who is the only way to eternal life.

Through God's Word (Rhema) Job had the opportunity to experience a type of being born again. He received his health back and his possessions and he also became the father of many children.

If you have friends who are suffering, pray for them so that they may have the supernatural manifestation of God's glory to change. Everyone who has this experience this will never be the same again!

MAIN SCRIPTURES
Job (all chapters)

REFERENCE SCRIPTURES
John 1:1-2; 11:25
1 Corinthians 2:4
Titus 3:9

TO MEMORIZE AND MEDITATE UPON
TITUS 3:9

BUT AVOID FOOLISH CONTROVERSIES AND GENEALOGIES AND ARGUMENTS AND QUARRELS ABOUT THE LAW, BECAUSE THESE ARE UNPROFITABLE AND USELESS.

QUESTIONS:

1. Is suffering necessarily the result of sin?
2. What is Rhema?
3. Can you make some comparisons between the lessons we learned and the story of Nicodemus and Jesus in John 3?

NOTES:

NOTES:

LESSON 23
Praise and Prayer

Psalms (all psalms)

INTRODUCTION TO THE BOOK OF PSALMS

The book of Psalms is one of the most popular books in the Old Testament. It is popular not only with Jewish and Christian believers but also with the secular world and people from other religions.

The name "Psalm" or "Psalter" is given by the Septuagint (Greek translation) which originally referred to the stringed instruments such as harp, lyre, and lute.

The original Hebrew name for Psalms is *TEHILLIM*, meaning "PRAISES." Even though the majority of the Psalms are PRAYERS, *THEPHILLOT*, they still call this book "Praises."

The book of Psalms is very essential for us Christians because:

1. It is filled with wisdom about God
2. It is filled with human feelings and emotions towards God and others.

Also, some Psalms should be understood in the historical context of previous Israeli history. There are also Prophetic or Messianic Psalms that deal with our Lord Jesus Christ. These Messianic Psalms are frequently quoted in the New Testament in reference to

Christ. The Messianic Psalms are: Psalm 8, 16, 22, 31, 40, 41, 45, 68, 69, 102, 110, and 118.

Many people refer David as the writer of the Psalms, but this is partly true; only seventy-three are written by David. Other writers include people like Asaph, Moses, Solomon, Heman, Ethan, and many others.

Originally the book of Psalms consisted of five books:

Book I (1–41)
Book II (42–72)
Book III (73–89)
Book IV (90–106)
Book V (107–150)

Psalms is very difficult to explain for a Bible study such as this, because it deals with various subjects unsystematically. This makes a clear-cut survey impossible. In this lesson, we will be studying some general teachings that are useful for our daily lives.

TODAY'S JOURNEY

As I just mentioned, the book of Psalms consists of two major things: Praises and Prayers.

The verb praise in Hebrew is *Halal*, the noun of this word is *Tehillah.*

Halal means "to praise" when we say Hallelujah. It means "let us praise YAH" (Yehovah). Halel comes from *Halal* and YAH comes from the word *Yehovah.* Praise means to glorify God, to give thanks for His greatness towards us. Praise can consist of words with or without music. It also means the way of life which is worthy of God.

Prayer is somehow different from praise. The Hebrew verb for prayer is *Palal*, the noun of this word is *Tephillah*. Prayer means to "talk to God," "to intervene," "to mediate," "to ask and request." In the Psalms prayer was often connected to music.

When we read Psalms, a very essential difference is seen between praise and prayer. In Praise, we read that man is speaking about God's greatness. The characters of God are mentioned with thankfulness. In praise, man speaks and thanks God for His characteristics. If you want to know what kind of God you are serving read the book of Psalms. His very character will be revealed to you.

In prayer-psalms, the man speaks to God, about himself. In these prayer-psalms the very character of man is revealed; man's emotions and feelings are noticeable.

Shortly said, praise-psalms show greatness, power, and love, while prayers often show the weakness of man and his need for God. I hope you will not make a formula out of this course. In prayer one can find the very character of God; in praise one finds the very character of man.

Praise-Psalms (Revelation of God's character and wisdom)

Normally, praise-psalms go together with thankfulness that is directed to God's character. "Thank you God that you love me!" This shows one of God's characteristics—love. This means we are worshipping a God who is love.

Let us analyze some of these psalms:

God is the creator of everything, (Psalm 8)
God is the creator of the heavens and earth. God is our beginning.
God is the maker of this world. (Psalm 8:3)
God is the miracle-making God (Psalm 9)

I will praise you oh Lord, with all my heart, I will tell you all your wonders. . . . (Psalm 9:1)

We must praise God because He is able to do great things in our lives. When every door is closed God will open it and make a way for you.

God is the everlasting Ruler and Judge (Psalm 9)

The Lord is the everlasting ruler. He rules over the world. He rules over your life. He is the one who gave you life. He is also the judge. He will judge the world one day through His Son Jesus Christ.

God is a Refuge and Shield (Psalm 11 and 46)

He is our refuge and shield. God loves His people and He protects them. Whenever we are weak and lonely, whenever we are dealing with a problem, we must remember that He is our shield and refuge.

The Lord is our Rock and Strength (Psalm 18 and 28)

The Lord is our Rock; only upon Him can we build our lives. Only upon Him can we have security and strength. Jesus Christ is the Rock. God gave us Jesus to build and base our lives upon. Jesus said, "Do not build your houses on sand, but build them on the rock" (Matt. 7:24).

The Lord our God is Faithful (Psalm 18:25)

In Psalms, we realize that no matter what happens in our lives, God remains unchangeable. He keeps His promises. Even though we leave Him and go far away from Him, He is still faithful to us. He is still caring for us. While people are unfaithful to one another, God remains faithful.

The Lord is Righteous (Psalm 18:20 and 33)

The Bible says no one is righteous because we all have sinned and we all come up short in the glory of God. Yet, God, in His righteousness, sent His Son Jesus Christ. By believing in Jesus, we too will be called righteous. Not because we are so but because the One who dwells in us is righteous. God is righteous. He knows you. He knows the very pain you are carrying in your life. He will answer you in His righteousness!

The Lord is our Shepherd, our Guide (Psalm 23)

Man always looks for guidance in life, like what kind of decision one must make. Man needs a guide. But the Bible is talking about a blind man leading another blind. How can it be? So do not trust people when they are guiding you. Put your trust in God's guidance. That is why He sent His Holy Spirit, the Spirit of all truth. He will guide you and shepherd you (John 16:1-16).

The Lord is the Comforter (Psalm 23:4)

Every person needs comfort in life. There is no greater comforter than the Holy Spirit (John 14). Whenever you need comfort, call His name He will be with you. People around us can put us down, but God and His Spirit will never leave us alone. Jesus is our comforter.

The Lord is Light and Salvation (Forgiving) (Psalm 27 and 32)

The Lord is my light and salvation, whom shall I fear? (Psalm 27:1)

Man still lives in darkness with so many lights and lamps being sold in shops. And even though we have the great sun, man needs that greater light for redemption and salvation.

Jesus said, "I am the Light of the world" (John 8:12)

You may think you live in light but if you do not have Jesus Christ, you live in absolute darkness. But once you have Him and accept Him as Lord and Savior, salvation waits for you. You are forgiven from your sins. This Light was nailed on the cross for you.

The Lord is our Healer (Psalm 30)

Lord I call you for help and you healed me (Psalm 30:2)

God says to us, *"I am the Lord who heals you."* His name is Jehovah the healer. When Jesus Christ came to this world, He healed everyone; the blind could see, the lame could walk, even the dead were raised, all because of Jesus' power. Even today Jesus is alive. In His name many sicknesses and diseases are healed. There is power in this name: **JESUS CHRIST.**

The Lord is our ever-present Helper (Psalm 30; 46)

God is our refuge and strength, an ever present help in trouble (Psalm 46:1)

Most of the time help is not there when we need it the most. This is what happens in the movies when the policemen arrive too late. But our God is an ever-present God. Anytime we need Him, He is there to help us. Our God never sleeps. He is always awake and watching over us through His Holy Spirit.

There is power in the Lord's Word (Psalm 33:6-7)

By the word of the Lord the heavens were made, their starry host by the breath of his mouth (Psalm 33:6)

In the last lesson in the book of Job, we learned about Rhema, which is the Word of God come alive. In God's Word, there is power. God can heal with His Word. God can set free with His word. God can create something that never existed. This Word became flesh and lived among us. God's word became visible in the person of Jesus Christ.

> *In the beginning was the Word and the Word was with God and the Word was God. He was with God in the beginning. Through Him all things were made, without Him nothing was made that has been made. In Him was life and that life was the light of man.*
>
> *(John 1:1-4)*

He is a Deliverer (Psalm 34:4)

I sought the Lord, and he answered me He delivered me from all my fears (Psalm 34:4)

God is our deliverer. He delivers us from every type of situation; He delivers us from the bondage of slavery and sin. That is why He sent Jesus to deliver us from eternal fire and condemnation. Jesus came to set the captives free and proclaim deliverance to the poor (Luke 4:18-19).

He Answers Prayers (Psalm 40)

Our God is a God who answers His children. Jesus said, *"Ask and it will be given unto you."* Give your desires to Him. He will answer you with more than you ask from Him (Jer. 33:3).

The Lord is Our Savior (Psalm 68:19)

Praise be to the Lord, to our God our Saviour, Who daily bears our burdens (Psalm 68:19)

Jesus Christ is called Savior; He is the Savior of the world. Only through Him can we be saved. Read Isaiah 9; Matthew 1:18-25; and Luke 1:26-38.

The Lord is Good, He is Love (Psalm 136)

Our God is a good God. He never wants His people to suffer. There is no evil in God. God is love. That is why in John 3:16 we read *"God so loved the world that He sent His only beloved son Jesus, whoever believes in Him will not perish and have eternal life."* God is good and He loves you no matter who you are.

Of course there are many characteristics of God that one must find out for himself. The above mentioned characteristics are only an example.

For instance, when someone reads Psalm 103 many characteristics of God are revealed. However, I want to remind you that sometimes praise and prayer are so close to each other that we cannot separate them. So when you are reading a psalm be open-minded. A psalm can be a mixture of praise and prayer.

All the above-mentioned characteristics are summarized in Jesus Christ and are demonstrated with power. As you read the four gospels of Jesus Christ, you will see that these characteristics were demonstrated by Jesus Christ.

WE SERVE A GREAT GOD, HALLELUJAH!

Prayer-Psalms (Man's Confession and Man's Need of God)

Like praise-psalms, prayer-psalms reflect God's character, but this time God's character is related to man's character. When we read prayer-psalms, we realize that we need God; we realize that we are not of our own lives. We are weak and we need God. In Psalms, various types of human characteristics come up. In prayer-psalms man asks God to intercede for him and others. Man deals with his emotions and heart towards God. Let us study some characteristics of man.

Man Is Weak and Needs God (Psalm 16:2 and 70)

The prayers in Psalms show us that every human is weak. We need God and to come to God we need Jesus Christ. Jesus said, *"He is the vine and we are the branches, apart from Him we will never bear fruits" (John 15:5).* No matter who we are, we need God in our lives; we are dependent of Him.

Fear of God (Psalm 38 and 51)

A godly man fears God. The book of Proverbs teaches us that the fear of God is the beginning of wisdom. No one can mock God. God can never be deceived.

Fear in General

One of the characteristics of man is being fearful: fears about tomorrow; fears about life; fears about the unknown. In the book of Psalms, all these fears are cast unto the Lord in prayers. For example, there is the fear of enemies (Psalm 27:12).

Man Is Complaining (Psalm 13 and 22)

Man is never satisfied. Man can get hurt by God just because of lack of understanding. In some Psalms man raises his voice and complain towards God. This is not wrong when we do not sin against Him and when we do not curse Him. But we can always empty our hearts to God's Spirit. He is there to listen to us.

Man Carries Anger Toward Others (Psalm 3 and 6:10)

Anger is also another feeling of man. Man gets angry that is why there are so many fights in the world. But we Christians must bring our anger towards others to God. We must ask God to help us deal with it. Sometimes the writer of a psalm wished his enemies to be destroyed, but this changed with the New Testament. We must love our fleshly enemies *because our fight is not against flesh and blood but against the powers of the air and the invisible world.* We can become angry with the invisible world and even curse it, but we must not do this to a fellow human being even if he or she is our fleshly enemy. Jesus said, "Bless those who curse you!"

Man Needs Love (Psalm 17:6-7)

Love is one of the greatest characteristics of man. We love one another; we love the things around us; we love our jobs, our car, etc. But still there is a greater kind of love that comes only from God. In the Psalms-Prayers we can see the writers describing how much love people like you and me seek during the whole cycle of human life.

LASTLY

We deal with these types of feelings and emotions daily. We must acknowledge our weaknesses and our total dependence upon God. We are allowed to ask God to rescue us from our fears. It is also possible to ask God regarding our sufferings. However, never blame God in your prayers. You can talk to Him and tell Him what you want or feel, but do not be angry with God or curse Him. That is why the Bible says, "In your anger do not sin."

SUMMARY

In this lesson we learned about praising and praying to God. There is a difference between these two. Normally, praise is a reaction of answered prayer. A praising tongue says, “Thank you Lord,” and a praying tongue says, “I need you Lord.”

We also learned some of God’s characteristics which are all united and gathered in Jesus Christ. Actually, Psalms is a book that describes The Father and Jesus.

We learned more about ourselves and our emotions. The book of Psalms is a gathering of every possible feeling that we may have in our lives. God loves us and He wants us to come to Him with all our burdens.

Lastly, the book of Psalms is filled with wisdom and whoever uses it will walk in the light.

MAIN SCRIPTURES
Psalms (all chapters)

REFERENCE SCRIPTURES
Isaiah 9
Matthew 7:24
Luke 1:26-38; 4:18-19
John 8:12; 16:1-16

TO MEMORIZE AND MEDITATE UPON
PSALM 46: 1

GOD IS OUR REFUGE AND STRENGTH, AN EVER-PRESENT HELP IN TROUBLE.

QUESTIONS:

1. Try to read some Psalms and find out for yourself some other characteristics of God.

2. Why do you think the book of Psalms is an important book for us Christians?

3. What is the difference between praise and prayer in the Psalms? What are the similarities?

NOTES:

NOTES:

LESSON 24
Wisdom

Proverbs and Ecclesiastes (all chapters)

INTRODUCTION TO THE BOOK OF PROVERBS

Sometimes the Jews speak of the entire Old Testament as the Law, the Prophets, and the Writings. The book of Proverbs, together with Job, Psalms, and Ecclesiastes, belongs to another category of writings. In our studies we will call these books Wisdom Books or Poetical Books. Personally, I prefer the term Wisdom Books because these books are filled with wise sayings that guide our lives. The book of Proverbs is a gathering of short and powerful statements which give us guidelines and truth about human behavior.

The Hebrew word for proverbs is *massal. Massal* is a statement that contains much truth in a few words, expressed in a particular way so that the reader will easily memorize it.

Many associate Proverbs only with the writings of Solomon which is wrong. The majority of the books are written by Solomon, but He is not the only writer of Proverbs. Chapter 30, for instance, is written by Agur and chapter 31 is penned by Lemuel. We do not have enough information about the identities or personalities of these men.

The book of Proverbs may have been written in the time of the United Kingdom of Israel around the tenth century B.C.

We can divide this book into the following outlines:

Benefits of wisdom and the disadvantages of folly (chapters 1–9)
The Proverbs of Solomon (chapters 10–29)
The Proverbs of Agur (chapter 30)
The Proverbs of King Lemuel (chapter 31)

INTRODUCTION TO THE BOOK OF ECCLESIASTES

Ecclesiastes is also a wisdom book. Many believe that Solomon is the writer of this book. Though we are not fully sure that Solomon is the writer, sections like 1:1, 12, 16; 2:4-9; and 7:26-29 give us great assurance that he is indeed the writer. To make this study simple, we will assume that Solomon is the writer. Solomon used his own personal life as a guideline to teach the reader. He used his life experiences, including his mistakes, to guide the reader. Of course, the Holy Spirit is the One who inspired these Scriptures and used Solomon's life.

The Hebrew name for this book is "The Teacher" or "The Preacher" derived from *qoheleth.*

I consider Ecclesiastes to be a continuation of Proverbs. Proverbs is the theoretical aspect of wisdom in life which expresses how we should and should not live. In Ecclesiastes, we read about the experience of the writer in practice, how he failed by using his own wisdom. Ecclesiastes, then, is the acknowledgement of Proverbs, the godly wisdom. The way Ecclesiastes is written makes it hard to give an outline or division for the book. This book consists of twelve chapters, and in this lesson we will study Proverbs and Ecclesiastes together.

TODAY'S JOURNEY

The Holy Bible is a book with varieties. The Bible is a deep ocean with many hidden gifts ready to be discovered by men through the guidance and revelation of the Holy Spirit.

The Bible is a book that has answers for everything once a ready heart is willing to know more. Many people think that the Bible only deals with spirituality and stories which took place a long time ago. Many believe that the Bible has no answers for society and for humanity. This idea is wrong once we study the books of Proverbs and Ecclesiastes. In these books there are no heroic stories unlike the book of Kings. The books of Proverbs and Ecclesiastes deal with Man and Society!

PROVERBS

Once a person reads Proverbs, he will learn how a person should live a life worthy of God. The reader will learn how to function in society and know what God expects from His people. Proverbs describes God's guidelines for a godly person, godly family, and a godly society. For a godly way of life, we need a higher knowledge that does not come from man; rather, we need that which comes from God. The book of Proverbs speaks to us and teaches us about godly wisdom.

> *Trust in the Lord your God with all your heart and lean not on your own understanding; in all your ways acknowledge Him, and He will make your path straight.*
>
> *(Proverbs 3:5-6)*

A. Straight Path

These days many people do not live on a straight path. They are lost in the subways and byways of life. They do not know where they are going; they do not know where they are. They are living in the slavery of broken families, drugs, and poverty both spiritually and physically. An average twenty-first century city is filled with these types of problems. Societies are simply sick.

But why? What is the reason? The answer is simple. Human beings do not lean on God's wisdom but on their own knowledge and understanding. God talks through the Bible to His people, but they do not listen. Humans think they know better and that they can do everything. Man thinks that he is the god of all creation. He does not need anyone else. Man thinks he is wise enough! There is something old and deeply rooted in man, and that is rebellion. The poison of the tree of knowledge is still circulating in the blood of every human being. In the beginning, God said to Adam and Eve, "Do not eat from the tree of knowledge or you will die!"

B. The Fear of the Lord

The people of the world do not live on the straight path of the Lord because they do not fear Him. The book says, "The fear of the Lord is the beginning of wisdom." Therefore, not fearing the Lord is the beginning of disorder, foolishness, anarchy, chaos, war, and many other evil things. Proverbs deals with unwise actions like adultery, sexual sins, stealing, lying, laziness, a foolish wife, rebellious children, a bad husband, and a wicked boss. All these things are described in Proverbs. The book of Proverbs teaches us that these things happen in a society due to lack of the fear of the Lord.

Some abuse their children sexually because there is no fear of the Lord. Some kill innocent people simply because there is no fear of the Lord. There is violence in the streets such as car accidents due to consumption of alcohol and gang violence. These are all the results of the lack of fear of the Lord.

In the original Hebrew language, "to fear" means "to revere," "to respect," and "to acknowledge the Lord." These days there's no more respect and reverence for God. Look at the TV programs. How many jokes are made about God and men of God? People are forgetting God's commands not to abuse His name! The fear of the Lord is the beginning of wisdom and godly life.

Actually, the book of Proverbs is the sociological and psychological book of the Bible. All the social and psychological issues are discussed there, and a great deal of the book deals with sexual sins, especially for young men.

C. Sexual Immorality

AIDS is one of the greatest issues of our century. Many children die because of AIDS but not by their own choice. They are victims of their parents' promiscuity! Billions of dollars are spent searching for a cure for AIDS. Besides this deadly disease, there are many other diseases that can be contracted due to illicit sexual practices, particularly among homosexuals.

The Bible is clear about these acts:

> *For the lips of an adulteress drip honey, and her speech is smoother than oil; but in the end she is bitter as gall, sharp as a double-edged sword. Her feet go down to death; her steps lead straight to the grave.*
>
> *(Proverbs 5:3-5)*

God is talking about a double-edged sword and death. Do we not have these today in our world? Is AIDS not death? Are the sicknesses not as sharp as a double-edged sword?

Prevention is always best. It is better to prevent rather than to solve a problem before it becomes so complicated. There is a greater type of prevention and that is spiritual or moral prevention. This prevention teaches the people about God and how to live according to God's guidelines. I believe with all my heart that if individuals start to obey what is written in Proverbs they will have a much better society than we have now!

Lastly, in the book of Proverbs there is much said about godly women. Proverbs 31:10-31 gives a very good description concerning how God wants a woman to be?

For example:

1. A good woman has her husband's full confidence (v.11). It is very common nowadays that husbands don't trust their wives and vice versa. There is no trust anymore between partners and, because of this, many families fall apart and many children grow up without a mother or a father.

2. A good woman is a good businesswoman (verses 14-19), providing food for her family. She considers a field and buys it, out of her earnings she plant a vineyard (verse 16). Thousands of years ago, God talked about the woman who works and who is good in her business.

3. A godly woman is clothed in strength and dignity (v.25).
Today, many women show their bodies as objects; they think they can get more attention through the garments they wear. But the Bible says being attractive comes from within. A lot of women have become objects and puppets for lustful men who look at them with sinful eyes. The media plays a very important role. By showing on TV its version of the ideal sexy woman, they create an image of a woman that the average woman cannot ever be.

What do we get then? We get frustrated women and men who cannot afford to be or look like those in the media! Also, some women try to act and dress like men. This is not good because it can bring confusion into a society. No one can distinguish who is whom anymore. But the Bible says that a woman should dress gently and with dignity.

ECCLESIASTES

As I said earlier, Proverbs is the sociological book of the Bible and Ecclesiastes is the philosophical book of the Bible. This book can simply be summarized in the following: everything is meaningless when it is not based upon God's Wisdom. In this book, the writer explains his experiences. He leaned upon his own understanding. He disobeyed God's command to not marry foreign women. He said all these are meaningless when your life is not based on God (Eccl. 1). The book of Ecclesiastes teaches us to relax and enjoy life in the Lord's freedom. It also teaches us that for everything there is a time (Eccl. 3:1-8). "A time to be born, a time to die. There is a time to weep and a time to laugh." Many people live hastily; they always run and rush to achieve their goals, but God said, "Everything has its own time."

THE CONCLUSION OF THE MATTER

Now that all has been heard, here is the conclusion of the matter:

> *Fear God and keep his commandments, for this is the whole duty of man. For God will bring every deed into judgment, including every hidden thing whether it is good or evil.*
>
> *(Ecclesiastes 12:13-14)*

According to the writer, the only duty of man is to fear the Lord and keep His commands. Only then are we able to enjoy life and have a better society and a better world with less sin!

God's Secret Wisdom

Since the conclusion of all this is to obey God's commands, we surely must do so by receiving Jesus Christ as our Lord and Savior. For if we do not receive Him as Lord the wisdom that Proverbs speaks of is useless. Nicodemus knew the Law and the Wisdom, but yet he could not gain eternal life because he was not born again (John 3:1-21).

The Bible teaches us that all the treasures of wisdom and knowledge are hidden in Jesus Christ (Col. 2:3). So if a man only keeps the words in Proverbs and denies the very fact that Jesus is the Messiah he is living in deception. That person only obeys on the surface and is not in the fullness of wisdom. Wisdom comes through Jesus Christ and not through rules and regulations!

The New Testament speaks to us about God's Secret Wisdom:

> *No, we speak about God's secret wisdom, a wisdom that has been hidden and that God destined for our glory before the time began.*
>
> *(1 Corinthians 2:7)*
>
> *. . . But God has revealed it to us by his Spirit (verse 10).*

The Bible teaches us that the Holy Spirit is only reflecting to us what Jesus has. The Holy Spirit did not come to this world according to His own will. He came to do the will of Jesus. Since Jesus has all the secret wisdom and knowledge of God, He passes them to the Holy Spirit and He passes them on to us.

> *He will send us the Holy Spirit the Teacher and the Counselor, for He will teach us into all the truth, if we obey Him.*
>
> (*John 14:15-31)*

The Holy Spirit is the Teacher. This is one of His names. Please compare this name with the Hebrew name of Ecclesiastes: *qoheleth* (The Teacher).

Unlike in the Old Testament, we now receive His teachings not just on paper. We ourselves are the temples of the teacher. This means that the teacher lives in us and guides us in all knowledge. Even Solomon and David did not experience this. This means it is only through the Holy Spirit's teachings, and through being a container of the teacher, that can we be able to have a life worthy of God. To become the container of the Holy Spirit, who is our Teacher, we must come to Jesus and be born again!

MAIN SCRIPTURES
Proverbs and Ecclesiastes (all chapters)

REFERENCE SCRIPTURES
John 3:1-21; 14:15-31
1 Corinthians 2:6-16
Colossians 2:3

TO MEMORIZE AND MEDITATE UPON
PROVERBS 3:5-6

TRUST IN THE LORD WITH ALL YOUR HEART AND LEAN NOT ON YOUR OWN UNDERSTANDING; IN ALL YOUR WAYS ACKNOWLEDGE HIM, AND HE WILL MAKE YOUR PATH STRAIGHT.

QUESTIONS:

1. It is written in Proverbs that there are six things which the Lord hates and seven which He detests. Where are these written and what are those things? Explain them.

2. Why do those who obey Proverbs but do not live in Christ not receive wisdom fully?

3. Why is the fear of the Lord the beginning of wisdom?

NOTES:

NOTES:

LESSON 25
Song of Songs

Song of Songs (all chapters)

INTRODUCTION TO THE BOOK OF SONG OF SONGS

Song of Songs was originally called "Solomon's Song of Songs." It was written somewhere in the tenth century B.C. Many believe Solomon wrote this song, however, it is not clear whether he is the real author. The name, "Solomon's Song of Songs," doesn't mean Solomon is the writer because it can also refer to a title of a song or just a song about Solomon!

It is quite interesting that the name of God is not clearly mentioned in this book. Nor can we find any reference to Israel, the covenant, or any other religious activities.

At first, you may not find any theological or biblical reason why this book has been placed among the canonical books. However, when you go deep in the Spirit in your reading many things will be revealed. However, we should not doctrinize the interpretations we get from the Holy Spirit because He can speak in various ways with His people.

TODAY'S JOURNEY

The Song of Songs, at first reading, shows the sexual love between the over and the beloved. In the Hebrew custom the lover is a man and beloved is the woman. What we read in this book is how the beloved, the most beautiful woman among others, longs and desires for her lover Solomon! The language used in these Songs is the language of love that goes with sexual desires. On the other hand, we read how the lover praises his beloved and how he desires to hear and meet her.

Many scholars consider this book as a handbook for (sexual) love between husbands and wives.

Man/Woman

After God created the world He saw that everything He made was good. But the Bible teaches us that there was only one thing in the eyes of God that was not good:

The Lord God said:

> *It is not good for man to be alone. I will make a helper suitable for him.*
>
> *(Genesis 2:18)*

The Lord caused the man to sleep, and while he was sleeping, He took one of his ribs and formed the woman as a partner for Adam. She was called woman because she was taken out of the man. In the Hebrew language, the word "woman" sounds similar to the word "man." Out of so many things God created none of them was a suitable partner for Adam; only the woman was suitable. Woman was called to existence because Adam needed a partner and a helper. This issue brought forth in the middle ages and the past centuries a wrong image of woman in Christianity and in society. Society believes a woman is under a man and a woman is not equal to the man. Her place is lower than the man's. Even in traditional Christianity people still think the same way. This concept of inequality between men and women is totally wrong!

When we study the word of God and look at the original terminology used for the name “woman” in Hebrew, we find that the term “woman” is actually the same as the term “man.” This means men and women have the same rights and are equal. Woman was not created as a slave, but as a friend! This was the perfect model God made for a man and woman before the fall. However, after the fall, things changed; sin entered into man, and because of sin, man abused the rights that God gave to the woman. So it was not God who took away the position of the woman as an equal friend and helper of man, but it was sin in the heart of both man and woman in the world that caused this gap.

Monogamy/Polygamy

Monogamy means to marry only one person of the opposite sex. Polygamy means to marry more than one partner.

When God created Adam, He chose Eve as his unique partner. Many people forces themselves to find a partner but fail in the end because they choose someone who simply is not for them. Every man can have an Eve and every woman can have an Adam. It is God who chooses our partners. Maybe as you read this study, your partner is hanging around somewhere in a different part of the world!

God gave Eve to Adam, not more and not less. The original marriage order requires one man and one woman as husband and wife; this means neither man to man nor woman to woman! Also, God do not want us to marry many people. But what about Solomon? He married more than one woman. Nevertheless, it was not God who was behind that choice. He did it and his sinful acts brought him his fall.

In the Old Testament times almost everyone was married, but today this has been changed. There are some people who are single today who have reached an age where it is unlikely that they will marry. It is still possible for God to have a great plan for them. But as I mentioned above, God saw that it was not good for Adam to be alone. God knew Adam better than Adam knew himself. God knew what was good for him. Likewise, God knows that being single and unattached can be better for some people. God's will should always prevail so that we can live in the blessings of God. However, He respects the choices we make. Also, we have the rights to ask Him for what we want. (see 1 Cor. 7:25-40).

The Song of Songs is written poetry about a lover and a beloved. Although the lover has many other beloveds (maids), there is only one who is desirable for him. In these songs you can read about the passionate feelings these two have towards each other. Some of these feelings are simply sexual feelings and desires. There is nothing wrong with having a good and desirable sexual relationship between those who are officially married before the Lord. This relationship is a gift from God, but once it is practiced outside the marriage covenant, it will bring curses upon them. Of course if the people come to Christ and deeply ask for forgiveness, God will remove this curse from them and will forgive them. Unfortunately, many married Christians consider sex as a taboo and as unholy. This is very wrong thinking. Once God has brought married couples together, it is their right to enjoy each other fully.

Sex is being commercialized through TV, magazines, and the like. They transmit to the viewers and readers many wrong concepts about sexual love. Men and women expect the ideal fantasy from each other, the Hollywood type of man and woman. The partners must never forget, though, that it is God who brought them together and they are made in the beauty of God's creation and not Hollywood's creation. The increase of pornographic movies changed God-given sex into demonic-given sex. There are some who practice sex in a way which is totally unbiblical. They even harm each other to the point of death to have full satisfaction. This is not godly sex but demonic sex.

The Jewish Interpretation

There is another interpretation of the Song of Songs. Some Jewish scholars believe that the book describes the unfailing love between Jehovah and Israel. This is not a surprising statement because many times God compared His relationship to Israel as a marriage relationship. Hosea 1–2 is a clear example. God commanded Hosea to go and marry an adulterous wife and have children of unfaithfulness because the land (Israel) was guilty of adultery (Hosea 1:2). Then He said to Hosea:

> *Rebuke your mother (Israel), rebuke her, for she is not my wife, and I am not her husband.*
>
> *(Hosea 2:2)*

According to some Jewish rabbis, "the beloved" in the Song of Songs is Israel and "the lover" is God. They say that when the beloved says in Songs 1:4, "Take me away with you-let us hurry! Let the king bring me into his chambers," it means the exodus of Israel from Egypt to the Promised Land. "His chambers" refers to the land of milk and honey.

I personally believe this interpretation because the Bible is multi-dimensional. In every epoch of human life and history the Holy Spirit uses the same verse and the same Bible text which has been read for centuries to give us new revelations.

Further, the beloved said,

> *Do not stare at me because I am dark, because I am darkened by sun. My mother's sons were angry with me and made me take care of the vineyards, my own vineyard I have rejected.*
>
> (Songs 1:6)

This shows the slavery of the Jews in Egypt for 430 years. They did not work on their vineyard but on the Egyptian ground.

The Christian Interpretations

After reading the Jewish interpretation you will not be surprised to read the Christian version.
Many Christians believe the relationship between the lover and the beloved in the Songs is comparable with the relationship between Christ Jesus and His church.

> *Wives, submit to your husbands as to the Lord. For the husband is the head of the wife as Christ is the head of the church, his body, of which he is the Savior.*
>
> (Ephesians 5:22-23)

> *Let us rejoice and be glad and give him glory! For the wedding of the Lamb has come, and his bride has made herself ready. Fine linen, bright and clean was given her to wear.*
>
> (Revelation 19:7-8)

Reading these verses reminds me of the essence of the Song of Songs. For instance, in Songs 1:4 the beloved asks the lover, the king, to take her away with him, to hurry, and let him bring her into his chambers. This reminds me of a praying church (beloved), who desperately prays for the coming of Christ who will bring His church, His bride, to the place of eternal life. He will bring them to His Father's house where there are many rooms prepared for her church.

> *In my Father's house there are many rooms; if it were not so, I would have told you. I am going there to prepare a place for you.*
>
> *(John 14:2)*

According to Romans 5, Christ is the second Adam. The first Adam failed because sin entered him through disobeying God. Through sin, death entered him and the generations to come. So through Adam, sin and death entered the human race. But Romans 5 teaches us that through Jesus, the second Adam, forgiveness of sin and life entered the human race. Through Jesus, the second Adam, they are made available to those who will believe in Jesus as the Messiah.

Genesis 2:21-24 is about the creation of the woman. After finding nothing in the creation to be good for Adam, God caused him to sleep and the woman was crated out of his rib. Since Jesus is the second Adam, His church is the second Eve. For out of Jesus' crucifixion, death and resurrection, the church of Jesus Christ was born through the coming of the Holy Spirit. The church of Jesus Christ was born out of the ribs of Christ which accounts for a holy relationship, a marriage relationship between Christ and His church. Jesus gained the victory by His death. He can never be challenged or tempted. That is why Paul said,

> *I promised you to one husband, to Christ, so that I might present you as a pure virgin to him. But I am afraid that just as Eve was deceived by serpent's cunning, your minds may somehow be led astray from your sincere and pure devotion to Christ. For if someone comes to you and preaches a Jesus other than the Jesus we preached, or if you receive a different spirit from the one you received, or a different Gospel from the one you have accepted, you put up with it easily enough.*
>
> *(2 Corinthians 11:2-4)*

So we as the Body of Christ must present ourselves clean, pure, and holy—a virgin unto our master. This cleanliness and love can be found in the Songs of Songs. If we imagine that we are the beloved and Jesus is the Lover we can come to the romantic passionate heart of God. We can also learn how the passionate loving heart of the "beloved" (the church) should be towards the Lord. Putting aside the sexual interpretation of the Song of Songs, by getting into Spirit, will lead you to the Holy of Holies: the Heart of God.

CONCLUSION

In this lesson we learned about the marriage relationship and the relationship of God (Christ) with His beloved ones. Reading this lesson brings us to a deeper meaning of love and marriage. Love is more than a physical act. The love between two hetero-married partners goes further than passion. Once two people are married, their bodies, their spirits, and their souls are connected to one another. Marriage is not about making a contract; it is about keeping that contract.

The relationship of Jesus with His church is a great example. Our relationship with Jesus is not a sexual relationship, but we are married to Him! This teaches us a great lesson about marriage life. Those who base their marriages on sexual attraction alone will not last forever! But those who build their marriage upon commitment, trust, patience, forgiveness, and love are the ones heading for a successful marriage. These kinds of marriages are quite rare nowadays.

MAIN SCRIPTURES
Songs of Songs (all chapters)

REFERENCE SCRIPTURES
Genesis 2:4-5
Hosea 2:1-2
John 14:2
Romans 5
1 Corinthians 2:25-40
2 Corinthians 11:1-4
Ephesians 5:22-23
Revelation 19:7-8

TO MEMORIZE AND MEDITATE UPON
(GENESIS 2:18)

THE LORD GOD SAID: "IT IS NOT GOOD FOR MAN TO BE ALONE. I WILL MAKE A HELPER SUITABLE FOR HIM."

QUESTIONS:

1. Is having sex prior to marriage a sin?

2. Read the Song of Songs and find two or more verses that can be compared with the relationship of Jesus to the church.

3. We learned at least three different interpretations about the Song of Songs. What are these interpretations and which ones do you accept the most? Specify your reasons.

NOTES:

. PART IV .

Journey With Prophets

LESSON 26

The Prophet of Gospel

Isaiah (all chapters)

GENERAL INTRODUCTION TO THE PROPHETS

The books from Isaiah to Malachi in the Old Testament are referred to as the Prophets. Isaiah, Jeremiah, Ezekiel and Daniel are called Major Prophets. This also includes Lamentations. The rest from Hosea to Malachi are known as the Minor Prophets. The terms "minor" and "major" are not based upon the importance of the prophets or the books they wrote. They refer to the length of the books. The major books are longer than the minor books.

Except for the book of Lamentations, the prophetic books are named after the prophet himself. For example, Ezekiel is named after the prophet Ezekiel. Isaiah is named for Isaiah.

Before we expose ourselves to the book of Isaiah, it is fruitful to first study the prophets and prophecies in general. This will make it easier to understand the book of Isaiah and the others. It will also help us to understand the prophets of our time.

Prophets and Prophecies

The word "prophet" comes from the Hebrew word *nabi*. Many scholars disagree about the roots of the word *nabi*. But in short, a prophet is a spokesperson of God. A prophet is one who receives a word from God and passes this divine revelation from the Lord to others. The prophets were basically the lips of God.

In Deuteronomy 18:14-21, God officially mentioned the office of prophet. In these verses, God spoke through Moses and said that the nations that the Israelites would conquer would be those nations that practiced magic, sorcery, and divination. He commanded the Israelites not to do the same since they were a holy nation, a separate nation to God.

> *I will raise up for them a prophet just like you (like Moses) from among their brothers. I will put my words in his mouth, and he will tell them everything I command him. If anyone does not listen to my words that the prophets speak in my name, I myself will call him to account. But a prophet who presumes to speak in my name anything I have not commanded him to say, or a prophet who speaks in the name of the other gods, must be put to death. You may say to yourselves, "How can we know when a message has not been spoken by the Lord?" If what a prophet proclaims in the name of the Lord does not take place or come true, that is a message the Lord has not spoken. That prophet has spoken presumptuously. Do not afraid of him.*
>
> *(Deuteronomy 18:18-22)*

In the Old Testament there were two types of prophets—the prophet with a book and the prophet without a book. For example, Elisha and Elijah did not write any books in the Bible, but they were as powerful as the other prophets who wrote books. There were also prophets in the old times, but their books were not included among the canonical books.

I believe the reason why these books of the prophets were divinely inspired to be placed in the Bible was because all of them spoke about Jesus Christ, including both His first and second comings. The prophets were chosen in the tribulation period of Israel. The prophets were those who had a message to kings and nations, and

especially to Israel. Most of the time, these messages were hard because the people of God had rebelled against Him by disobeying Him.
In the New Testament, the meaning of prophet changed. Now the prophet specifically comes through Jesus Christ. If a prophet does not come in the name of the Lord Jesus Christ, he is not a true prophet. Paul speaks often about himself as a prophet of Jesus Christ. In the New Testament times until today, a true prophet speaks the word of the Lord only through Jesus Christ and through His Holy Spirit.

This is the only way we can be sure if a prophet is from God or not.

He acknowledges the Godhood of Jesus Christ and everything written in the Holy Bible concerning Jesus without manipulating it or misinterpreting it.

He acknowledges the Triune God: God the Father, God the Son, and God the Holy Spirit.

He acknowledges Jesus Christ as the only way to salvation.

A true prophet of God never mixes Christianity with other religions, cults, or new age ideologies and practices.

A true prophet calls the people for salvation and acknowledges the existence of hell for those who deny Christ and also the existence of heaven for those who believe and obey Jesus Christ as their Savior.

Lastly, a prophet is recognized by the fruits of his work. This includes the way he or she lives and the way his or her private life is considered.

INTRODUCTION TO THE BOOK OF ISAIAH

The book of Isaiah is named after the prophet Isaiah, who wrote the book under the inspiration of the Holy Spirit. The prophet Isaiah's ministry took place during the reigns of the four kings of Judah: Uzziah, Jotham, Ahaz, and Hezekiah. He ministered when the Kingdom of Israel was captured by the Assyrians in 722 B.C.

The book of Isaiah is one of the most important prophetic books. It has great value for us Christians because of its great revelations about Jesus Christ. Many people call this book "the gospel of Isaiah," because of its clear-cut testimony about Jesus. In reading this book, one might think Isaiah could have been one of the eye witnesses of Jesus. But this, of course, is not true. Isaiah lived almost seven hundred years before the physical birth of Christ.

The name "Isaiah" explains a lot about the nature of the book itself. Isaiah means "the Salvation of Jehovah." The main issue of this book is not only the salvation of Israel by Jehovah, but rather, the salvation that comes through Jesus Christ for the Jews and the Gentiles!

The book of Isaiah can be divided into two parts:

God's Judgement (chapters 1–39)
God's Salvation (chapters 40–66)

TODAY'S JOURNEY

In order to understand the book of Isaiah and its prophecies, it helps to know a little bit about its historical background and the political setting of the period Isaiah ministered in. After looking at the historical-political background of that time, we will focus on the prophecies of Isaiah. Normally, I categorize the prophecies of Isaiah in the following way:

-Historical Prophecies
-Christ-centered Prophecies
-End Times Prophecies

Historical Background

In lessons 18 and 19 we explained a little about Israel's history. We learned that if someone wants to understand the prophets properly, he or she should have a good foundational knowledge about the books of Samuel, Kings, and Chronicles.

We also explained that after the death of Solomon, the United Kingdom of Israel was divided into two kingdoms that each had a king of its own: the Northern Kingdom, which is also called Israel, and the Southern Kingdom, which is also called Judah. All the kings who reigned in the Northern Kingdom were cruel, harsh, and rebellious. But since some of the kings of Judah were the descendants of David, not all of them were bad. Out of the nineteen kings of Judah, eight were men of God.

We also learned that the Kingdom of Israel lasted until 722 B.C. when it fell to the Assyrians. The Kingdom of Judah lasted until 586 B.C. when the Babylonians captured Jerusalem (read lesson 19).

Isaiah's historical background goes back to the time when the Assyrians captured the Northern Kingdom of Israel. Judah was somehow independent under the protectorate and influence of the Assyrians. Assyria was the superpower of the world. It actually brought Egypt to her knees. They were conquering region by region and added to its territories.

The growing power of the Assyrians terrified the Northern Kingdom of Israel and the whole world. In those days, the king of Israel and Aram tried to persuade King Ahaz of Judah to form a coalition in order to fight the Assyrians. King Ahaz did so in spite of the fact that God commanded him to choose for the Lord His God, rather than the Assyrians or Israel. Through the Prophet Isaiah, God rebuked and condemned the action of King Ahaz (Isa. 7).

Assyria worked alongside the Kingdom of Judah to conquer the Northern Kingdom of Israel. But after a while, Assyria threatened Judah and wanted to conquer Jerusalem (chapter 36). But because of the prayers of the godly king, Hezekiah, the Assyrians were confused and could not conquer Jerusalem.

In those days the Northern Kingdom was ruled by ungodly kings. Israel was not worshipping God with all its heart. They were mixing their faith with idol-worship and other practices from the east. Also, in the Southern Kingdom not all the kings were good. Some kings, like Ahaz were ungodly. However, Judah was brought back to the Law to follow the decrees of the Lord. They were then called to return to their roots.

The Prophet Called Isaiah

Isaiah was a contemporary of Amos, Hosea, and Micah. He began his ministry in approximately 740 B.C., the year of King Uzziah's death. Every prophet of God had a supernatural encounter with God. Isaiah had such personal experiences with the Lord. Isaiah 6 describes a wonderful testimony of Isaiah, when God called him to the ministry and how the man of unclean lips saw the King (I believe this King was Jesus Christ.) and how without ceremonial rules and regulations he was cleansed and forgiven. Isaiah saw Jesus. He believed in Him and was forgiven even before Jesus ever came to this world. Today you can look to Jesus and be saved. After seeing Jesus, Isaiah had an encounter with the burning coal, the fire which cleansed him, the Holy Spirit. He became holy, because he saw the Holy Lord and the Holy Spirit. He was set apart and had experienced a type of being born-again. When we are baptized in the Holy Spirit, we become holy because the Holy Spirit dwells in us.

After the burning coal touched the lips of Isaiah, the voice of the Lord said, "Whom shall I send? And who will go for us?" God was looking for someone who would tell the truth; someone who could stand for the Lord, who could raise the flag of God.
Today, God is calling His church, His body, and His people into a ministry. He is sending us into the world to tell it about Him. Whom shall He send to preach the gospel, the message of deliverance and truth? Many ignore God's calling to the ministry. I personally believe every born again Christian is a messenger of God through Jesus Christ. I believe every born again Christian is a full time minister. But many are sleeping today! God has called us to share our testimony of the Gospel to the entire world, and then the end will come.

Isaiah's answer to God's question was, "Here I am. Send me." The response of Isaiah was an immediate answer. He did not say, "Let me go back and arrange things, then use me." Or, "Let me go and study theology for six years and then use me." No! He said, "Here I am. Send me." As you hear God's voice today do not harden your heart, just be willing and obedient to whatever God asks you to do. Do not wait for an angel to come down from heaven to tell you what you should do. Jesus already told you:

SHARE YOUR TESTIMONY OF THE GOSPEL.

Historical Prophecies

Under historical prophecies, the spoken words from God through the prophet Isaiah tell us about what is going to happen to Israel, Judah, and the other nations of the world in the years to come. In

these passages, Isaiah prophesied about the fall of Israel, Aram, Judah, Assyria, and even about the captivity period of Israel. Judah was clearly mentioned too. Even King Cyrus of Persia, who lived many years after the death of Isaiah, was mentioned by name. Because of this, some theologians believe the book of Isaiah was not written by one man, but by two or more, simply because Isaiah did not live during the time of the Persian King. I believe Isaiah was the only author because He prophesied what God said in His word, *"See the former things have taken place, and new things I declare: before they spring into being I announce them to you."*
God knows everything. He knew you by name even before you were born. He has a plan with your life. He will make sure His plans will be fulfilled if you also believe and trust in Him.

As I explained earlier, the kings of Israel and Aram allied against the superpower, Assyria. In Isaiah 7, we read that the kings of Aram and Israel and other allied forces wanted to attack and capture Judah, but God used the prophet Isaiah to tell Ahaz, the King of Judah, not to be afraid:

> *"If you do not stand firm in your faith, you will not stand at all."*
> *(Isaiah 7:9)*

God wanted King Ahaz to trust Him and not lose his faith. We must also stand firm in our faith. There are many temptations, challenges, and difficulties, so we must be on guard and be faithful to our Lord. Otherwise we will fall.

Prophecies to Israel

The Northern Kingdom became a wicked nation with wicked kings. They forgot the Lord and worshipped idol gods. Pride and arrogance were all over the kingdom. There was no righteousness in the land (Isaiah 9:8; 10:1-4; 48:1-11). Therefore, Isaiah prophesied that Israel would be handed over to captivity. Assyria conquered Israel in 722–721 B.C.

Prophecies to Judah

After allying with Assyria to defeat Israel, Judah became the target of Assyria itself! In that time, King Hezekiah was king over all Judah. He heard that the Assyrians were coming to destroy his kingdom, and he was terrified and distressed. But the Lord promised Hezekiah to deliver them and not allow the Assyrians to attack Judah. After Hezekiah received the letter from the messengers, he went up to the temple and prayed to the Lord. In turn, God did what He promised. God confused the King of Assyria, Sennacharib. While he was preparing his army to attack Judah, the angel of the Lord came and slew 185,000 of his soldiers. He returned to Nineveh and could not attack Judah anymore. Later, he was killed by his own son while he was worshipping his idol god (chapter 36–37).

When we pray, God will help us. It doesn't matter how bad the news is that the messengers have given you, God is able to change bad news into good news and impossible situations into possible ones.

A short while after this event, the Babylonian king who was an enemy of the Assyrians, sent gifts and representatives to King Hezekiah. King Hezekiah was enthusiastic. He showed all his palaces and everything he had. In those days, Babylon was not yet a superpower, but it was soon to become one.

> *Hezekiah said to Isaiah, "There is nothing in my kingdom that I did not show them."*
>
> *(Isaiah 39:4)*

But the Lord did not like what Hezekiah did, so through Isaiah the Lord said:

> *The time will surely come, when everything in your palace and all that fathers have stored up until this day, will be carried off to Babylon. And some of your descendants, your*

own flesh and blood who will be born to you will be taken away and they will become eunuchs in the palace of the King of Babylon.

(Isaiah 39:5-7)

Isaiah prophesied about the Babylonian invasion of Judah and Judah's captivity. These events happened long after Isaiah's ministry in 586 B.C. During Ezekiel's ministry, the Babylonians captured the Southern Kingdom.

Sometimes enthusiasm and emotion will lead us into captivity too. We become so enthusiastic that we give away a lot of information to people we do not know, and later we reap the consequences. We must not base our actions upon emotions, but we must be wise.

Remnant

The concept of the remnant has a special meaning in the history of Israel. When God made His promise to Abraham, He promised him not to destroy his descendants even if they were unfaithful to Him. The remnant means those selected ones among the Israelites and Judah whom God chose to save. They are normally those who remained faithful to Him. Isaiah prophesied that Babylon would capture Judah, however, some would also return to their land. These are the chosen ones who are saved and who will build up Jerusalem and Israel again.

In that day the remnant of Israel, the survivors of the house of Jacob, will no longer rely on him who struck them [this means Assyria and Babylon], but will truly rely on the Lord, the Holy One of Israel. A remnant of Jacob return to mighty God.

(Isaiah 10:20-34)

This took place when people like Ezra and Nehemiah returned back to build their nation.

Isaiah also prophesied that a nation would rise up to become a new superpower. King Cyrus of Persia (today Iran) was the chosen one of God. He would defeat Babylon and set the Jews free to go back to their nation (Isaiah 44; 45; 47).

Other Nations

In Isaiah we read the prophecies about other nations such as Egypt, Assyria, and Babylon. God predicted exactly what would happen. Indeed, everything took place during Isaiah's ministry and some things took place later after his death.

Christ-Centered Prophecies

Isaiah not only prophesied the exact events that were going to take place in Israel's history, but he also prophesied the exact coming of Jesus Christ including His life, His ministry and His death. All these things were prophesied by Isaiah. It seems that he saw a vision. That is why I believe Isaiah was the first evangelist. Even before the Gospel officially started, he preached the Gospel. The book of Isaiah is often used as a reference for the Gospel. Even Jesus, when He started His ministry, read from Isaiah 61, proclaiming that its prophecy was fulfilled today (Luke 4:14-21 with Isaiah 61).

The birth of Jesus was prophesied in Isaiah 9:6:

> *For unto us a child is born, to us a son is given, and the government will be on his shoulders. And he will be called Wonderful Counselor, Mighty God, Everlasting Father, Prince of Peace.*

The most important part of Isaiah is chapter 53 which tell us about the death of Jesus and the fulfilment of His mission. How amazing is our God because at least seven hundred years before Jesus was born, Isaiah prophesied about Him (read Isaiah 53).

-He was rejected (v. 3)
-He was despised (v. 3)
-He took our infirmities and sorrows (v. 4)
-He was pierced for our transgressions and crushed for our iniquities (v. 5)
-By His wounds we are healed (v. 5)
-He died among the wicked (v. 9)
-He rose (v.11)
-He bore our sins (v. 12)
-Jesus is still alive today,

He heals us today,
He forgives our sins.
He can also do it for you.

End Times Prophecies

Many Spirit-filled scholars and leaders are agreed that the end times began with the birth of Jesus Christ. When you read Isaiah regularly you will be confronted with the end times and the prophecies about Jesus Christ. Therefore, from the time of Jesus until today we are living in the process of the end times. These were the things Isaiah prophesied during and right after Jesus Christ: *The New Remnant, Remnant for the Gentiles.*

The New Remnant

Isaiah prophesied salvation that comes through Jesus Christ, not only for the Jews, but also for all the nations of the world. Isaiah prophesied that God would choose a remnant from among the Jews. This new remnant took place by the coming of Jesus Christ. The

Jews who believed Jesus was the Messiah were the new Jewish remnant. Those who recognized Him as the Messiah were the remnant that is saved eternally through the redemption of Jesus Christ. Isaiah 11 is a very clear description of this Jewish remnant:

> *A shoot will come up from the scum of Jesse; from his root a branch will bear fruit. The Spirit of the Lord will rest on him (v.1).*

Jesus said that He is the vine and we are the branches (John 15). He also said the Spirit of God was upon Him. The shoot of the branch that Isaiah talked about was Jesus Christ because Jesus was the descendant of David. Further, in Isaiah 11:10-12, Isaiah spoke about the future remnant, the Jews:

> *In that day the Root of Jesse will stand as a banner for the peoples; the nations will rally to him, and his place of rest will be glorious. In that day the Lord will reach out his hand a second time to reclaim the remnant that is left of his people from Assyria, from lower Egypt, from upper Egypt, from Cush, from Elam, from Babylonia, from Hamath and from the islands of the sea. He will raise a banner for the nations and gather the exiles of Israel; he will assemble the scattered people of Judah from four quarters of the earth.*

During Jesus' ministry and after, the Jews were scattered to every corner, to the above mentioned regions, far and beyond. The Jews who heard the Gospel received it were the new remnant of Israel.

The book of Hebrews for example was written for the Messianic Jews, the Hebrews who believed in Christ. The book of Romans was written for the Jews who lived in Rome and received Jesus Christ as their Lord and Savior.

Remnant for the Gentiles

After the Gospel was preached to the Jews, it was preached to the Gentiles and to the entire world. The gospel is reaching different parts of the world, different nations. Isaiah wrote in chapter 56 about salvation for the non-Jews. Verse three says, "*Let no foreigner who has called himself to the Lord say: 'The Lord surely excludes me from His people.'*"

These foreigners are the people of the world who have received Jesus as Lord and Savior. They are the remnants of the Gentiles. You are called a remnant because you are set apart and saved by Jesus Christ. You are a remnant because you chose to follow Jesus. Isaiah 65 talks about the Gentiles who are called to the Lord.

> *I revealed myself to those who did not ask for me; I was found by those who did not seek me. To a nation who did not call on my name, I said, "Here am I, here am I."*
>
> *(Isaiah 65:1)*

One very interesting issue in the book of Isaiah is the phrase, "Mountain of the Lord." The Jews believe this mountain is Zion. Originally, Zion was a Jebusite fortress captured by King David (2 Sam. 5:6-9) in the city of David, Jerusalem.

In Isaiah, God speaks about the remnant who took refuge in the mountain of the Lord; this mountain is Jesus Christ and His church.

> *In the last days the mountain of the Lord's temple will be established as chief among the mountains; it will be raised above the hills and all nations will stream to it.*
>
> *(Isaiah 2:2)*

God also speaks about those who will not take refuge in this mountain of the Lord. They will be banned, destroyed, and punished (Isa. 65:11-14).

Some people believe the mountain of the Lord is the New Jerusalem that will come from above. All the remnants of nations will stream to it but those who do not will be destroyed (read Revelation 21).

Closing of the Book

The book of Isaiah closes with a great promise from God for all who believe, but it also has a dangerous warning for those who are rebellious:

> *"As the new heavens and the new earth that I make will endure before me," declares the Lord, "so will be your name and descendants endure. From one New Moon to another and from one Sabbath to another, all mankind will come bow down before me," says the Lord. "And they will go out and look upon the dead bodies of those who rebelled against me; their worm will not die, nor will their fire be quenched, and they will be loathsome to all mankind."*
>
> *(Isaiah 66:22-24)*

WHAT CAN WE LEARN?

In the book of Isaiah we learn about the prophecies given about Jesus Christ almost seven hundred years before He was even born. Isaiah is an Old Testament gospel because it talks about the salvation that comes through Jesus Christ.

One of the greatest things you can learn while reading this book is that rebellion against God leads to captivity. The Israelites lost their love for God and they worshipped other gods and idols. The Israelites offered empty sacrifices, fastings, and prayers. God disliked them (Isaiah 58) because their hearts were not with Him.

There are many nations in the world today that rebel against God. They hear His voice but they still worship idols and follow traditional rules and regulations. Therefore, they are slaves of poverty, hunger, war, and many different crises. But among these are the chosen people (the remnant) who are the Spirit-filled Christians. Though they are hungry, they never die; though they are persecuted, they are never defeated.

God promised them:

> *Fear not, for I have redeemed you;*
> *I have summoned you by name;*
> *You are mine.*
> *When you pass through the waters,*
> *I will be with you;*
> *And when you pass through the rivers,*
> *They will not sweep over you.*
> *When you walk through the fire,*
> *You will not be burned;*
> *The flames will not set you ablaze.*
>
> *(Isaiah 43:1-2)*

You are the remnant for your nation. You must tell the truth about Jesus Christ to set others free from the curse of poverty and calamities. God wants to use you to change the nations of the world. Whom shall He send? You!

MAIN SCRIPTURES
Isaiah (all chapters)

REFERENCE SCRIPTURES:
Deuteronomy 18:14-22
2 Samuel 5:6-9
Luke 4:14-21
John 15
Revelation 21

TO MEMORIZE AND MEDITATE UPON
ISAIAH 42:9

SEE, THE FORMER THINGS HAVE TAKEN PLACE, AND NEW THINGS I DECLARE; BEFORE THEY SPRING INTO BEING I ANNOUNCE THEM TO YOU.

QUESTIONS:

1. In which chapter of Isaiah can you read about the death and resurrection of Jesus Christ?

2. What does "Jewish Remnant" mean in the context of the Babylonian captivity and in the New Testament era?

3. When did Isaiah live?

4. What is the difference between Old Testament prophets and New Testament prophets?

NOTES:

LESSON 27
Jeremiah *"Jehovah Establishes"*

Jeremiah and Lamentations (all chapters)

INTRODUCTION TO THE BOOKS OF JEREMIAH AND LAMENTATIONS

The book of Jeremiah is the longest prophetic book in the Bible. It describes the prophecies of Jeremiah concerning the fall of Judah into the hands of the Babylonians. It has a prophetic side but even more so, it discusses the miserable scenarios of the prophecies being fulfilled such as the fall of Judah and the siege of Jerusalem.

Jeremiah is the writer of this book. God called Jeremiah into prophetic ministry when he was very young. He preached the Lord's message for about forty years. He saw with his very eyes how all the prophecies he gave concerning the fall of Judah and Jerusalem came to pass. He started his ministry during the reign of King Josiah (620 B.C.) and he was still prophesying when Babylon captured Jerusalem during the reign of Zedekiah (580 B.C.).

Jeremiah means "Jehovah Establishes." I believe every prophet's name has to do with the message he preaches. Later on in this lesson we will learn that which Jehovah establishes through Jeremiah's message.

Jeremiah is called the "Weeping Prophet" because God chose him to preach the horrible prophecies against the nation of Judah because of their idolatry.

Jeremiah was always despised, rejected, and hated by the people. Many times he was almost killed by the people of Judah. He wept for his countrymen and Jerusalem. When you read Jeremiah and the book of Lamentations you will understand his grief and his love for his people. For many times he wanted to resign from his prophetic ministry, but God did not let him. Jeremiah was always dependent upon God's love.

Reading the Lamentations of the Weeping Prophet shows his tremendous grief. No other book in the Bible expresses such grief and sadness. In Lamentations you can read the feelings of Jeremiah as a person and as a prophet, as well as the Lord's anger towards His people.

I believe the book of Lamentations and the book of Jeremiah are strongly connected to each other. Understanding the book of Jeremiah is important in order to understand Lamentations.

In this foundational Bible study, we will not only focus on the prophecies concerning the fall of Judah, but we will also enter a journey to find Jesus Christ. As Christ was revealed unto Isaiah, Christ was also revealed unto Jeremiah. Further, we will learn how to apply this wonderful book to our own personal lives.

We can divide this book into the following outlines:

The Call of Jeremiah and the Prophecies against Judah and Jerusalem (chapters 1–45)
Prophecies concerning the nations (chapters 46–51)
Historical Summary (chapter 52)

TODAY'S JOURNEY

In the last lesson we learned about the sin of Israel and Isaiah's prophecies against the Northern Kingdom. We saw the political situation and the danger the Israelites were going through because they disobeyed God.

Jeremiah's Call

I the Lord Formed You

Jeremiah was very young when God called him into the ministry. He was the only prophet God deliberately asked not to marry but to fully devote himself to the ministry. Chapter one describes his calling. God already chose Jeremiah as a prophet to the nations even before he was formed in the womb (Jer. 1:4-5).

Yes, God has a plan with every individual in the world. Even before birth, God established His plan in our lives. In the same way, you are born for a purpose just like Jeremiah was born for a purpose. The only thing is whether we will choose for the plan of God or not.

Weakness

In response to God's calling, Jeremiah became fearful and saw his weakness because he was young and not an adequate speaker. Jeremiah said: "Oh Lord I do not know how to speak and I am a child" (1:6). But God said to him, "Do not say that you are young, just do what I tell you."

God never looks at the age of a person. He can use everyone, old or young, man or woman.

God can use you. He does not look at your weaknesses. He looks on how He can use your weaknesses for glorifying His name. God commanded Jeremiah: "DO NOT SAY you are a child." In other words, do not confess it. Many people have an inferiority complex, even in the body of Christ. In place of confessing our weaknesses it is better for us to follow God's plan.

The Touch

After Jeremiah confessed his weakness to God, God reached out with His hand and touched Jeremiah's mouth and promised to put His words in Jeremiah's mouth,

> *Now I have put my words in your mouth. See today I appoint you over nations and Kingdoms to uproot and tear down, to destroy and to overthrow, to build and to plant.*
> *(Jeremiah 1:9-10)*

God touched the mouth of Jeremiah. Jeremiah, the inadequate speaker, got the power in his words. The hand of God represents the Holy Spirit and the touch represents His anointing. Whenever the Holy Spirit touches you, you will be a different person; your weakness changes into power; your fear changes into boldness. If you want to be used by God start to seek His touch. The touch of God in the Old Testament was only for prophets, kings, and God's servants. It was kept from ordinary men. Two thousand years ago, when Jesus Christ died on the cross, He destroyed the gap between the ordinary man and the Eternal God. The curtain between the Holy Place and the Most Holy Place was destroyed. On the day of Pentecost, God reached His hand and touched the mouth of the weak church and the church was empowered with burning tongues.

Today, the same touch of God's hand is ready for you and me.
After God touched the mouth of Jeremiah, he received power over every power and dominion. He received power to build and also to destroy. Jeremiah was now ready! He also received the power over

the nations of the world. Thanks be to God that this power is not only given to a specific people like the prophets or the priests, but this power is also available to everyone who is saved and believes in Jesus Christ as Lord and Savior through the Holy Spirit. That is why Jesus said that all power and authority had been given to Himself who freely gives to everyone who asks. Whatever we bind on earth will be bound on heaven. You and I have the power to influence our nations, the circumstances of our lives, and everything that comes along our paths. We have received the touch of God and His power!

Jeremiah's Message

I believe the entire book of Jeremiah, including its message and the reason why God decided to punish His people, is summarized in Jeremiah 25. Jeremiah was called during one of the darkest times in Israel's history. Jeremiah's message was a message of doom and God's anger and grief to both the Israelites and the people of Judah.

Jeremiah was lonely; he was one of the few prophets in those times who preached God's anger and doom. He was in the middle of hundreds of false prophets. The false prophets preached that everything was alright and that God was not angry with what the nation was doing. Jeremiah, on the contrary, preached a different message about God's anger. Jeremiah proclaimed it because of Judah's sin and because God would use Babylon to destroy them.

Before we focus on Jeremiah's message let us see why God was angry with Judah. What did they do that so grieved God's heart?

Jeremiah 25 categorizes three major causes for God's anger against Judah. The first was "the evil ways and practices" of the nation (25:5). God called them for almost twenty years to repentance but they refused to do so. Let us examine these evil ways and practices.

The Evil Ways and Practices

In Jeremiah 7 God gives a deeper description of their evil ways and practices:

> *If you change your ways and actions and deal with each other justly, if you do not oppress the alien, the fatherless or the widow and do not shed innocent blood in this place and if you do not follow other gods to your own harm, then I will let you live in this place, in the land I gave your forefathers for ever and ever.*
>
> *(Jeremiah 7:5-7)*

Israel and Judah gradually became unjust and oppressive. They did not care about justice; they lived in lies and forgot the widows and the fatherless children. They become rude, careless, and egoistic. Each person thought only about himself. Individualism and self-gratification became the norm of the society.

Our world looks a lot like the society Jeremiah lived in. Corruption has covered our world; the rich become richer and the poor become poorer. The capitalistic world-system has introduced poverty and oppression to the world. So-called freedom turned into an evil weapon that destroys our family morals that were once based on God's law. In the name of "Freedom," which the false prophets were teaching, man was able to do abusive things such as, terrorism, drug trafficking, flesh-trade, alcohol abuse, and so on and so forth. These are increasing day by day. Innocent blood is being shed everyday. There is cruelty and war between nations, apathy, and racial discrimination. The end of the twentieth century has witnessed the Kosovo wars and Yugoslavian bloodshed. In Africa we witnessed Rwanda, Sudan, Uganda, and much other violence and bloodshed.

Jesus Christ is coming back and He will deal with every act of unrighteousness that is taking place. God is not sitting down! God is looking at the world and He is still waiting for its people to repent.

This time He is not using Jeremiah the prophet, but He is using you and me to tell the world about the second coming of Jesus Christ. I believe that every born again, Spirit-filled Christian is a full-time prophet unto the world.

I deliberately say unto the world and not unto church because we have a message to preach to the world. The prophets unto the church are those who have the gift and the mandate of apostleship and leadership.

Worshiping Other Gods

One of the major reasons for God's anger was idolatry by Judah and Israel, particularly the worship of Baal and the Queen of Heaven. The Queen of Heaven was a female goddess who gain popularity among the women in Judah and to whom they offered baked cakes and different sacrifices (7:18).

Baal was the most important male god of the Canaanite people. Baal had an extra attractiveness and charisma to the adulterous Israelites. Baal was one of the greatest enemies of our Lord. Baal became the national god of Israel during the reign of King Ahab and his wife, Jezebel (1 Kings 16:29-34). Elijah was the one present when God destroyed the four hundred prophets of Baal at one time.

Baal was the god of fertility and productivity. Baal worshippers offered many animals and some even sacrificed their own sons by passing them through the fire as an offering to Baal. During this worship, male and female prostitution was available to encourage the fertility of both the land and people.

In those times, Baal-worship took its extreme form. The Israelites and the people of Judah forgot what the Lord had done for them. They followed the evil desires and ways of Baal. They engaged in sexual sins, religious sins, and child-sacrifices. These all grieved the heart of the Lord. In Jeremiah 7 we read:

> *"The people of Judah have done evil in my eyes," says the Lord. "They have set up their detestable idols in the house that bears my Name and have defiled it. They have built the high places of Topheth in the valley of Ben Hinom to burn their sons and daughters in the fire."*

"Something I did not command nor did it enter in my mind" (7:31).

Today, the same evil god is working in our world. His name might be different, but his works and the results are the same: homosexuality and prostitution are increasing in our world. Idol worship and turning to other gods are also increasing daily. Think of the New Age Movement. In Africa some still worship their ancestors. Even worse, the killing of children still continues. This time it is not done by passing them through the fire but by advanced medical technology like abortion. They are aborted from the womb of the mother where God formed the child. God formed Jeremiah in the womb and spoke His plan for his life. It's a pity that our societies still kill unborn children in the name of humanity and free choice in a "free world." In some countries abortion is legalized and even encouraged by some authorities.

But we Christians have a message of God's wrath and anger upon such activities. God's heart is grieved when He sees the world in such a mess. God wants to use YOU for calling the world to repentance.

There is no greater sin than to turn our face to other gods like the Israelites did back then. But still God was patient with them. God was waiting. He was still hoping that His people would return to Him. For forty years, Jeremiah preached God's patience and mercy so that lost people might change, but they did not hear and did not obey God's words.

Jeremiah Prophesied

Jeremiah's mission to deliver the message of God's anger to Israelites and the people of Judah was not easy. He prophesied that God would bring disaster upon the two nations, the chosen ones of God. Because of their sins God would hand them over to Babylon. For seventy years God would keep them captive. He also prophesied that Jerusalem would be destroyed and everyone who remained there.

The problem with Jeremiah's prophecy was that God commanded the people of Judah and Jerusalem to go with the Babylonians and be taken as captives. But those who remained and wanted to fight back against the Babylonians would be killed. This provoked the anger of the nationalistic Jews and they considered Jeremiah a collaborator, a betrayer, and a false prophet.

God always has His different ways that are far beyond human understanding. Through sending that certain group of Jews into captivity, He wanted to save them from sword and discipline them for seventy years and then send them back again to their land.

Many people go through difficult times in their lives. Life may look so grim and miserable, but God has a plan to save them, discipline them, and restore them. God may even bring some people into the desert before He waters them. God may bring some people into 'slavery' for the purpose of discipline. As Christians, we must realize that our lives are no longer in Satan's hand but they are under the control of the Lord. He will use every possible situation, whether positive or negative, and turn them for our benefit.

As Christians, we must know that we are always on the winning side even if everything looks like defeat and failure.

The Remaining Jews Will Die

Jeremiah prophesied that those who still wanted to fight for their country in spite of its prophesied defeat would all die. These Jews blindly followed their own honor and pride.

Many people do not want to listen to God because of their pride and doctrine. These kinds of people can be the hard-headed Christians who refuse to get into God's new moves. Instead, they continue to hold on to their old-fashioned rules and traditions for which they are ready to die. These types of people are those who honor their man-made doctrines more than the God-given plan. They love their constitution book more than the voice of God. This type of Christianity will not survive any longer. That is why many traditional churches are "dying" because they do not want to move beyond their traditions. They are just like those Jews who did not want to go to Babylon.

Other Nations Will Also Perish

Just like Isaiah, Jeremiah also prophesied the word of God against specific nations. You can find these in chapters 46–51. You can find in these chapters prophecies against the Philistines, Moabites, Babylonians, and many other nations. These verses will make you realize how God can raise up even ungodly nations to fulfil His purposes.

Famine, Sword and Plague

Jeremiah 14 describes God's anger against the nation of Judah:

> *Although they fast, I will not listen to their cry, though they offer burnt offerings and grain offerings, I will not accept them. Instead, I will destroy them by sword, famine and plague.*
>
> *(Jeremiah 14:12)*

Even today, almost three thousand years after Jeremiah, these three things are the major killers in the world. Some parts of the world are dying from drought and famine. Like never before in the history of humanity, we have witnessed severe famine and drought in the world. The Sahara in Africa is moving southward and the greens are changing into dry deserts. Almost 25% of the world's population lives below the poverty level and experiences malnutrition.

As long as the nations of the world worship other gods and demonic forces, which they consider holy, there will be drought and famine in the world. What we see in the world is only the surface. Famine is caused when a nation disobeys God and worships other spirits. As long as India is worshiping their gods and as long as Africa worships ancestral powers and magic, there will be drought and famine. Maybe it seems harsh to say this because there are also spirit-filled Christians who become victims. I assure you, though, that a Christian is never a victim even though it looks that way! A Christian is already on the winning side; nevertheless, a Christian must rescue his or her nation from these calamities by telling the truth and by offering intercessory prayers.

The sword is also the second killer in the world. We live in the beginning of the twenty-first century. With all the modernization we have gained, and with all the achievements of "peace talks," we still have killings and wars. Kosovo, Yugoslavia, Latin America, the Middle East, Africa and all over the world, people are being massacred, killed, and destroyed systematically.

There is war and killing because man does not want to listen to God's call through Jesus Christ. The world lives in anger and hate which are against the law of Jesus Christ. This disobedience and harshness of man have brought the sword and killings to the world.

Plagues may seem like an old fashioned term for our modern world. But even in our modern world we have modern plagues. Every time we think we have found a solution for a certain sickness or plague, we find another one that is harder and more dangerous than the previous one. The human race cannot play games with God Almighty. Look for instance at AIDS; this new 'tumor' of death destroys our world today. Even innocent children are victims of the mistakes others.

A New Covenant and the Coming of the Messiah

Lastly, Jeremiah prophesied about the coming of the Messiah, our Lord Jesus Christ, and the covenant that will be established upon His throne. The word "covenant' has a central place in Jeremiah. The importance of every prophetic book is that they reflect the coming of Christ. God spoke through Jeremiah and said:

> *"The days are coming" declares the Lord,*
> *"when I will raise up to David a righteous branch,*
> *a King who will reign wisely*
> *and do what is just and wise in the land.*
> *In his days Judah will be saved and Israel*
> *will live in safety. This is the name by which he will be called:*
> *The Lord Our Righteousness."*
>
> *(Jeremiah 23:5-6)*

In those days, King David's royal family was almost destroyed. But still, God promised that out of David's house a righteous branch would come. This was the same thing God had promised to David himself. Jesus is the one who fulfilled this prophecy (Luke 1:32-33). Jesus saved the people of Judah and Israel from their sins (Matt. 1:21). And Paul says the following:

> *It is because of him (God) that you are in Christ Jesus, who has become for us wisdom from God-that is, our righteousness, holiness and redemption."*
>
> *(1 Corinthians 1:30)*

Also, in Jeremiah 33 God promised the restoration of Israel and Judah through Jesus Christ.

Once again we can see God's love and grace to His people. Even in the time of discipline and punishment He confirms that He doesn't forget His promise to His servant David. He will make sure every spoken word will come to pass for He loves His people even in the times of sin and adultery.

However, in Jeremiah 11 we read that the covenant was broken by God's people. God told them this because of their disobedience. They destroyed the covenant God made with their forefathers to give them the land of milk and honey. But just like their forefathers, they sinned and broke the covenant. Then the Lord said to me (Jeremiah):

> *There is a conspiracy among the people of Judah and those who live in Jerusalem. They have returned to the sin of their forefathers, who refused to listen to my words. They have followed other gods to serve them. Both the house of Israel and the house of Judah have broken the covenant I made with their forefathers.*
>
> *(Jeremiah 11:9-10)*

God's covenant was broken in every way because they broke the Law of Moses. They disobeyed God's commands. Therefore, every blessing and promise that went with this covenant of Moses was broken and curses were brought to the people. Read Deuteronomy 28. The entire chapter speaks about blessings and curses.

God spoke through Jeremiah about the One who would come in the future, who would establish a new kingdom, a new branch. This new branch is Jesus Christ, and truly He brought forth the New Covenant. As I mentioned earlier, the name Jeremiah means "Jehovah establishes." Jeremiah the prophet prophesied about the establishing of God's New Covenant through Jesus Christ.

> *"The time is coming" declares the Lord, "when I will make a new covenant with the house of Israel and with the house of Judah. It will not be like the covenant I made with their forefathers when I took them out of Egypt, because they broke my covenant, though I was a husband to them," declares the Lord. "This is the covenant I will make with the house of Israel after that time. I will put my law in their minds and write it on their hearts. I will be their God and they will be my people. No longer will a man teach his neighbor, or a man his brother, saying 'Know the Lord,' because they will all know me from the least of them to the greatest," declares the Lord. "For I will forgive their wickedness and will remember their sins no more."*
>
> *(Jeremiah 31:31-34)*

Read also Hebrews 8. The writer of Hebrews says in verse 13, "By calling this covenant 'new' he (the Lord) has made the first obsolete; and what is obsolete and aging will soon disappear" (Heb. 8:13).

Jesus Christ brought us this New Covenant which is God's salvation and everlasting love.
You and I are also among those who follow this covenant. This covenant is not anymore written on tablets of stone but on the flesh of our hearts, through the Holy Spirit our teacher.

LASTLY

Even though the book of Jeremiah is filled with the grief and anger of God, we can still find beautiful verses that give us hope among the lines and between the words of punishment that are written. These are good and effective for meditation and prayer. I will just give you two or three of them, but I pray that you will have the spiritual eyes to find more of these for your own benefit and growth. Here are some examples:

> *Return, faithless people; I will cure you of backsliding.*
> *(Jeremiah 3:22)*

> *Heal me oh Lord, and I will be healed; save me and I will be saved, for you are the one I praise.*
> *(Jeremiah 17:14)*

> *Call to me and I will answer you and tell you great and unreachable things you do not know.*
> (Jeremiah 33:3)

THE BOOK OF LAMENTATIONS

This is a poetical book written by the prophet Jeremiah himself who was grieving over the fall of Jerusalem. Lamentations consists of five sad songs. Song 1 describes the city after being captured. Song 2 describes the reason when it happened, and song 3 explains why God allowed this punishment to take place. With Song 4, Zion remembers the crying and lamenting of the former days.

Eventually, in Song 5, Zion is pleads with God for a return and forgiveness:

> *Restore us unto you oh Lord, that we may return.*
> *(Lamentations 5:21)*

MAIN SCRIPTURES:
Jeremiah and Lamentations (all chapters)

REFERENCE SCRIPTURES:
Deuteronomy 28
Matthew 1:21
Luke 1:32-33
1 Corinthians 1:30
Hebrews 8

TO MEMORIZE AND MEDITATE UPON
(JEREMIAH 17:14)

**HEAL ME OH LORD, AND I WILL BE HEALED;
SAVE ME AND I WILL BE SAVED,
FOR YOU ARE THE ONE I PRAISE.**

QUESTIONS:

1. Explain five major series that Jeremiah prophesied.

2. Explain why Judah should be taken captive in Babylon for seventy years.

3. Find out some other verses that might reflect on the coming of Jesus Christ or the New Covenant.

NOTES:

NOTES:

LESSON 28
Ezekiel

Prophet of Judgements and Restoration
Ezekiel (all chapters)

INTRODUCTION TO THE BOOK OF EZEKIEL

During the first Babylonian invasion of the Southern Kingdom of Judah, Ezekiel was taken captive. During this period, the prophet Jeremiah was preaching in the Southern Kingdom of Judah and Ezekiel was preaching to the exiled Israelites in Babylon.

Ezekiel was transported to Babylon along with other Israelites; a few years later Ezekiel received his call from God to be a prophet. The ministry of Ezekiel was a two-part ministry.

In the first part of his ministerial life, he prophesied Jerusalem's destruction. This occurred in Ezekiel 32. After Jerusalem and the temple were destroyed by the Babylonians for thirteen years, Ezekiel kept his silence. Then the prophet took up a new message in his ministry: the message of hope, comfort, and promises of restoration for the exiles. These messages start with Ezekiel 33 and go to the end of the book.

The book of Ezekiel can be divided into the following parts:

Prophecies against Judah and the nations: (chapters 1–32)
Prophecies of restoration (chapters 33–39)
Prophecies of the restoration of the temple (chapters 40–48)

The book of Ezekiel has very pictorial types of prophecies; this means that God asked him to use illustrations to explain his prophecies. There are also apocalyptic prophecies similar to the books of Revelation and Daniel. This makes the book of Ezekiel quite difficult to understand unless one has the guidance of the Holy Spirit. There are various passages in the book that are interpreted differently by different people. The goal of this lesson is to give the reader background information that he or she can use for practical situations and daily life.

What you read in this lesson is not the commentary explanation of the book of Ezekiel but one way to understand this book. So please do not try to make a doctrine of what you read so that you may have a broader understanding of the book of Ezekiel.

TODAY'S JOURNEY

Introduction

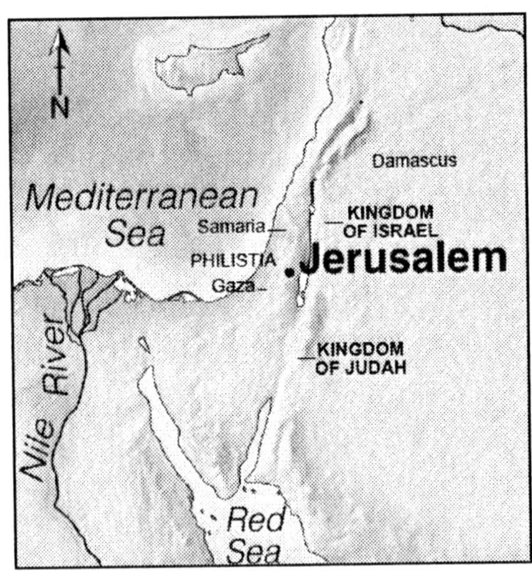

As I mentioned earlier in this lesson, while Jeremiah was preaching in Judah, Ezekiel was ministering in exile. Though they were far from each other, their messages were compatible and almost the same. This shows that there are many prophets, but the message is the same if it comes from God. A prophecy must be confirmed and this shows that God is one and His message is one. We must also keep in mind that God has different times. In a certain era, God can prophesy doom, restoration, and blessing. But one thing is for sure. Even if the messages are not the same they come from the same source: GOD.

Ezekiel's Prophecies

In the book of Ezekiel we see three ways in which the prophecies were brought forth to the Jews.
1) Action Prophecies
2) Vision Prophecies
3) Verbal Prophecies

Action Prophecies

God had extraordinary ways to bring His messages to the Jews by using Ezekiel as the literal illustrator of these prophecies. By "action prophecies" I mean that God asked Ezekiel to act or do certain things to illustrate to the Jews what God wanted them to do.

Let me give you an example:

In chapter five we read that God asked Ezekiel to take a sharp sword and use a barber's razor to shave his head and his beard. After shaving his head and beard, he carefully weighed and divided his hair into three parts. He burned the first part in his sandbox city. The burned hairs represented those Jews who would die when the Babylonians came and laid siege the city of Jerusalem.

The other part of his hair was spread around the city ground and attacked with a sword. He took the last part of his hair and tossed it into the air to be scattered by the wind. This symbolizes the Jews who will be scattered to the four corners of the world. Here we can see the strange things Ezekiel did to declare God's prophecies to the exiles in Babylon.

There are other action prophecies that Ezekiel did. Read them carefully and try to place them within the context of the book and history.

Vision Prophecies

Another important part of Ezekiel's prophecies are the vision prophecies. Before explaining this, you should be aware that there is a spiritual dimension connected to the materialistic world. There is a spiritual world (the unseen) and the world in which we live. That is why Paul said:

> *Our struggle is not against flesh and blood, but against the rulers, against the authorities, against the powers of dark world and against the spiritual forces of evil in the heavenly realms.*
>
> *(Ephesians 6:12)*

While there is a battle going on between us and these forces, there is also a battle going on in the heavenly realms between the forces of God and the forces of evil.

Likewise, when there is rejoicing among the people of God, there will also be joy among the spiritual forces of God including angels. So what we read about in the book of Ezekiel simply shows us what was taking place in the spiritual world at that time concerning the Jews and other nations. This will also take place in the near and far future.

The "vision prophecies" are those prophecies of Ezekiel when the Spirit of God literally took his spirit and transferred him to a spiritual world. He even saw visions of God's plan for the future. In some of these vision prophecies, Ezekiel was transferred into the current times of the spiritual situation of the Jews. These visions were there to show Ezekiel how wicked the nation of Israel, including their priests, were at that time. *"The Spirit lifted me up . . . and in the visions of God he took me to Jerusalem,"* says Ezekiel in 8:3-4. Please notice that when Ezekiel was in Babylon, God brought him in the Spirit to Jerusalem. The Spirit of God took Ezekiel and brought him in the "Spirit" into God's temple at that time. Ezekiel saw in the spiritual world what these leaders and priests did in secret in the temple of God.

Ezekiel also saw how the glory of God departed from the temple (Ezek. 8–10). Through these visions, Ezekiel prophesied about the departure of the Lord from the temple in Jerusalem. The Jews in Judah were left alone. (Notice Judah, the Southern kingdom, was not fully captured by the enemy; they were still free).

In other vision prophecies, Ezekiel also travelled through time. The Spirit of God brought him to the future and showed him what would happen.

Scholars still debate whether these events were already fulfilled or yet to be fulfilled in the end times. I personally believe some of these prophecies are already fulfilled. But some are still to come in connection with the book of Revelation.

Verbal Prophecies

Verbal prophecies are what the Lord directly said through Ezekiel to the Jews. Normally these prophecies start like this: *"Now this is what the Lord says,"* or *"Thus says the Lord."* Verbal prophecies could also be the explanation for the visions Ezekiel saw and/or the explanation of these action prophecies.

Important Things to Know

There are many important and outstanding facts in the book of Ezekiel that cannot be explained in a single lesson. As born-again Christians, there are three major things we should know when we read Ezekiel or speak about it to others: disobedience and idolatry leads to captivity and distraction.

The second part of the book of Ezekiel is the promise of restoration of Israel as a nation and the spiritual restoration of Israel through Jesus Christ: the promise of the Holy Spirit and the new birth (being born again).

One more time, the word of God confirms in Ezekiel that idolatry and spiritual adultery will bring human beings into captivity. Even now, many live under the curse and wrath of God because God has left them.

We read in Ezekiel how God longed to get rid of the hypocritical leaders of Israel and their evil practices in the temple of God and their nation in order to create a new covenant with the people He loved.

If we want God to bless us, and if we want God's grace in our lives, we must repent from our evil practices and come to Jesus Christ our Lord. Only then can God's promises cover us.

In this lesson, I do not want to focus much on the issue of disobedience and spiritual adultery for I believe I have sufficiently explored the results of these kinds of acts of man against God in the previous lessons. God also spoke about the punishment waiting to fall on the other nations of the world.

ISRAEL'S RESTORATION

(Physical and Spiritual)

After proclaiming that the Jews would be scattered to the uttermost corners of the world because of their sins and transgressions, Ezekiel saw several visions about the restoration and the return of the Jews back to their land. This is not only about the return of the

Jews from Babylon, or later from Persia, but it goes even further in time than that (although scholars debate this).

This lesson is a proper opportunity to share with you a short sketch of Israel's history from ancient times until recent events.

I believe every born again Christian should know some basic information and background about the nation Israel. We must never forget that Israel is still loved by God and we should pray for Israel and the peace of this nation.

Recent History of Israel

In order to understand some of the visions Ezekiel described in the book, it is beneficial to know a little bit about the history of Israel.

Since the fall of the two kingdoms, Judah and Israel, the Jews entered into captivity. Over this period of time, the Jews were spread to different parts of the world. From that time onward the Jews never had a king again. The Jewish nation came into the hands of different kingdoms such as the Babylon, Persian, Greek, and Roman Empires respectively. Even the geographical territory of Israel came under the influence of these nations.

But the promise of God to the Jews was fulfilled when they got a king, Jesus Christ. However, many did not recognize Him as the king promised by God; that out of the throne of David, there would be a king and His kingdom would be everlasting. That is also why Jesus Christ often spoke about "Kingdom of heaven" and the "Kingdom of God."

The apostle Paul used an interesting illustration about this kingdom in Romans 11:11-36. The apostle speaks about a tree, which is Israel, and some fallen branches which are those who rejected the call of Christ. In place of them were wild branches engrafted on the tree. These engrafted branches are Gentiles and non-Jews. But today, because of the Kingdom of Jesus Christ, we are joined together. However, those who reject Christ, either Jew or non-Jew, will never belong to this kingdom unless they are born again.

Until 1948, Israel was ruled by different nations. At the end of the nineteenth century, Israel was a part of Turkish Ottoman Empire. The Turkish kingdom was spread from the Middle East up through Europe, and Israel was a part of this Empire. After the weakening of the Turkish Ottoman Empire, and later its fall, the superpowers of the time such as France, Britain, and Russia all had eyes on these massive territories of the fallen Turkish Empire.

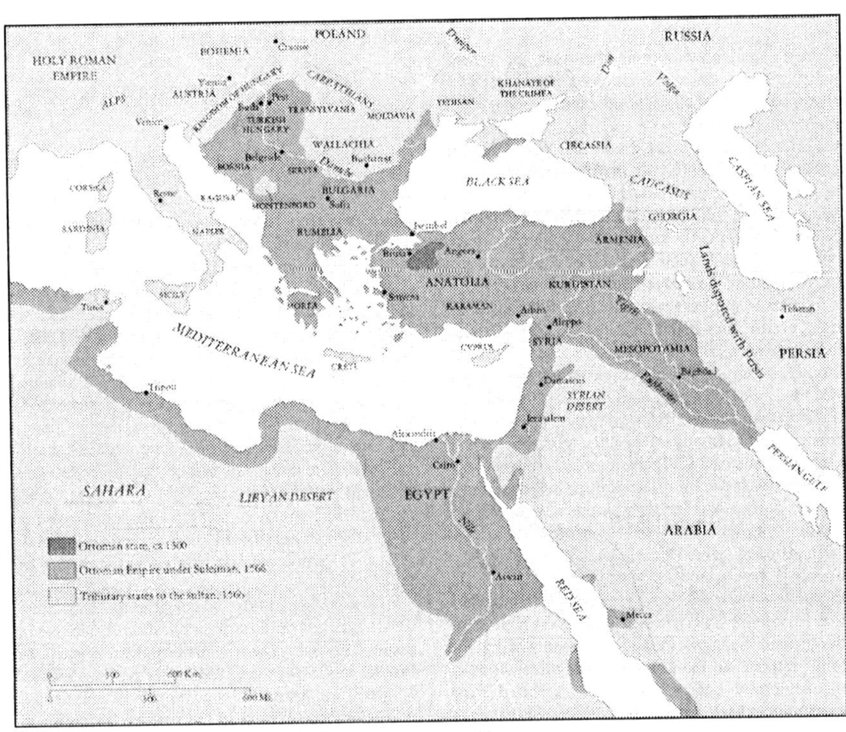

The Ottoman Empire

The twentieth century witnessed two world wars. The First World War was from 1916–1919. During this war, France and England had eyes on the territories of the Turkish Empire, so Britain and France divided the Ottoman Empire. Israel came under the influence of the British Empire. In those days that region of Israel was called "Philistines," and there lived the Arabs for more than one thousand years.

From the time of Jesus until those days, the Jews were spread all over Europe, Russia, the Middle East, and even America. They were travelling, migrating, and moving. Many of them were also more prosperous than the native Europeans. In those times of poverty in Europe many Jews were rich. This caused a lot of hatred toward the Jews especially in Russia and Europe. The Jews were discriminated against. Some were killed and abused. This hate and anger grew more intense in Germany, Austria, and other nations in Europe. In 1933, a terrorist named Adolph Hitler became the national leader of Germany. Germany became one of the strongest nations in the world. The first thing Hitler did was gather Jews from Germany and kill them in concentration camps. Later in 1939, Germany attacked Poland, captured the country, and started the Second World War. In 1940, Germany entered into war with the neighboring countries and captured them one by one. France, England, Russia and later the United States, joined hands to destroy Hitler's Nazi kingdom. What Hitler did was terrible. He captured every nation and took the Jews by killing them in concentration camps. Historians say that more than six million Jews died during this period.

Many scholars believe that these scenes were shown in the book of Ezekiel. However, many others disagree. It depends on what you believe.

Let me bring you to one of the most powerful places in Ezekiel where I believe he saw with his eyes what happened almost 2500 years later. Ezekiel 37:1-14 refers to the "valley of the dry bones." In this passage, Ezekiel says the hand of the Lord was on him, and the Lord brought him out by the Spirit and brought him into a valley of many bones, "the valley of dry bones." He said these dry bones were the Jews. They were dead.

Now this valley of dry bones is a very familiar picture in the Second World War (1939–1945) where the Jews were massacred. He starved them, killed them, and then made valleys of them. Their bodies (their bones) were moved by bulldozers to the fire for burning. Many believe this was what Ezekiel saw 2500 years before these things happened.

Human bones found in Second World War mass grave

In Ezekiel 37, God promised the Jews restoration. God asked Ezekiel to speak to the dead bones. When he did so, flesh and skin started to form. The wind blew and the dry bones received breath and stood up. God said these are the people of Israel. In the last days He restored them.

He also said the Jews will return to their land:

> *I will take the Israelites out of the nations they have gone. I will gather them from all around and bring them back into their own land. I will make them one nation on the*

mountains of Israel. There will be one king over all of them and they will never be divided into two nations.

(Ezekiel 37:21-22)

After Hitler lost in battle in 1945, many Jews do not want to live there again. Many Jews in Europe, Russia, America, and other places wanted to return to Israel. In that time, the land was called Philistine which was still under the control of Britain.

In 1948, the prophecy of Ezekiel came to pass. Israel became one nation: Britain took back his commissioner from Philistines, and in May 1948, David Ben Gurion proclaimed the new State of ISRAEL. In those times, the Jews came to Israel from the North, South, West and East. This was not easy because for one thousand years the Arabs lived there. This started a conflict with the nations around Israel who chose the side of the Arabs. They attacked this new born Israel, and until today, the conflict goes on.

Today Israel is a nation with its president as the head of the state. Israel is one of the developing countries in the world.

Other Explanations

Many people disagree with the above-mentioned interpretations. They say the dead bones were the Jews who suffered during the Roman Empire. The wind describes the Holy Spirit; the one nation describes the Kingdom of God and Jesus Christ as its King. I personally believe these explanations do not need to oppose one another, but they complement each other: first the physical and then the spiritual. This brings us to the next interpretation which says, Israel as a nation was born, and now is the time when the whole Israel will be saved through Jesus before the end time. This is also one of the promises of God.

Israel's Spiritual Restoration

In the first part of the book of Ezekiel, we read how God's Spirit left the temple and how the Jews will receive punishment because of their unfaithfulness. However, there is a certain group called the remnant to whom God promised restoration. In the second part of the book, we read about the spiritual transportation of Ezekiel into the New Temple, the temple which God promised to be restored (Ezekiel 40–44).

He literally saw and entered into the New Temple. Some people have taught that this was fulfilled through Zerubbabel and Nehemiah, but the map of this temple is not the same as the temple that was restored by Zerubbabel and Nehemiah. On the other hand, many believe this promise is yet to be fulfilled when Israel comes under the lordship and kingship of Jesus Christ. Then this temple will be literally built. However, we must be very careful with our interpretations and keep them for ourselves for issues like this can confuse many people.

But one thing is sure. Israel, sooner or later, will come under the rulership of Jesus Christ for this is the promise of God. Many things that Ezekiel saw can be found in the book of Revelation, too. Ezekiel saw a vision of the New Jerusalem (Ezek. 40:1-2), the same things which were seen by the apostle John in Revelation 21:10.

Here are some parallels between Ezekiel and Revelation:

Visions for New Jerusalem (Ezekiel 40:1-2) (Rev. 21:10)
Measuring the temple (Ezekiel 40:3) (Rev. 11-1)
Voice of rushing waters (Ezekiel 43:2) (Rev. 1:15)
Flowing waters and fruit trees (Ezekiel 47:1, 12) (Rev. 22:1-2)
12 gates of the city (Ezekiel 48:30-35) (Rev. 21:12-13)

There are many other parallels that are interesting but not suitable to be mentioned in this particular lesson.

Holy Spirit Was Prophesied

Lastly, the most important thing in the book of Ezekiel is the prophecy about the outpouring of the Holy Spirit upon the people of God in the future:

> *For I will take you out of the nations; I will gather you from all countries and bring you back into your own land. I will sprinkle clean water on you, and you will be clean. I will cleanse you from all your impurities and from all your idols. I will give you a new heart and put a new spirit in you. I will remove from you your heart of stone and give you a heart of flesh. And I will put my Spirit in you and move you to follow my decrees and be careful to keep my laws.*
>
> *(Ezekiel 36:24-28)*

This passage clearly prophesies the experience of being born again through the sprinkling of the clean water which is the Holy Spirit. In Old Testament times, people followed the Law written on tablets of stone, but since the coming of Jesus Christ and the outpouring of the Holy Spirit, man is not bound by the law written on tablets of stones, but the written law in the hearts of man.

This can only be fulfilled through the born-again experience. Jesus explained to Nicodemus in John 3 that a person must be "born again." A person can only be born again through believing in Jesus Christ. Believing in Jesus Christ will be the gate through which the Holy Spirit can enter a person's life. From that moment on, a person will be new; he/she will receive a new heart and he/she will fear the Lord not because of the law written on stones but because of the Holy Spirit, who is the composer of law within the heart. The Holy Spirit will make it possible to follow God's decrees. The promise of this experience in Ezekiel was fulfilled and is being fulfilled today.

Another interesting issue is the relationship between the books of Ezekiel, Isaiah, and Jeremiah. Many times Ezekiel spoke about the "Spirit of the Lord." By careful study of these facts, I can easily say that in the book of Ezekiel, the Spirit of the Lord gets the attention and the glory, while in Isaiah the focus was mostly concentrated on the Son of God, Jesus Christ, and His coming. In addition to this, by reading Jeremiah, we will encounter the heart of the Father. In short, Jesus Christ is the center in Isaiah, whereas in Jeremiah, the Father is glorified, and in Ezekiel, the Holy Spirit. However, this doesn't mean the other triune personalities of the Godhead were totally neglected in the other two books, not at all! (I only generalize the books). In Ezekiel we also read about the promise of the coming of Jesus Christ. For example, God promised His people a great shepherd:

> *"I myself will tend My sheep and have them lie down," declares the Lord. "I will search for the lost and bring back the strays. I will bind up the injured and strengthen the weak."*
>
> *(Ezekiel 34:15-16)*

This shepherd is Jesus Christ Himself. Remember what Jesus said:

> *I am the good shepherd. The good shepherd lays down his life for the sheep.*
>
> *(John 10:11)*

IN SHORT

Ezekiel is a very complicated book to understand unless the Spirit of God reveals to us the secrets of His wisdom in this prophetic book.

As born again Christians and workers of Jesus Christ, we must know that the book of Ezekiel prophesies about the Holy Spirit, Jesus Christ, the restoration of Israel as a nation, and the establishment of the New Temple and the New Jerusalem.

MAIN SCRIPTURES
Ezekiel (all chapters)

REFERENCE SCRIPTURES
John 10:11
Romans 11:11-36
Ephesians 6:12
Revelation 21

TO MEMORIZE AND MEDITATE UPON
EZEKIEL 36:27

AND I WILL PUT MY SPIRIT AND MOVE YOU TO FOLLOW MY DECREES AND BE CAREFUL TO KEEP MY LAWS.

QUESTIONS:

1. Name at least three important things we should know about the book of Ezekiel.

2. Where in this book did God promise the experience of being born again?

NOTES:

LESSON 29

Daniel
The Kingdom Prophet

Daniel (all chapters)

INTRODUCTION TO THE BOOK OF DANIEL

Daniel was one of the very first exiles who was brought to Babylon. He was brought to this place to serve. Later, Daniel became one of the administrators in the empire of Nebuchadnezzar. The interesting thing about Daniel is that he experienced the fall of Judah and lived throughout the time of the Babylonian Empire until it was overthrown by the Persians. He actually lived in the period of three kingdoms: Judah, Babylon, and Persia.

The book of Daniel is very easy to divide because it is systematically composed. This is the division of the book:

The personal history of Daniel (chapters 1–6)
Daniel's prophetic visions (chapters 7–12)

The first part of the book (the first six chapters) is easy to read because each chapter is a complete story. These first six chapters of Daniel should also be placed in the context of history and time. The last six chapters discuss the vision about the end times and the future events that are going to take place in the world before the end.

Some parts of the book were written in the Aramaic language and other parts were written in Hebrew. That is why many non-born again Christians doubt its reliability. But for us, we believe fully in its divine inspiration and that it was given by the Most High God and His Spirit.

TODAY'S JOURNEY

The first part of the book (1–6) took place in the empire of Babylon and it focuses mainly on the dreams of Nebuchadnezzar and the interpretations of Daniel regarding these dreams.

The Prophet of the Kingdom

Daniel was a "prophet of kingdom." As Isaiah prophesied about the coming of Jesus Christ, Daniel prophesied about the kingdom that Jesus Christ was going to establish. In the first six chapters, Daniel gave us a greater revelation of God's Kingdom.

Let us take Daniel 2 as the main topic for the first part of the book. King Nebuchadnezzar of Babylon had a tremendous dream that was troubling him. He would not tell the dream to any magician, sorcerer, or astrologer unless they first revealed the dream to the king. Otherwise, they would be killed. How can a man say what another man dreamed? This is a very funny request. No one could change the king's mind until a man called Daniel asked the king not to kill the people for he would pray to the Most High God to ask what the king's dream was and its interpretation.

Daniel the Only Man of God Who Could Reveal the Dream.

Only God can answer and reveal mysteries. God uses His people to bring forth the message He wants the world to know.

Daniel's answer to the king was:

> *No wise man, enchanter, magician or diviner can explain to the king the mystery he asked about, but there is a God in heaven who reveals mysteries. He has shown king Nebuchadnezzar what will happen in the days to come.*
> *(Daniel 2:27)*

These days many people look for mysteries and other sources to know more about their lives and how to achieve their goals. That is why magicians, astrologers and many false demonic teachers pollute the worldwide web, magazines, newspapers, and books.

As Christians, we should avoid such things for we have someone who reveals to us all the mysteries according to God's will, and that person is the Holy Spirit.

The Dream

Knowing the dream of the king is very essential to understanding the book of Daniel. What was the dream? The king saw a statue. The head of the statue was made from gold, the chest was made from silver, its belly was from bronze, and its legs were partly iron and partly clay.

While the king was watching this enormous statue, a rock was cut out, not by human hands. It struck the statue on its feet of iron and clay and the statue were broken into pieces. (Dan. 2:32-34)

Then, the wind swept them away without leaving any trace. But the rock that struck the statue became a huge mountain and filled the whole earth (Dan. 2:35).

The Interpretation

In 2:39-45, Daniel interprets the dream: the golden head is Babylon, but another kingdom will rise and defeat it which is the chest of silver. Then the third kingdom will come which is the bronze and it will rule the world. Finally there will be a fourth kingdom as strong as iron and as weak as clay. During this fourth kingdom the God of heaven will set up a kingdom that will never be destroyed and that is the rock which was made by God's own hands.

History proved the interpretation of Daniel to be true because what he said came to pass. This is the account: God was just revealing history to Daniel.

The golden head was the kingdom of Babylon, and then came the silver chest, represented by the Persian kingdom. After that came the bronze belly which represented the Greek Empire. The iron/clay legs represented the Roman Empire.

Daniel also said during the time of the fourth kingdom (the Roman Empire) there would come a kingdom, a Rock that would last and reign forever. This is a truthful fact, for just during the Roman Empire, God sent His Son, Jesus Christ, to establish the everlasting Kingdom, the Kingdom of God. The Rock that king Nebuchadnezzar saw was Jesus Christ Himself.

Once again we see how precise God was about the coming of Jesus Christ and the kingdom He was going to establish.

The Rock became a Mountain (v. 35).

The Rock became a mountain and filled the whole earth.

Once the Rock crushed down the power of Satan, out of the Rock came forth a mountain. That mountain grew and grew and spread to the whole world. The mountain in the dream is the everlasting kingdom, the Church of Jesus Christ.

In the dream, the wind came and swept all the pieces away, and after that, we read that the rock was changed into a mountain. This is the evidence of the Day of Pentecost, the day when the Holy Spirit came down like a mighty rushing wind and gave birth to this mountain: the church (Acts 2:1-28).

Since the coming of the Rock, Jesus Christ, kingdoms have come and gone, but they were all defeated. But until today, the Kingdom of God is growing stronger and stronger. Kings have come and gone and their kingdoms are just a mere part of history, but the Kingdom of Jesus Christ is fresh and new forever.

There Was Only One Mountain

When you read the dream carefully, you notice that there was only one solid mountain. The church can only be effective and successful when we are united. There is no kingdom that can stand against the love of Jesus Christ in us. This was the prayer of Jesus:

> *May they (the believers) be brought to complete unity to let the world know that you (the Father) sent me and have loved them even as you have loved me.*
>
> *(John 17:23)*

The Kingdom

In reading the words of Jesus in the four gospels of the New Testament, we notice that Jesus Christ regularly spoke about the kingdom He was about to establish. Sometimes He used the name "kingdom of heaven" and sometimes "the kingdom of God," but according to the scholars they are the same. In this paragraph, I only want to focus on the kingdom that Jesus established, that which still goes on and will grow more and more as the end of the ages comes near. Daniel 7 describes the kingdom that Daniel saw in a vision.

Daniel Saw a Vision: Four Beasts Each Different from the Others

The first was a lion with eagle's wings. The second was a bear. The third was a leopard with four wings on its back and four heads. The fourth beast was a terrifying beast. It was a powerful one with large iron teeth and ten horns. Suddenly, among these ten horns arose a small horn which uprooted the three horns. Daniel says he continued to watch and he saw the Ancient of Days take His seat. His clothing was as white as a snow; the hair of His head was as white as wool. Thousands upon thousands stood before him. The court was seated and the books were opened. He kept looking and he saw that the fourth beast was destroyed and thrown into the blazing fire.

Then he saw:

> *And one like the Son of man, coming with the clouds of heaven. He approached the Ancient Days and was led into his presence. He was given authority, glory and sovereign power; all peoples; nations and men of every language worshiped him. His dominion is an everlasting dominion that will not pass away, and his kingdom is one that will never be destroyed.*
>
> *(Daniel 7:13-14)*

What Daniel saw was Jesus Christ ruling on the throne. He saw that all authority and dominion were given to Him. Remember the words of Jesus:

> *All authority in heaven and on earth has been given to me.*
>
> *(Matthew 28:18)*

Daniel also saw nations and different races before Him. Jesus Christ came and reconciled us with the Father. Through Him the vision Daniel saw came to pass. Every nation, every race, and every language were worshipping Christ. This is the greatest sign of the Kingdom of God. That is why Jesus urged us in Matthew 28:19:

Therefore go and make disciples of all the nations.

In short, the Kingdom of God is an Everlasting Kingdom. It is made of people who believe in Jesus Christ regardless of race, nationality and geography. This kingdom has divine power and authority. These are the signs of the kingdom that Jesus Christ spoke to us in the four gospels.

Daniel saw that for a short period the saints would be handed over to the small horn that grew among the ten horns. He persecuted the saints but this power would be taken away and destroyed. Then all the kingdoms would be submitted and handed over to the saints of the kingdom. They are the believers, the people of the Most High. God will rule.

Yes, we, too, are going to rule the world. Jesus said:

Blessed are the meek, for they shall inherit the earth.
(Matthew 5:5)

The Seventy Weeks of Daniel

Another interesting thing is the vision of the Seventy 'Sevens' or 'Weeks':

"Seventy 'sevens' are decreed for your people and your holy city to finish transgression, to put an end to sin, to atone for wickedness. . . .
From the issuing of the decree to restore and rebuild Jerusalem until the Anointed One, the ruler, comes, there will be Seven "sevens" and sixty two "sevens." After sixty two "sevens" the Anointed One will be cut off and will have nothing."

(Daniel 9:24-26)

History has shown us that "seven" or "week" is made of seven years. In total there are 70 x 7, this equals 490 years.

The angel Gabriel said to Daniel that in a period of 7 x 7, or 49 years, exactly 49 years from the vision of Daniel, the temple and Jerusalem were restored (Read lessons on Ezra and Nehemiah).

Then the angel Gabriel said that after the restoration of Jerusalem and the temple there will be 62 x 7 years until the Anointed One will be cut off (62 x 7 is equal to 434 years).
Exactly 434 years after the restoration of Jerusalem and the temple, Jesus Christ was crucified exactly according to the calculations which were given to Daniel by the angel Gabriel. This makes it a total of 69 "weeks." There is a huge gap between the 69th "week" and the 70th week. From the death of Jesus Christ (week 69) there is not much to know. But according to the Scriptures the 70th "week" will start after the rapture (1 Thess. 4:15-18).

The seventieth week will be called "The Great Tribulation."

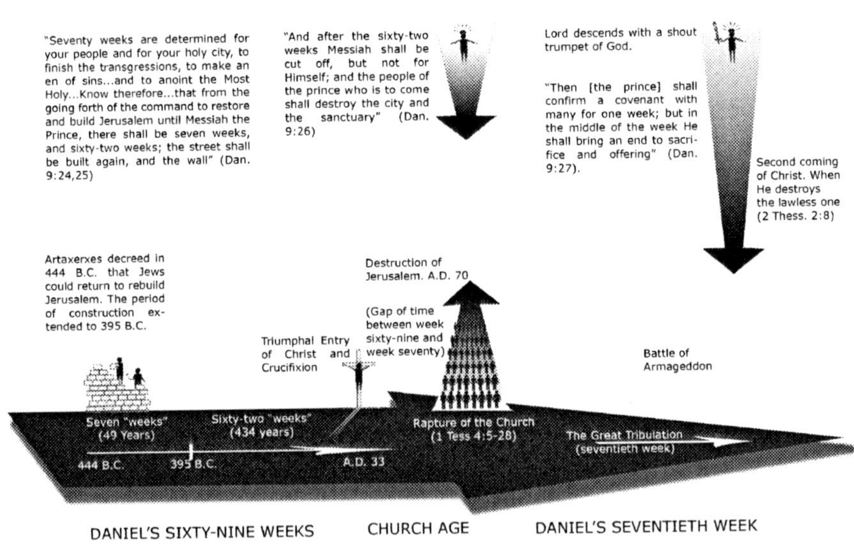

ΑΩ The Seventy Weeks of Daniel (Dan. 9:24-27)

LASTLY

The book of Daniel is the forerunner of the book of Revelation. At the end of the book, Daniel was commanded to close up the book and seal it:

> *But you, Daniel, close up and seal the words of the scroll until the time of the end.*
>
> *(Daniel 12:4)*

I believe centuries later, when the Apostle John opened the scroll, God revealed to him the continuation and addition of the book of Daniel.

Further, the book of Daniel gives us a lot of information within only twelve short chapters. This information is about:

-The World's history- the events that are going to take place
-The Coming of Jesus Christ and the Establishment of the church
-The Second coming of Christ and the Everlasting Kingdom

The End Times

Lastly, as I mentioned in the previous lesson on Isaiah, Jesus Christ receives the center attention. In Jeremiah the Father plays an important role, and in Ezekiel, the promise of the Holy Spirit was the focus. In the book of Daniel, the Kingdom of God gets the center attention which started with the birth of the church two thousand years ago.

MAIN SCRIPTURES
Daniel (all chapters)

REFERENCE SCRIPTURES
Matthew 5:5; 28:18-19
John 17:23
1 Thessalonians 4:15-18
Acts 2:1-28

TO MEMORIZE AND MEDITATE UPON
Daniel 2:22

HE (THE LORD) REVEALS DEEP AND HIDDEN THINGS,
HE KNOWS WHAT LIES IN DARKNESS,
AND LIGHT DWELLS WITH HIM.

QUESTIONS:

1. Explain the importance of the book of Daniel.
2. Describe the Everlasting Kingdom which Daniel saw. How did it look?
3. When did this Kingdom start and with whom did it start?

NOTES:

NOTES:

LESSON 30

Hosea ~ Joel ~ Amos Adultery, Calamity and Injustice

Hosea- Joel- Amos (all chapters)

TODAY'S JOURNEY

THE BOOK OF HOSEA (SALVATION)

Hosea means "Salvation." This is the name of the prophet who ministered in the Northern Kingdom of Israel just before the period of captivity.

In those days, Israel was going through a period of material prosperity, but inwardly the nation was decaying because of the spiritual adultery and unholy practices of the people.

Hosea ministered during the reign of King Uzziah, Jotham, Ahaz, and Hezekiah. During that time, Isaiah and Micah ministered in Judah while Hosea ministered in Israel.

Hosea can be divided into two parts:

The personal experience of the prophet (chapters 1–3)
God's judgement and mercy (chapters 4–14)

The book of Hosea is the story of adultery and deception by a nation towards Almighty God. At the same time, it is a parallel story about the personal life of the prophet Hosea with his unfaithful and adulterous wife. While Hosea was suffering because of his wife's adultery, the Father's heart was also bleeding because of Israel's unfaithfulness.

In the book of Hosea, God asked the prophet to go and take for himself a prostitute called Gomer and marry her. The Lord compared Israel to Gomer for they both lived in adultery. God considered Israel as His own spouse; He was the husband. After all the goodness and love He showed to Israel from the very beginning, the Israelites forgot His love.

In Hosea, we read about the bleeding heart of the husband who loved his adulterous wife and wanted to give her a chance to come back to him. And so was the Lord's heart toward Israel and everyone who is far away from Him. In the book of Hosea, we can see two opposite feelings fighting in the heart of God: mercy versus anger; salvation versus punishment; and love versus grief.

But eventually, God chooses for mercy, love, and salvation for His people even though they neglected Him.

The Lack of Knowledge

Hosea 4 is the focal point of the entire book:

> *Hear the word of the Lord, You children of Israel, for the Lord brings a charge against the inhabitants of the Land: There is no truth or mercy or knowledge of God in the Land. By swearing and lying, killing and stealing and committing adultery.*
>
> *(Hosea 4:1-2)*

The Lord also said:

> *My people are destroyed for the lack of the knowledge. Because you have rejected knowledge, I also will reject you as my priests because you have forgotten the law of your God, I also will forget your children. The more they increased the more they sinned against Me.*
>
> *(Hosea 4:6-7)*

The greatest ignorance of every person, every family, and every nation is lack of knowledge about God and His Law. God said His people are destroyed because of lack of knowledge about Him. God also said that the more they increased the more they forget God. This is a fact even in our time today. The more people increase in health and worldly knowledge, the more they forget God. Many people rely on their own increase; they rely on the little scientific knowledge they have gained; or, they rely on their own power and say things like, "There is no God." Or "God is an old-fashion word. God does not exist."

The reason why many in the developed countries have no interest in God is that they are proud of their achievements and their increasing science and technology. They have forgotten the knowledge of God.

This lack of knowledge of God and His laws and commands brings destruction to the families, cities, and nations of the world.

Today, not many people know about God and His moral standards of living. We live in societies where a child takes a gun and goes to school to shoot his teachers and classmates. All these things happen because we lack knowledge of God. In order to have godly knowledge, we must come on our knees and repent and cry to Almighty God. Accept Jesus Christ as Lord and Savior and be baptised in the Holy Spirit who is the Spirit of all truth. He shall write the laws of God on our hearts and empower us to obey them.

God Will Save in the Wilderness

Disobeying God and lacking His knowledge leads us into God's disciplining period. God allows us to be disciplined. For through His discipline He leads us to mercy and salvation.

The discipline of God might be hard but it gives life and guides us to a better life. It brings us back to our senses. Therefore, God said to the Israelites:

> *I will punish her for the days of the Baals to which she burned incense. She decked herself with rings and jewelry, and went after her lovers, but Me she forgot. Therefore, behold, I will allure her, will bring her into the wilderness and speak comfort to her.*
>
> *(Hosea 2:13-14)*

This is one of the most interesting verses in the book of Hosea: "In the wilderness, I will bring comfort to her." God is speaking about Israel who had turned to the gods of Baal. Then God says He will surely punish her and bring her into the wilderness and comfort her.

Please notice that God disciplines His people when they disobey Him. However, comfort from God always comes during the wilderness period. So if you are going through some wilderness in your life, know that God's comfort is available for you.

He promised the Israelites that He would comfort them:

> *Then I will plant her (Israel) for myself in the Earth, and I will have mercy on her who had not obtained mercy; then I will say to those who were not my people, "You are My people!"' And they shall say: "You are my God."*
>
> *(Hosea 2:23)*

God's hands are always open to everyone no matter how great the sins of that person are. God knows how to handle people. He disciplines them and then restores them. The verse above speaks about God's mercy and salvation. For God said He will have mercy on her who has not obtained mercy. Yes, no one had ever obtained mercy, not even you. But God gave us mercy because it is a gift from Christ. The mercy that God spoke of in the verse above is Jesus Christ Himself. While we were sinners Christ died for us (Rom. 5:6-8).

Through God's mercy not only the Jews will be saved but so will everyone who believes in Jesus Christ regardless of race, color, gender, or nationality.

Hosea means "salvation" and that is indeed the subject of the book; though the Israelites sinned in those days still God promised to save them.

The name of Jesus is "Yeshuah" or "Joshua" and the word "Hosea" comes from the same Hebrew root. The name of Jesus consists of (Joshua, Yeshu) and (Yah which is Yahweh). That is what Jesus means in the original language: "Yahweh is Salvation." Let all men come back to the knowledge of God through Jesus Christ and His Holy Spirit.

THE BOOK OF JOEL (Jehovah is God)

The book of Joel is famous because of chapter 2. The apostle Peter used these verses to proclaim the outpouring of the Holy Spirit upon the disciples on the Day of Pentecost.

It is not clear when the prophet Joel lived. The only thing we know is that during this period, a great devastation in the land occurred caused by a massive invasion of locusts to the land. The book of Joel is a short book; therefore, I will not divide the book into different parts.

Devastations

The book of Joel starts with the terrible report of a great natural calamity, the invasion of locusts upon the land. The whole land was plundered and everything was eaten up. The fig trees and other types of trees withered and the grain fields dried up (1:1-12).

In short, the land was going through a devastation period.

I personally believe that whenever a region or a country is hit by a natural calamity such as drought, flood, quake and things like that, God wants to tell something to that nation. God wants to call that nation to repentance.

Many regions and countries are suffering from calamities and devastations simply because of ungodliness, unrighteousness, injustices, lawlessness, idol/shamanistic worship, and the rejecting of Christ as the Messiah.

I know some people might be sensitive to these convictions, but this is what I believe. As long as India is not turning to Almighty God, through believing in Jesus Christ, and as long as there is a caste-system among the people, and idol-worshipping, there will be constant calamities and various disasters in that nation bringing death to thousands of innocent children and people who may never have had the chance to choose for Jesus. Therefore, we Christians must rise up the banner of Christ no matter what. We must preach the gospel and call the nations to repentance.

Repentance

Joel did the same thing; he used the calamity and the devastation of that time to call the people to repentance (Joel 1:13-20; 2:1-17).

We must know the signs of the times; we must be watchful, prayerful and alert about the things that are happening in our nation and in the world. Therefore, in times such as devastations and natural calamities, God wants to use us to proclaim His Gospel, just like Joel did in those days. He called the people to repentance. What about your family, village, city, or nation? God wants to use you to call the people to repent.

Restoration

Repentance will lead to restoration. After Joel called out the people to repent, God promised them the restoration of their devastated land (Joel 2:18-32); He promised them that the Land would be fruitful again and He would send abundant showers of rain and blessing.

Not only did God promise the restoration of Israel's land, we also can take it as a spiritual refreshment and revival. God said:

> *I am sending you grain, new wine and oil, enough to satisfy you fully.*
>
> *(Joel 2:19)*

God speaks about three things: grain, new wine, and oil. Two thousand years ago God sent us His Son, Jesus Christ: His blood was the new wine poured out for us for the New Covenant, the covenant of love and forgiveness to all who believe in Him. This New Covenant is the refreshing Word of God in the New Testament. This represents the grain.

He also promised the oil which is the Holy Spirit of the living God who came down officially after the ascension of Jesus Christ.

When we have these three things, the oil, the grain, and the new wine we shall never thirst or hunger. For in Jesus Christ there is fullness of joy. In His words there is fullness of wisdom and comfort, and in His Holy Spirit there is guidance and peace.

Holy Spirit Specified

The famous part of the book of Joel is the passage which the apostle Peter used to proclaim the outpouring of the Holy Spirit on the Day of Pentecost in Acts 2.

Peter quoted the verses from Joel 2:28-32. (Read Acts 2:14-21)

> *I will pour out my Spirit on all people. Your sons and daughters will prophesy. Your old men will dream dreams, Your young men will see visions. Even on my servants, both men and women, I will pour out my Spirit in those days.*
> *(Joel 2:28-29)*

Peter quoted these verses from Joel 2:32:

> *And everyone who calls on the name of the Lord will be saved.*

This indicates that the title "Last Days" does not mean that a specific day is the last day. The "Last Days" is a process that started with Jesus Christ right after the day of Pentecost when Peter officially announced the beginning of the Last Days. Please notice that Peter did not quote the entire prophesies of Joel, but he stopped with “Everyone who calls on the name of the Lord shall be saved.” This is the great task and commission for all Christians around the world, and that is to make known the name of Jesus Christ so that the unbelievers can call on His name. How can they call on His name if they never heard about Him?

Jo-El

Jo-el means “Yahweh is God.” In other words “God is God” and this is the exact theme of the book. God shows here that He is the One who has the power over all the nations, and in the end He will judge the whole world for the evil deeds it committed (Joel 3).

THE BOOK OF AMOS

Amos lived during the time of his colleague, the prophet Hosea. Amos prophesied against the Northern Kingdom of Israel.

Amos can be divided into 3 major parts:

Listing the sins of Israel (chapters 1–4)
Amos' warnings and call to repentance (chapters 5–7)
Destruction and Restoration (chapters 8–9)

Social Injustice

While Hosea prophesied against idolatry in Israel, Amos prophesied against the ongoing social injustices in Israel. In those days, just before the fall of the Assyrian Kingdom, Israel was enjoying a period of prosperity and economic growth. For this reason, the people forgot the real meaning of righteousness and justice. Their attitude towards the poor was changed; the people became corrupt and they abused many for their own advantage. The Lord said in Amos 2:6-7:

> *They (Israel) sell the righteous for silver, and the needy for a pair of sandals. They trample on the heads of the poor as upon the dust of the ground and deny justice to the oppressed.*

When societies become rich and prosperous they often forget about justice and righteousness. For the sake of prosperity man compromises the basic rights of the people especially those who cannot defend themselves. Social injustice is prevalent; the poor become poorer, and the rich become richer. When an economic policy is not based on godliness and righteousness, that country will not receive the fullness of God's blessings.

In our present economic system, we are being persuaded or "forced" to buy things we do not need or we are coerced to do things that are even unhealthy and immoral. Many times when I travel, mostly to poor countries around the world, I have noticed how the West has influenced the lifestyle and choices of the people living there. Some people who do not even have enough money to buy bread would do everything to have an image of being modern or "high-tech."

Here in Europe there are families who get by on a day to day basis, but because of the system some parents are forced to buy things their children ask for even though the parents cannot afford them. They resort to using the credit card or asking for bank for loans and the system goes on and on.

Somehow the way we live our lives now is the same as the way the Israelites lived before.

Unaccepted Worship

As I mentioned earlier, Israel was going through powerful and stable economic growth. In the meantime, Israel's religiosity was going on. They feasted and assembled together to worship the Lord. More than before they made sacrifices and offerings while at the same time social injustice was growing day by day. Therefore this is what God told them:

> *I hate, I despise your religious feasts; I cannot stand your assemblies. Even though you bring me burnt offerings I will not accept them. Though you bring choice fellowship offerings, I will have no regard for them. Away with the noise of your songs! I will not listen to the music of your harps. But let justice roll on like a river, righteousness like a never-failing stream!*
>
> *(Amos 5:21-24)*

This is one of the horrible passages every believer should have as a nightmare. The Lord does not accept our sacrifices and our worship. This is a description of a failed church and hypocritical Christianity. God spoke to the Israelites and said: “But let justice roll on like a river, righteousness like a never-failing stream!”

God not only spoke to the Israelites, He is also speaking today to the so called Christians and churches who have all the right formulas, the right songs, and technically are alright in every aspect of worship. They are even receiving so much money regularly in the name of God and tithing. However, they never feed the hungry either spiritually or materially. They never evangelize or invest in supporting the poor and the oppressed. I long for the Church of Jesus Christ to intervene in every aspect of society. Christians must not be religious people but people who will stand for righteousness in society, in politics, in education, in business, in science, and in technology. The church must show the power of the Holy Spirit which was manifested in the first decades of the church. God will never accept an exclusive and closed Christianity. God will never rejoice in our praises unless we stand for righteousness and justice; this starts within us.

Imagine you have a friend who is in danger and in desperate need. He knocks on your door but you don’t open it because you are praying to God. God will never accept these types of prayers! Here we learn something great. Worship, prayer, music, and Christianity in general, go far beyond religious activities. It is a way of life. What we do in the name of our Lord to expand the kingdom and help others is also called “PRAYER and WORSHIP.”

Punishment of Repentance

Because of all these things, God used Amos to preach repentance to the Northern Kingdom. There is a very short and powerful verse in Amos, where God says to the Israelites:

Seek me and live
(Amos 5:4)

God is asking His church to seek Him with an upright heart and repent from its iniquities. Some churches are so rich and their pastors enjoys such enormous monthly salaries while there is no burden to share with the brethren from poor countries who are fighting with empty stomachs and bare hands to preach the Gospel so that the Kingdom of God might be expanded. Some churches, leaders, and Christians must repent today!

Through Amos, God gave the Israelites a chance to repent from their way of life, but they did not listen. Therefore, God prophesied through Amos and also through Hosea that Israel would be captured and handed over to the enemy. There is a famous verse in Amos that says:

> *Surely the sovereign LORD does nothing without revealing His plan to His servants the prophets.*
> *(Amos 3:7)*

And so, once again captivity was prophesied to Israel because of disobedience to God. This prophecy came to pass thirty years after Amos. The Northern Kingdom ended in 722 B.C., and Israel was handed over to the Assyrian Kingdom (2 Kings 17).

Christ in Amos

The clearest prophecy about Christ in the book of Amos is found at the end of the book where it predicts that Jesus Christ will judge and also restore His people. All nations will bear His name and seek the LORD (Amos 9).

MAIN SCRIPTURES
Hosea – Joel – Amos

REFERENCE SCRIPTURES
2 Kings
Acts 2:14-21
Romans 5:6-8

TO MEMORIZE AND MEDITATE UPON
AMOS 5:4

SEEK ME (THE LORD) AND LIVE.

QUESTIONS:

1. Against which specific sin did Amos preach against?

2. Why might Joel be called the prophet of the Holy Spirit or the Pentecost? Explain.

3. In Hosea, God says His people lack the knowledge of God. Explain what the consequences are for lack of godly knowledge.

NOTES:

NOTES:

LESSON 31

The LORD above the LAW

Obadiah – Jonah – Micah – Nahum (all chapters)

TODAY'S JOURNEY

THE BOOK OF OBADIAH

Obadiah is the oldest book of all the prophetic books, and at the same time it is the shortest book of the Old Testament.

The prophet Obadiah was specifically called to prophesy against Edom. Edom was a neighbor nation. The people of Edom were the descendants of Esau, the brother of Jacob. The origin of the conflicts between Edom and Israel can be traced to the conflicts between Jacob and Esau (see Gen. 25:19-34, 27, 32).

The Root Diagnosis

Every problem and conflict has a root cause. This is certainly the case with the conflict between Edom and Israel. They were two nations but the conflict started with two people.

In the same way, we can interpret the events and happenings in our world. They all originate and have their roots in the sin committed by Adam and Eve.

Whenever there is a problem in your life try to find out when it started and why it started. In other words, know what the root of the problem is. After that, pray against it and bind it in the name of the Lord Jesus Christ.
In the book of Obadiah God is angry at Edom. He promised to punish and destroy it because of their pride, violence, and aggression against Israel. The Lord promised to cover Edom with shame:

> *Because of the violence against your brother Jacob you will be covered with shame; you will be destroyed forever.*
>
> *(Obad. 10)*

And further the Lord said:

> *You should not march through the gates of my people in the day of their disaster, nor look down on them in their calamity, in the day of their disaster nor seize their wealth in the day of their disaster.*
>
> *(Obad. 13)*

Edom looked down on Israel; pride had covered Edom's eyes and it rejoiced every time Israel failed. This reminds me of some so-called Christians who look down on their fellow brothers and sisters and fellow churches. Some people even rejoice when a church falls apart or an evangelist is caught in scandal. Some people rejoice about the failure of their fellow Christians to prove their doctrines or faith are better than others. They use other people's failures to justify their own ways of worship and doctrines.

I remember the words Jesus said to His disciples:

> *However, do not rejoice that the spirits submit to you but rejoice that your names are written in heaven.*
>
> *(Luke 10:20)*

Jesus says we should not rejoice when the spirits submit to our prayers and commands, but we should rejoice that our names are written in the Lamb's Book of Life. Likewise, we must be careful about how we treat our own brothers and sisters or other churches in the Lord. We should never rejoice in other people's failures.

THE BOOKS OF JONAH AND NAHUM

The book of Jonah describes on one side the love of God for a wicked city, and from the other side the life of a man of God who justified his own personal ideas and tried to run away from God's plan. God called the prophet Jonah to go to Nineveh, the wicked and sinful city in Assyria, to call them to repentance because the distraction and the anger of God was coming.

However, Jonah disobeyed God and went to Tarshish, a city probably in Spain. Imagine this: Nineveh was located in the Northeast and Tarshish was in the West. Instead of Jonah moving towards the Northeast he moved to the West. This is also how we as Christians disobey God. God asks us to move a certain way but we move the totally opposite way.

Jonah Flees from the Lord (chapter 1)

One of the funniest events in the Old Testament is when a man of God chooses to run away from God. Can a man run away from God? No way! Because God is everywhere, we can never hide from Him. Many of us try to run away from God's calling; God asks us to fulfil a certain task, but we do our own will anyway. Jonah is an example of human stubbornness.

God Is More Than the Law

But why did Jonah run away from God? It was because Jonah disagreed with God in giving grace to the Ninevites. First, they were gentiles, and second, they were wicked and sinful. Jonah could not accept the fact that God wanted to give Nineveh a chance to repent. He wanted God to punish them according to the Law for their sins.

As Christians, we must evaluate our lives through the guidance of the Holy Spirit. Are we considered as Christians because of our doctrines? Are the things we do for our own sake or our church's sake? Every believer must ask these questions.

If you are a pastor, an evangelist or even a worker in the Body of Christ, you should ask yourself why you are doing the things you do. Are you doing those things for the sake of your own ideas? For the sake of the law? Or because God asked you to do so?

Let me give you an example. Imagine you are an evangelist and you want to make a very big crusade. Are you conducting the crusade for the sake of the crusade or are you doing it because God asked you to do it. Sometimes, we want our crusades to be so successful, but in the process we neglect to love the souls, those people who are coming to the crusades. We should not treat them as numbers but as individual souls. We use people so that in the end we can say, "We had a great crusade!"

In the same way, Jonah grabbed the Law and the punishment that came with it. He forgot the very basis of it all: THE GRACE AND LOVE OF GOD.

The church must realize that it is all about God's grace and love to lost and sinners. The church must realize the Great Commission that the Lord Jesus Christ gave us in Matthew 28. This is a duty and it must be fulfilled. As long as the church is hanging on man-made rules and regulations based upon false revelations it will never be able to fulfil the Great Commission.

Jonah loved the Law more than anything else and this kept him from going to Nineveh. The church must repent from its spiritual arrogance and obey what the Lord asks. "Thus says the Lord." (This is a prophecy). If you live such a life as this, you need to repent today and come back to the Almighty, Omnipotent and Omnipresent God.

Jonah in the Fish

Jonah took the ship and fled from God towards Tarshish. On his way, God sent a big storm to the sea and everybody in it was in great danger until Jonah realized that it was his fault. Therefore, the people threw him into the sea and the sea calmed down. However, God sent a huge fish that swallowed Jonah. For three days and three nights he stayed in the fish's belly until he repented and surrendered to the will of God.

Many people today live in a "fish" simply because they do not want to submit to the will of God. Whatever God asks you to do—do it and you shall prosper.

Jesus Christ used Jonah's experience inside the fish as an illustration of his death, burial and resurrection (see Matt. 12:40; 16:21).

This experience of Jonah can have more revelations for you as you study it. The Holy Spirit will reveal to you more when you meditate and pray about it. One of the interpretations is that Jonah's fish experience is an illustration of being born again of water and spirit. It means we are dead in sin, just as when Jonah was inside the belly of the fish. We are dead in sin and we will rise again just like Jesus came out of the tomb and Jonah came out of the fish. Being in the belly of the fish in the sea or water represents the water baptism that happens along with repentance.

God's Mercy

Upon repenting, Jonah went back to Nineveh and called upon the people to repent. Many people heard the message and eventually the whole nation repented. God saved them from the disaster and calamity He intended for them. Therefore, Jonah got angry with the Father again (Jonah 4). But God answered him by saying He is concerned about Nineveh (read Jonah 4).

In the same way, God is concerned about your city, village, or country. As a Christian, do your uttermost best to speak about Jesus Christ to many people. If you are a church leader or a Christian worker, I challenge you to pray for your city or village. Go to different government institutions, and if you are led by the Spirit of God offer them your prayers.

Nineveh Was Still Punished (the Book of Nahum)

From the book of Jonah we will jump to the book of Nahum simply because the book of Nahum shows that Nineveh's repentance was only a temporary repentance, and, therefore, God sent them another prophet called Nahum. He prophesied concerning God's anger and Nineveh's plunder and final destruction. I recall the words of Jesus when He said:

> *When an evil spirit comes out of a man, it goes through arid places seeking rest and does not find it. Then he says 'I will return to the house I left'. . . then it goes and takes seven other spirits more wicked than itself, and they go in and live there. And the final condition of that man is worse than the first.*
>
> *(Luke 11:24-26)*

This is exactly what happened in Nineveh; they repented but only for a short period of time. Therefore, God punished them according to the warnings He gave through Jonah. This time God prophesied through Nahum that the city would be fully destroyed and plundered. This prophecy was fulfilled when the Babylonians invaded Nineveh and plundered it.

God gave Nineveh a chance because God is patient with every person and every nation until they repent. Unfortunately, in Old Testament times it was somehow different. God gave sinners a chance but when they did not repent, He punished them either through the Law or through direct punishments such as invasions, wars, and natural calamities. This is one of the most important verses in the book of Nahum:

> *The Lord is slow to anger and great in power, the Lord will not leave the guilty unpunished.*
>
> *(Nahum 1:3)*

However, this has been changed in the New Testament era. Today we live in the time of God's grace. God is more patient with the people of the world than in Old Testament times. That is why Jesus said,

> *I stands behind the door and knock, if anyone hears my voice and opens the door, I will enter in.*
>
> *(Revelation 3:20)*

However, our chance will finish when we die. After the body has died, there is no more chance to choose for God. This choice should have been made during the time we were alive.

Repentance

Many people repent out of their own emotions such as fear of punishment or temporary feelings, but after a few days they fall back again to their sins.

True repentance must be rooted in Christ alone. Once a person experiences being born again through the Holy Spirit, that person will automatically kneel down before the Father and repent from the heart. What about you? Do you repent out of fear of punishment or because you are really convinced that what you are doing is wrong and you want to please God with your life.

Repentance means a realization of the sinful life you lead coupled with a decision to turn away from that sinful life. This is only possible when we are born again through believing in Jesus Christ and by the conviction of the Holy Spirit.

THE BOOK OF MICAH

Micah was a prophet from the Southern Kingdom of Judah. He prophesied in the last days of the Northern Kingdom of Israel. Just like all the other prophets, Micah prophesied against the growing wickedness, injustice, and unrighteousness in Judah. The book of Micah is a somber prophecy against the unfaithful leaders and prophets in those days.

This is one of the important passages in the book of Micah against the false prophets:

> *This is what the Lord says: "As for the prophets, who lead my people astray, if one feed them, they proclaim peace; if he does not, they prepare to wage war against them."*
>
> *(Micah 3:5)*

Bethlehem

Probably one of the most outstanding prophecies in the Old Testament is the prophecy about the place where the Messiah would be born, namely Bethlehem.

More than seven hundred years before the birth of Jesus Christ, this was clearly prophesied in the book of Micah:

> *But you, Bethlehem Ephrathah, though you are small among the clans of Judah, out of you will come for me one who will be ruler over Israel, whose origins are from old, from ancient times."*
>
> *(Micah 5:2)*

Our God is a God of divine plan and design; He already proclaimed to His people that the Messiah would be born in Bethlehem, and indeed, He was born there.
In answer to the false prophets and corrupt leaders, God promised to make Jesus the shepherd over all Israel and the whole world. In the book of Micah, Jesus Christ was prophesied as the Great Shepherd.

> *He will stand and shepherd his flock in the strength of the LORD, in the majesty of the name of the LORD his God. And they will live securely, for then his. Greatness will reach to the ends of the earth, and he will be their peace.*
>
> *(Micah 5:4-5)*

Yes, Jesus Christ is our shepherd and He is also our peace. Everyone who believes in Him shall live securely and has protection from the lover of our souls, Jesus Christ.

SUMMARY

In this lesson we learned that we should not look down at our fellow brothers and sisters or other churches. We also should not rejoice in their failures (Obadiah). We also learned to live a life of obedience and not to place the Law higher than the Giver of the Law—God Himself. He is greater than the Law. We also learned that repentance should be rooted in Christ and through the conviction of the Holy Spirit. It must not be based upon human emotions or fear of punishment (Nahum).

Lastly, we learned that the birthplace of Jesus Christ was prophesied in Micah. It was also prophesied that Jesus Christ would be the Great Shepherd over the entire world.

MAIN SCRIPTURES
Obadiah
Jonah
Micah
Nahum

REFERENCE SCRIPTURES
Genesis 25:19-34, 27, 32
Matthew 12:40; 16:21
Luke 3:20
Revelation 3:20

TO MEMORIZE AND MEDITATE UPON
NAHUM 1:7

THE LORD IS GOOD,
A REFUGE IN THE TIMES OF TROUBLE.
HE CARES FOR THOSE WHO TRUST IN HIM.

QUESTIONS:

1. Why shouldn't we look down on our brothers? Give Scripture references.

2. Why is the experience of Jonah, when he was inside the belly of the fish, considered a type of being born again with water and the spirit? Explain.

3. What are the main themes of the books Nahum and Micah?

NOTES:

LESSON 32

Habakkuk and Zephaniah

(all chapters)

TODAY'S JOURNEY

THE BOOK OF HABAKKUK

Habakkuk was probably written during the reign of King Jehoiakim (2 Kings 23 and 24). Habakkuk wrote about the coming disaster upon Judah. Just like his fellow prophets, Habakkuk spoke about injustice and the rising unrighteousness in Judah.

The book of Habakkuk is a book of "WHY GOD?" In this book Habakkuk asks God why He allows sin and injustice to grow in His nation and in the world.

These questions of Habakkuk are being asked today by many people. Let us see what questions he asked.

> *How long oh LORD must I call for help, but you do not listen? Or cry to you "violence!" But you do not save? Why do you make me look at injustice? Why do you tolerate wrong? Destruction and violence are before me; there is strife, and conflict abounds. Therefore the law is paralyzed, and justice never prevails. The wicked hem in the righteous So that justice is perverted.*
>
> *(Habakkuk 1:1-4)*

And we read further in verse 13:

> *Your eyes are too pure to look on evil; you cannot tolerate wrong.*
> *Why then do you tolerate treacherous? Why are you silent while the wicked swallow up those more righteous than themselves?*

These are common questions people ask God today: "Lord if you exist, why do you let these things happen"; "Why does unrighteousness increase?"; "Why does sin goes on and on?"

In one sense, Habakkuk is a man like Jonah. Both of them claim the hard side of the Lord (THE LAW). That is why Habakkuk declared, "The law is paralyzed" (1:4). Habakkuk wanted the unrighteous to be punished immediately. For this reason, he said to God, *"Why then do you tolerate the treacherous?"* (1:13).

Here we see a man too "righteous" who plays the role of God! This seems so familiar to our ears today. Many of us try to play God. We judge more than God Himself even though we are also sinners.

That is why Jesus said:

> *Do not judge or you too will be judged. For the same way you judge others, you will be judged, and with the measure you use, it will be measured to you.*
>
> *(Matthew 7:1)*

Some of us preach God's punishment and judgment in place of His mercy, salvation, and love. In 1 Corinthians 4:3, the apostle Paul says he himself does not judge, so who are we to judge others? We must let God judge everything at His appointed time. We must realize that we cannot be more righteous than God Himself.

There are some people who pray for punishment for the sinful world so that they can get to heaven. This is one of the most egoistic statements I have ever heard. These kinds of Christians think only about their own selves and do not care about the new souls being saved into the kingdom.

I do not intend to create a negative image of the prophet Habakkuk because he was a powerful man of God. But I only want to use this opportunity to teach you these things: we must desire mercy and not judgement for our neighbours so that many souls can still be saved; we must ask God to delay His judgement and wrath so that we can bring more souls into the kingdom.

God's Response

God had a powerful response to Habakkuk's prayer:

> *Write down the revelation and make it plain on tables so that a herald may run in it. For the revelation awaits an appointed time; it speaks of end and will not prove false. Though it linger, wait for it: it will certainly come and will not delay.*
>
> *(Habakkuk 2:2-3)*

In other words, God told Habakkuk to wait because God had His own time to judge Judah and the world. Even if it seems that God is delayed in reality He is not. He loves the world and He wants to give everybody a chance to repent. God gave Habakkuk one of the incredible revelations about the end times; He will judge the world according to His own planning (read Habakkuk 2).

God also gave one of the most famous verses in the Bible which says:

> *but the righteous will live by his faith.*
>
> *(Romans 1:17)*

This means that only the righteous will be saved by their faith. They will not be saved because of their own righteousness, but they will be saved because of their faith and this faith comes by believing in Jesus Christ. Whoever believes in Him shall be saved and live eternally.

Let us work harder and tell many people about our faith in Jesus Christ. Let us not judge in the flesh but give hope to this dying world through the Gospel of Jesus Christ so that many souls might be saved before the end comes!

THE BOOK OF ZEPHANIAH

Zephaniah means "the LORD has hidden." Zephaniah prophesied God's judgement during the reign of King Josiah. The main theme of this book is: "The Day of the Lord" is near. However, the book ends up with hope.

The book starts with a very terrifying and threatening statement. The Lord said:

> *I will sweep away everything; from the face of the earth. I will sweep away both men and animals; I will sweep away the birds of the air and the fish of the sea. The wicked will have only heaps of rubble. When I cut off man from the face of the earth.*
>
> *(Zephaniah 1:2-3)*

Then God's prophecy turned to Judah and all the other neighboring nations. God told them that even their silver and gold would not be able to save them and sudden destruction would come upon the world. (1:18) Yes, the world's riches cannot save the world from the coming wrath of God and no wealth can bring any person to heaven. So let us not trust in our own wealth and money but let us put our hope in Jesus Christ.

Finally, God prophesied to Jerusalem in chapter 3. In this chapter, there are five things that Jerusalem did that hurt the heart of God:

> *She obeys no one and accepts no correction* (3:2).

The LORD sent many prophets to correct the people of Jerusalem, but they did not listen and they did not obey. They despised the messages of the prophets. Just as Jesus said:

> *O Jerusalem, Jerusalem, you who kill the prophets and stone those sent to you.*
>
> *(Matthew 23:36)*

Correction from God is a light to our path. When God tries to correct you through the Holy Spirit, the Bible, preaching, or a godly friend, you must listen and obey. Do so because God knows what is best for you.

In those days, Judah tried to find refuge in the neighboring countries because of political pressures. In place of putting their faith and trust in God, they exerted human efforts without trusting the LORD their Creator and without drawing near to Him.

The opposite of this act is the secret to success and prosperity: **trust and prayer.**

Sometimes we are so busy with our own things and we try by our own power to make things happen. We rely on our own power and forget to focus on God's Word and prayer. Prayer and reading the Bible will give us more wisdom and knowledge. Through God's power we shall prosper and succeed. Psalm 130:5 says:

I wait for the Lord, my soul waits, and in His word I put my hope. Her officials are roaring lions, her rules are evening wolves, who leave nothing for the morning.

Here, God talks about the rules and the officials who were abusing the people's money. This reminds me of the situation where Jesus was preaching the "seven woes" on the teachers of the law and the Pharisees (Matt. 23:1-39).

There are churches, leaders, and church officials who are abusing money in the church for their own interests.

God will deal with these types of people according to His righteousness. If you are a leader of a church and you are playing with the money of your people, it is better for you to repent today before it is too late.

> *Her prophets are arrogant, they are treacherous men.*
> *(Zephaniah 3:4)*

God was talking about those false prophets, the so-called men of God who prophesied to the nation what their itching ears wanted to hear. They were arrogant and hard-headed. Arrogance is never from God. One of the characteristics of a false prophet is his or her arrogance. These types of people do not listen to anybody and they think they are the only ones God uses. They are also treacherous; you cannot trust them and they change day by day.

> *Her priests profane (blaspheme) the sanctuary and do violence to the law.*
> *(Zephaniah 3:6)*

God talks about those Pharisees and priests who blasphemed the temple by twisting the law for the sake of their own evil understandings and desires.

Many people use verses of the Bible and twist them to justify their evil ways of life. Even today, there are church leaders who are profaning the sanctuary by violating the law. For example, they marry two people from the same gender, man and man or woman and woman, and they justify their actions by twisting the Word of

God. This is a sin and God does not tolerate this; moreover, God wants to heal the people from this. There are hundreds of examples of these types of leaders who are misinterpreting the Word of God for their own sakes. Therefore, God promised destruction to Judah and Jerusalem and to all other nations, but after this something good will happen: Restoration.

Restoration and the Remnant

> *God promised that He will purify the lips of the peoples, all of them may call on the name of the Lord and serve him shoulder to shoulder.*
>
> *(Zephaniah 3:9)*

I believe God is talking about the great revival on the day of Pentecost! He purified the lips of the peoples in different nations through the fire of the Holy Spirit. All of them worked hand-in-hand to preach the gospel of Jesus Christ. From that day on, everyone who was purified through the Holy Spirit was called a minister and worked to advance the Gospel. This means every Spirit-filled person in Christ Jesus shall be used in one way or another by the Lord and for the Lord. In other words, this means every Spirit-filled person is a minister.

Ephesians 4:11 says:

> *It was he who gave some to be apostles, some to be prophets. Some to be evangelists and some to be pastors and teachers, to prepare God's people for works of service so that the body of Christ may be built up until we reach unity in faith and in knowledge of the Son of God and become mature, attaining to the whole measure of the fullness of Christ.*

Please focus on the word "service," this means ministry! So the work of a pastor, evangelist, teacher, prophet or an apostle is to train the people of God to be a minister. You are a minister of God so that in unity (like Zephaniah says: hand in hand) we can be built up in the faith and knowledge of Christ Jesus our Lord.

Lastly, the Lord prophesied restoration and blessing to Jerusalem. He said before her very eyes that He shall restore her fortunes (3:20). There will be a remnant of Israel in these last days.

> *The remnant of Israel will do no wrong; they will speak no lies, nor will deceit be found in their mouths. They will eat and lie down and no one will make them afraid.*
>
> *(Zephaniah 3:13)*

Whatever blessing God has prophesied to Israel is also available to us today! Through the blood of Jesus we became the descendants of Abraham. Thus, we will also eat and lie down with our Shepherd. His name is Jesus. He brings us to the green pastures and leads us to clean waters. We shall not be afraid.

MAIN SCRIPTURES
Habakkuk
Zephaniah

REFERENCE SCRIPTURES
2 *Kings 23*
Psalm 130:5
Matthew 7:1
Matthew 23

TO MEMORIZE AND MEDITATE UPON
PSALM 130:5

I WAIT FOR THE LORD, MY SOUL WAITS, AND IN HIS WORD I PUT MY HOPE.

QUESTIONS:

1. In the book of Habakkuk God condemns idol-worship. Which verses do they refer to?

2. There are five things God despised in Jerusalem. What are they?

NOTES:

LESSON 33

Haggai ~ Zechariah ~ Malachi

(all chapters)

TODAY'S JOURNEY

THE BOOK OF HAGGAI

You probably can still recall Lesson 20 (Ezra and Nehemiah). We learned that after the crushing of the Babylonian Empire the king of Persia allowed religious freedom in the captured territories. The Jews were allowed to return to Jerusalem and rebuild the temple and the city. A group of Jews returned to rebuild the temple, however, their works remained unfinished. As soon as they were back in their land, they focused on their own business and life and they forgot the purpose of why God sent them there. During this period, God raised a prophet called Haggai. He prophesied against the Jews who neglected the Lord and focused on their own things.

The prophet Haggai returned with the first group of Jews under the leadership of Zerubbabel who continued to live in Jerusalem.

Priorities in Life

Haggai is a book of priorities in life especially towards God and His divine plan. In Haggai, we read about the people who returned to Jerusalem and did not straighten their priorities. They were too busy with their own things. The Lord said:

> *Because of my house, which remains a ruin, while each of you is busy with his own house. Because of you the heavens have withheld their dew and the earth its crops.*
>
> *(Haggai 1:9-10)*

The heart of God was grieved because He saw that His people did not fulfil the very purpose for which they were sent to Jerusalem. Therefore God said:

> *Give careful thought to your ways.*
>
> *(Haggai 1:5)*

This story is not a new issue, especially in the body of Christ. God has created you and me in this very specific time so that we might fulfil His purposes here on earth. There is a very specific and universal purpose for every born again Christian and that is to give witness about Jesus Christ. Also, churches with various denominations are placed in different countries, cities, and villages so that God's plan may be fulfilled through the church and believers.

Today, we must thank God for so many Spirit-filled, anointed, and powerful churches, missions, ministries, and individuals who are fulfilling God's purposes in their lives. On the other hand, there are also many Christians who are busy with their own lives and do not care about God. They do whatever pleases them first and then place God at the second, third or even the tenth place of their priorities.

There are even some Christians who are so busy with their cats and dogs at home that they have no time to do what God has asked them to do. There are also a lot of businesses going on in the churches that neglect the very call of God. There are so many festivals and activities "for Christ" that they lose their actual calling in Christ.

If you are a born again Christian reading this book, please re-evaluate your life. Make God your top priority. Pray carefully and ask God what His plans and purpose for your life are. If you are a pastor, remind yourself about the very purpose why God assigned you to your church. Do not let your church be busy with so many things God did not ask the church to do. Rather, motivate, encourage, and mobilize your people to fulfil godly purposes.

I believe with all my heart that the Church of Jesus Christ must rise up and not fall asleep. The Body of Christ must be focused like never before. We must act as sharp as possible and be as alert as we can. For Jesus Christ is coming back for a focused and straight church.

The Glory of the New House

After they heard the prophecy of Haggai, they repented and started to build the temple. The Lord told them that He would be with them and He would provide every need for building that temple. The Lord said:

> *Silver is mine and gold is mine.*
> *The glory of this house shall be greater*
> *than the glory of the former house.*
> *(Haggai 2:8-9)*

The Lord promised that the rebuilt temple would contain more glory than the first. I personally believe this refers to the fact that the Messiah will personally visit the place during His worldly life here on earth. In the time of Jesus, this temple was called Herod's Temple because Herod renovated the temple which was made by Zerubbabel.

It was in this temple where Jesus Christ was presented after He was born. This is where God revealed to the old man, Simon, that he would see the Messiah before he died (Luke 2:21-32). Again it was the same temple where Jesus as a teenager spoke the words of the heavenly Father and amazed the teachers in the temple. Further, it was in the same place where Jesus got furious and turned everything upside down in the temple court because the people turned the Lord's House into a den of thieves.

And lastly, it was the very same temple where Jesus prophesied that not even one stone would remain on each other. In other words, the temple would be destroyed! (Matt. 24:2). And truly, about thirty five years later, the temple was totally destroyed and plundered by the enemies. Indeed, the prophecy of Haggai came to pass because Jesus was seen personally in fleshly form teaching and preaching the words of God in the place. The temple witnessed important historical moments with the Messiah which Moses and Elijah desired to witness. The temple saw the glory according to the prophecies, the glory who was Jesus Christ Himself:

Christ in you, the Hope of Glory.
(Colossians 1:27)

The New Temple

Jesus came down and literally destroyed the religious systems and cursed the hypocrisy of the Pharisees. He also said to His disciples that not even one stone would remain from this temple because Jesus knew the plan of God. Jesus knew what would take place soon after His crucifixion, resurrection, and the outpouring of the Holy Spirit. He knew that the era of God's temple as a stony building would be over and it would be a spiritual temple. This new temple will never be destroyed and no one will be able to plunder it. That is why He said to the people who asked for a sign: "*Destroy the temple and I shall build it for you in three days!*" (John 2:19).

The writer of Acts quoted what Paul preached in Athens:

> *The God who made the world and everything in it is the Lord of heaven and earth and does not live in temples built by hands"*
>
> *(Acts 17:24)*

And further in the book of 2 Corinthians 6:16, the apostle Paul said:

> *We are the temples of the living God.*

If Jesus Christ in His bodily form was present in that stony temple, how much more shall we receive the Lord's glory in our lives? This time we are the temple of God and Jesus Christ, through His Spirit, is permanently within us. This means the power of God is in us. The truth is in us. The miracle-making power is within us permanently. We are the temple of the living God. The glory of the newest temple (the Body of Christ, you and me) is even greater than the temple which was built in Haggai's time. This is the Church of Jesus Christ and you are His temple! The church is not anymore an organization based on the Law and the curses of God. Nor is it a temple of religious practices and beliefs. The church is now a living organism which grows day by day. With this kingdom there shall be no end!

Man-made church organizations are groups of people who exist out of formulas and are not led by the consequences of their actions whether successful or not.

A God-made church is an organism, composed of people who act out of love to the Lord Jesus Christ and love for the people. Let us not be an organization but an organism for God. Organization is dead, but organism lives and moves. It is alive!

THE BOOK OF ZECHARIAH

Zechariah was a contemporary of Haggai. He also prophesied to the Jews who returned to the Promised Land. Reading the book of Zechariah reminds me of the book of Isaiah. If I were asked to give a new name to the book of Zechariah, I would call it "Second Isaiah" because just like Isaiah, Zechariah describes some scenes about Jesus Christ which we can find parallels to the four gospels in the New Testament. Zechariah describes them clearly and specifically. In the following paragraphs we are going to learn the most important fact about this book. Zechariah had, in total, eight prophetic visions through which the Lord spoke to him and His people. In this lesson I will not go into detail about these visions. I recommend that you read them on your own.

Christ Revealed in Zechariah

The book of Zechariah is quite interesting because many of the prophecies concentrate on the last week of Jesus' life in Jerusalem: His entry, His betrayal, and His death. These are some of the prophecies:

Christ shall come and live among us. In chapter 2 Christ reveals Himself to Zechariah and says:

> *Shout and be glad, O Daughter of Zion. For I am coming. And will live among you, declares the Lord.*
> *(Zechariah 2:10)*

Indeed, God came and lived among the Jews. His name is Jesus Christ. He became human and suffered in our place. God was among His people and yet His people did not receive Him.

> *For in Christ all the fullness of Deity lives in bodily form.*
> *(Colossians 2:9)*

The Branch (chapter 3)

The Lord promised the coming of a Branch. This Branch is Jesus Christ Himself who through Him, the Branch, all sins will be removed on a single day! (read Zech. 3:8-10).

Jesus shall enter Jerusalem on a donkey and will teach and preach there (Zech. 9).

In the gospels we read about the glorious entry of Jesus Christ to Jerusalem. They shouted "Hosanna, to the Son of David" as Jesus entered Jerusalem riding on a donkey (Matt. 21:1:11). Zechariah the prophet prophesied this particular event hundreds of years before:

> *Rejoice greatly, O Daughters of Zion! Shout daughters of Jerusalem! See, your king comes to you, righteous and having salvation, gentle and riding on a donkey.*
>
> *(Zechariah 9:9)*

The God whom we serve is the God of purpose and plan. Everything that comes out of His mouth shall come to pass, just like the prophecies to the Jews centuries before Jesus was born. The prophecy concerns the Messiah entering Jerusalem riding on a donkey.

These prophecies took place because it was the plan of God and because Jesus chose to be in the Father's plan. If you stay in the Father's plan, then you too will see the fulfilment of every plan God has in your life and every godly prophesy which has been given to you shall come to pass exactly 100% according to the spoken Word.

We read further in Zechariah 9:10 that the Messiah will enter Jerusalem and will teach and proclaim peace not only there but also to all the nations. Remember the Gospel officially started to spread from Jerusalem and beyond after the outpouring of the Holy Spirit!

The Messiah Will Be Betrayed for Thirty Pieces of Silver (chapter 11)

One day in a vision God asked Zechariah to become a shepherd of the flock but his flock detested him and betrayed him. Then he resigned from his job as a shepherd and asked for his wage. So they priced Zechariah for thirty pieces of silver which was the wage of a slave. The Lord told Zechariah to throw the thirty coins to the potter.

What happened here was a foreshadowing of what would be done to Jesus Christ. First, the same people in Jerusalem who called Him their King and sang Hosanna for Him, now have deserted Jesus. Worse than that, His own disciple, Judas, betrayed Him for thirty coins of silver. After being sorry, he threw the money to the potter and so the chief priests bought the Potter's Field with that money. It became a burial place for foreigners (Matt. 27:1-10).

The Death of Jesus Was Prophesied

> *And I will pour out on the house of David and the inhabitants of Jerusalem a spirit of grace and supplication. They will look at me, the one they pierced, and will mourn for him as one mourns for an only child, and grieves bitterly for a first born son.*
>
> *(Zechariah 12:10)*

Remember those words of Jesus when He told the weeping mothers in Jerusalem not to mourn for Him but for themselves (Luke 23:26-28).

Indeed Jesus was the first born son!

The night before the arrest of Jesus in Gethsemane was also prophesied by Zechariah:

> *Awake, O sword, against my shepherd, against the man who is closed to me! Strike the shepherd and the sheep will be scattered and I will turn my hands against the little ones.*
> *(Zechariah 13:7)*

Read Mark 14:43-50. After Jesus was arrested, the disciples were scattered and some ran away. Even Peter disowned Jesus three times before the rooster crowed. Mark 14:27 states:

"You will all fall away" Jesus told them (the disciples). "For it is written: I will strike the shepherd and the sheep will be scattered." These were the words of Jesus Himself during the Last Supper to His disciples, and He quoted from Zechariah the prophet.

A Temple Built Not by Might or by Power

One of the most famous verses in the Old Testament quoted by many believers in many services is Zechariah 4:6

"It is not by might, nor by power but by my Spirit," says the Lord.

However, there is a lot behind this powerful Bible verse because the Lord wants to tell us a little about the characteristics of a spiritual temple that is going to be established.

To place this Bible verse in its context will make things much easier and understandable. This verse is spoken by the Lord in the context of the vision Zechariah had. Zechariah explained that the angel of the Lord woke him from his sleep and showed him a solid gold lampstand with a bowl at the top, seven lights on it, and seven channels to the lights. There were also two olive trees, one on the right of the bowl and the other on the left.

Zechariah then asked the angel what they were and the angel answered, "It is not by might nor by power but by my Spirit says the Lord." Zechariah asked about the two olive trees connected with the two golden pipes that poured out golden oil. The Lord said they were the two anointed ones who were going to serve the Lord. Probably, God mentioned Zerubbabel as the appointed governor and Joshua as the appointed priest to build the temple.

But there is more than what the vision itself tells us:

The lampstand with its branches of light represents the church. In the Bible, lampstands often represent the church. For instance, in the book of Revelation, we read about the seven lampstands that represent the seven churches.

When Zechariah saw the two trees, the angel answered, "Not by might or by power." The "might" represents one olive tree that represents kingly authority and the other olive tree represents the "power" which was the priestly power.

And when the Lord said: "Not by might nor by power, but by my Spirit." The oil represented the Spirit. In other words, the Lord is saying that this time the temple He is going to build shall not be built by any kingly or priestly authority, but it shall be built by His HOLY SPIRIT. In Jewish history, God blessed only two types of authority: the priestly and the kingly. By this God is saying, the new temple, or the new church, shall not be influenced by the kings or by the priests but by the anointing that comes through the Holy Spirit in their lives.

In other words, you can be a priest, a pastor, and a leader, but if you do not seek His Spirit, and if you are not a vessel of His oil, you shall never be a part of the living temple. He also means that the new church or the new temple is going to be established through Jesus Christ. The leaders are not doing the job, but it is the Spirit within them who does the job.

If you are a traditional church leader, a pastor, or just an ordinary Christian who never had the experience of getting to know the Holy Spirit, I am urging you to do so. I am asking you to simply invite the Spirit to come and show you things you have never seen before. And then you will be just like the olive tree which contains the spiritual oil. The Holy Spirit will light the lampstand in your life. We Christians can never move even one step without His Spirit.

What use is a king or a priest without the Holy Spirit? Nothing!

THE BOOK OF MALACHI

Eventually we have arrived at the closing book of the Old Testament— *Malachi.*

Malachi lived during the time of Nehemiah. Just like Nehemiah, Malachi condemned the practices of the Jews who returned to the Promised Land after the King of Persia allowed them to return. Malachi condemned the people for forgetting the Law of Moses, the Sabbath, tithes, and many other things.

The book of Malachi is frequently used to teach the people about paying tithes and offerings to the house of God. However, there are more things to be learned in this book than tithes and offering.

The book of Malachi, unfortunately, describes a beloved nation who is trying to cheat God through God's given law and doing it as if they loved Him. Hypocrisy!

Here are some of the ways that generation tried to cheat God!

The Blemished Sacrifices

God was angry with the way they sacrificed to Him:

> *When you bring blind animals for sacrifice, is that not wrong? When you sacrifice crippled or diseased animals, is*

that not wrong? Try offering them to your governor! Would he be pleased? Would he accept you?
(Malachi 1:8)

As you can read, they followed all the ceremonies according to the Law, but God was not pleased. They thought God was as blind as the cattle they sacrificed to Him. This is a way of cheating God, doing what has the form of godliness, but denying the very fact of His power (2 Tim. 3:5).
There are many Christians who play around with God. They go to church (this is an act of worship) but afterwards they do what they desire. Many people offer sacrifices to fool themselves!

They go to church and then do whatever their hearts desire. They pay their tithes and offerings, but they continue to live in disobedience.

The Tithes and the Offerings

Malachi 3 is the most famous chapter of the book because it describes how people can rob God through neglect of the tithes and offerings. As you read this teaching, I pray the Lord will open up your heart to receive this and be faithful to do it. The Lord was angry with the Israelites because they robbed Him by not paying tithes and offerings. Therefore, God proclaimed that they were under a curse unless they brought their money to the house of God. Only then will God open the heavens and pour out on them such blessings where there will not even be enough room for the blessing. Their cup shall overflow! (Mal. 3:6-13).

All Scriptures are breathed by the Spirit of God; even this Scripture from Malachi is part of God's commands. Sad to say, there is so much money-worshipping in the Body of Christ. Repentance is called for today, most especially by those who are leading the flock. There are countless numbers of churches and leaders who preach curses to their people so that tithes and offerings will come. Christ came to accomplish the Law, therefore, not only 10% of our income belongs to God, but our entire income, life and being belongs to Him. We belong to Jesus because He bought us with His blood.

Many people are victims of careless and curse-oriented messages that come from the pulpits. They preach curses to the people while Christ took out the infirmities because of His blood shed on the cross. He removed all the curses to those who believe in Christ.

Have you ever had the feeling of guilt at a conference when you felt led to give a specific amount, but yet you couldn't do so because you didn't have the ability? If so, then I have good news for you. Do not listen to the voice of that man behind the microphone, but listen to the Holy Spirit inside of you. He will tell you what to do. Maybe you need to give more.

Please do not misunderstand me; I am not against tithing. In fact God said to tithe so that "In my house there may be food" (Mal. 3:10). Food means Gospel. The church must realize that the bottom line of every Christian activity is saving souls. The house of God must always have "food" in the house; having the Gospel in the house! To preach the Gospel and to reach the people in our villages, cities, countries, and even the world, needs money. The tithe in the church is not only for paying the rent or electricity, but it is there to reach out and to feed the hungry souls who need the Gospel.

Unfortunately, it has been taught for a long time that through our giving we shall be blessed. Of course this is a fact and I agree with it fully. I only disagree when our motivation to give is to gain more in return. What if Jesus doesn't bless you? What if you receive nothing? We must tithe because we love Jesus; we give because we love Jesus; we offer because it comes from our hearts and love for Jesus. We should not do these things to buy a blessing.

Lastly, there are people who give to God because of the Law; their 10% is paid monthly to their local church. Because of this they justify their evil actions and they think they can buy God off with their money. The Israelites robbed God by not paying their tithes. Some of the so-called Christians cheat God by paying their tithes so that they can compensate their evil actions with their 10% offering. Let me say it clearly, cheating God is worse than robbing God. Robbing God is from the pocket, but cheating God streams from the heart.

Do you want to be prosperous? Then do what the Spirit asks you to do. Be sure that in whatever He asks you to do, there is prosperity and assurance of gaining. God is not behind your 10% income. He is more concerned about you as His child and everything that concerns your life!

I also want to warn every leader and pastor. Do not preach curse to your people on money issues such as the tithes and offerings. Do not preach out of your own knowledge or copy another man's teachings about being blessed. My advice for you is to teach them to give from their hearts in obedience to the Spirit of God.

Teach them what a tithe is and what an offering is to God. Do not harden your eyes unto your members' tithes or offerings but give them the chance to move freely and to give with joy! Teach them by revelation and not by law. The apostle Paul said:

> *I do not set aside the grace of God, for if righteousness could be gained through the law, Christ died for nothing.*
> *(Galatians 2:21)*

CLOSING VERSES

See I will send you the prophet Elijah before that great and dreadful day of the Lord comes. He will turn the hearts of the fathers to their children and the hearts of children to their fathers, or else I will come and strike the land with a curse.

(Malachi 4:5-6)

Many believe Elijah came in the spirit of John the Baptist. (Matt. 11:13-14; 17:12-13). However, some still believe that before the end time, Elijah will come again as one of the two witnesses in Revelation 11:3-9. Nevertheless, whether he came already or is still yet to come is not the issue of this paragraph.

The issue here is that God closes the whole Old Testament Era with an option to curse. From that time on it took 450 years before the incarnation of Christ to fulfil His mission to bear our sins and give us eternal life. Therefore, a person without Christ shall live under the curse which was spoken about in Malachi and the Old Testament in general.

MAIN SCRIPTURES
Haggai
Zechariah
Malachi

REFERENCE SCRIPTURES
Matthew 24:2; 27:1-10
Mark 14:27
Luke 2:21-32; 23:26-28
2 Timothy 3:5
Colossians 1:27

TO MEMORIZE AND MEDITATE UPON
ZECHARIAH 4:6

IT IS NOT BY MIGHT, NOR BY POWER BUT MY SPIRIT, SAYS THE LORD.

QUESTIONS:

1. The book of Haggai is about priorities in life. Why was God angry with the Jews who returned to Jerusalem?

2. The book of Zechariah described a lot about the life of Christ before He was crucified. Give your insights on this.

3. Malachi gave instructions on tithes and offerings. Why is it important to tithe? Is it for the sake of a blessing or because we love God?

NOTES:

NOTES:

. PART V .

Journey to Grace

LESSON 34
Closing Lesson

(Old Testament)

TODAY'S JOURNEY

You and I have finished a long journey throughout the Old Testament. What did you learn? How did it change your life? I hope during the past thirty three lessons you did not learn theology, but you learned something more than that.

As Christians we learned about our root, our origin. From Genesis to Malachi, we learned the background and root of God's chosen nation, Israel and how we, the chosen people of God through Jesus Christ, can learn from their mistakes.

We also saw from the very beginning of the book of Genesis to the ending verses of Malachi how Christ Jesus was revealed in details and how He showed the character of the Father. He is the God of divine plans and purposes for the human race through Jesus Christ. We also learned about the entrance of man into the New Testament Era in which we are today.

If I could summarize the entire Old Testament in one word, I would use the word: **LAW**.

The Old Testament is the Law by which we were all bound. Disobeying that LAW brought the people curses and death. LAW was for the stony hearts. They knew the consequences of disobeying God. Therefore many obeyed Him not out of the heart, but out of concern for the Law and its punishments.

God promised in the Old Testament to give man a heart of flesh and to write His laws in their hearts so that they can worship Him out of love (Ezek. 36:24-27). To fulfil this mission, man needs to have the born-again experience (John 3:1-21), and this was only possible through His Son, Jesus Christ. By becoming the ultimate sacrifice we can be saved. By believing in Him we shall not be judged by the Law anymore but loved by Grace. Therefore, if I may summarize the whole New Testament in one word, I will call it "**GRACE**!"

> *For it is by grace you have been saved, through faith-and this not from yourselves, it is the gift of God-not by works, so that no one can boast.*
>
> *(Ephesians 2:8)*

Law versus Grace. Christ came because of Grace and Mercy. The Old Testament shows us how much we have sinned and the New Testament shows us how much we are forgiven by His grace! As you have finished this course, remember that you are saved not because of your good deeds or because you know a lot from the Old Testament. Rather, you are saved because you were born again through believing in Jesus Christ and worshipping Him in Spirit and in Truth. Therefore, have mercy on those who are weaker than you in faith. Demonstrate the love of God through the love you have received from God.

Lastly, I see both the Old Testament and New Testament as phases in the history of humans, and at the same time, a phase of growth in our spiritual journey in Christ Jesus.

Let me explain it to you:

From the time you were a baby until a certain period in your life, you were under the authority of your mother and father. In order to teach you obedience and to show you their authority, they put certain sanctions on your way. They would say, "If you do so and so, then this and that will take place." Or "If you do so and so, there will be punishment." Most of the time, these sanctions and punishments were physically-oriented.

I remember when I was a little boy of six years old I learned a terrible dirty word from the kids on the street. My mother commanded me not to speak that word ever again. But I didn't listen. She told me she would punish me if I spoke that word again. However, I tried to tease my mom. I repeated that particular dirty word again and immediately my mom took a bottle of white pepper, opened my mouth, and threw all the white pepper inside. My mouth burned for more than a day and I cried a lot. From that day on, I never uttered any dirty words again. Not because I became a gentle boy but because I knew the consequences.

When I became an adult, I fully realized that what I did was wrong, not out of fear but out of love and respect to myself and to the people around me.

The Bible says, "When the time was fully ready, Jesus Christ came to this world." From the time of creation until the time of Jesus' ministry, death, and resurrection, the people of God was in the premature, pre-adolescence period. The religious man was not ready for grace. The religious people were only Law-oriented, especially the Jews. The Law was written on their hearts of stone, just like the Law of Moses was written on tablets of stone.

But things changed when the Holy Spirit officially came down and lived in the heart of man. This was the time when the religious people, especially the people of God, got a chance to come out of the law-oriented life to a born-again, grace-oriented life through Jesus Christ the Savior. The outpouring of the Holy Spirit is available to all since the Pentecost day onward!

Everyone who has an encounter with Jesus Christ and His Spirit lives by the grace and love of God and is not anymore under the Law.

The past is not valid anymore. Rather, it is fulfilled in us through the Spirit of God who grants us to live without condemnation and also to live in grace and truth.

On the other hand, those who have no understanding of how grace and love work still live in the pre-adolescence time. They are people who live under the Law with all its systems and traditions. They shall be judged by the Law.

The Old and New Testaments reflect a person's experience when he or she receives the Lord. Somehow his or her life is a bit law-oriented in terms of discipline in the faith. That is why Jesus said to go and make disciples. The word "disciple" comes from the word "discipline."

I remember when I just became a born again Christian, I learned I must have time with the Lord every morning. Consequently, each day when I wake up in the morning, and before I go to sleep at night, I discipline myself to pray. This was my routine; failing to do so brought me sadness and emptiness. After many years this pattern changed. Now I do not pray only twice a day as my routine, but I pray in the Spirit whenever and wherever He leads me. I have a peaceful relationship with His Spirit.

The first was needed to be able to come into the second condition. If I did not discipline myself to pray based on a routine in those early years, I was not able to train myself with listening to the Holy Spirit. I needed the discipline in order for me to understand His ways.

If you are just a new-born Christian, I suggest you try to make every effort to have a routine in your Christian life until you become a mature Christian who can hear the voice of the Holy Spirit clearly.

In short I will summarize again the Old and New Testaments like this:

> *As long as we have no personal relationship with the Holy Spirit through faith in Jesus Christ, we still live by the Law (the Old Testament) and shall be judged by it accordingly. However, by having a personal relationship with the Holy Spirit and by being obedient to His voice, we shall live under the grace of God (New Testament) and enter a life of victory, power, and freedom in Jesus Christ.*

Samuel Lee

RESOURCES

For more information or to schedule
Dr. Lee for ministry engagements, contact:

SLWE
P.O. Box 12429
1100 AK Amsterdam
The Netherlands

www.slwe.org
www.foundationuniversity.com
www.apostolicintegrity.net

Additional Works by **SAMUEL LEE**

ANOINTED *for* CALLING

DISCOVER YOUR CALLING IN LIFE AND TRANSFORM THE WORLD

ISBN: 90-76077-04-8
Published by
Ministryhouse

Christianity becomes relevant to a society when Christians are anointed for their calling. Our consuming passion for Jesus is great, and will yield greater works when we live and function according to God's actual design for us. "Anointed for Calling" is a helpful tool for those who desire to pursue serving God correctly, joyfully and strategically absent from regret or disillusionment. This book will help you discover your calling in life and will reveal to you how you can live for God in its fullness, build up the church and enlarge the harvest.